TOWARD WORLD LITERACY

The Each One Teach One Way

Frank Laubach teaching the first chart in Hausa, near Zaria, Nigeria. When these men learn, some may teach others; thus in 96 countries and 274 languages Each One Teach One may be quietly, steadily going on.

TOWARD WORLD LITERACY

The Each One Teach One Way

Frank C. Laubach

and

Robert S. Laubach

In Two Parts

Part I TEACHING ILLITERATES

Part II WRITING FOR NEW LITERATES

SYRACUSE UNIVERSITY PRESS

Library of Congress Catalog Card 60-10108
© 1960 by SYRACUSE UNIVERSITY PRESS

*Manufactured in the United States of America by
Book Craftsmen Associates, Inc., New York*

FOREWORD

This text is offered with the hope that the experiences, the techniques and the suggestions within its covers may be of aid to the men and the women in many lands who are gallantly seeking ever better to serve their illiterate fellowmen.

We wish to pay special tribute to the scores of students, from more than thirty countries, who have been much more than "students" in the Writing for New Literates classes at the School of Journalism of Syracuse University and summer sessions at the University's Chautauqua, New York, center, and other places where we have been privileged to teach. Some will find their "by-lines" in this book; to all of them goes our gratitude for their expressed needs, their earnest questions, their hard work and their deep dedication.

Through seven years of fellowship in the classes and correspondence with those in the field, this text has grown. Whatever enthusiasm for the cause of the new literate may reflect from its pages is truly a reflection: of the zealous glow on the faces of many of these former students, as they are now engrossed in one of the world's most thrilling tasks--bringing the printed word and its myriad messages to the world's billion illiterates.

F. C. L. and R. S. L.

January 1960

Note: The pronoun "I" in Part I generally refers to Frank Laubach, and in Part II to Robert Laubach.

IN APPRECIATION

Grateful thanks is hereby expressed to the following individuals and publishers who gave permission for the use of material included in this book:

Dr. Davida M. Finney, Miss Halana Mikhail and Miss Marjorie Dye, for "Carrying on the Literacy Campaign at Manhari, Egypt."

Miss Betty Mooney, for "Literacy House, Allahabad, India," and "Tin Trunk Libraries."

Robert C. Likins, for "The Story of Baylor University Literacy Center."

Mr. J. R. Shaw, for "How to Make It Easy for People to Get Helpful Books."

Mr. Edwin C. Carlson, for "Getting Good Reading out to the People in the North Sudan."

Brandt & Brandt, for portion of "God's Word," from The Collected Poems of Edna St. Vincent Millay, Harper & Bros., copyright 1913, 1941 by Edna St. Vincent Millay.

Mary Gibson and The Saturday Evening Post, for the cartoon on page 169.

Joseph Samba, for his plea for the mother tongue, on page 170.

Miss Sally Anstey, for her comments on translating the Bible into Telegu, on page 174.

Charles Scribner's Sons, for the opening passages of Cry, The Beloved Country, by Alan Paton.

Harvard Alumni Bulletin, for a version of the "Gettysburg Address," by Prof. Richard D. Fay, of the Massachusetts Institute of Technology.

Johnny Hart and The New York Herald Tribune, Inc., for the cartoon on pages 194, 195.

Dr. Rudolf Flesch, for description of his Reading Ease and Human Interest formulas, published in his The Art of Readable Writing and How to Test Readability, Harper and Brothers.

"Smilby" and Punch (Copyright Punch, London), for the cartoon on page 215.

Dr. Seth Spaulding and Modern Language Journal, for description of his two readability formulas in Spanish.

Mr. Robert Gunning, for description of his Fog Index formula, which appears in The Technique of Clear Writing, published by McGraw-Hill.

Walt Disney Music Company, for the use of verse, chorus (and permission to write a new verse) and melodic line of "The Ballad of Davy Crockett," copyright 1955, Wonderland Music Co., Inc.; verses by Tom Blackburn and set to music by George Bruns.

Miss Alice Grant, for including fifteen of her original poems for new literates.

Mr. Hall Duncan and World Outlook, for "What Do Africans See in Pictures?"

Teachers College, Columbia University (Bureau of Publications), for including the first 1,000 words of the Thorndike-Lorge Teacher's Wordbook of 30,000 Words.

Journal of Applied Psychology (Vol. 33, pp. 275-278), and James N. Farr and James J. Jenkins, for tables for use with Flesch Reading Ease and Human Interest formulas.

- - - -

Miss Margaret Lee Runbeck died in the fall of 1956, before permission was obtained for the use of her passage, "Dramatic Story Telling." She was a wonderful friend of the illiterates, having taught them, and writers for them, both in India and in the United States. So we used her material in confident assurance that this would be her wish.

- - - -

The younger of the authors feels his indebtedness to the elder, for pointing out the road ahead in literacy, and for the inspiration to go on and on down that road. The younger of the authors also wishes to express his appreciation to his colleagues, especially Prof. Roland E. Wolseley and Prof. Robert Root, for their continuing encouragement.

For long hours of typing, we both thank Frances Laubach and Joanne Meadows, and for proofreading, our thanks to David Whieldon and George Prasad.

TABLE OF CONTENTS

PART I

TEACHING ILLITERATES

PART II

WRITING FOR NEW LITERATES

SUPPLEMENT

First Lesson in English, with Instructions
First Lesson in "Engliddish," with Instructions
(See Folded Sheet in Back of Book)

CHARTS, TABLES AND FORMULAS

Part I

TEACHING ILLITERATES

Chapter 1

How Each One Teach One Began

Will "each one teach one?"

The late Professor Edward L. Thorndike of Columbia University, in a prefatory note written to my book, Toward A Literate World, raised the question:

> Can we depend upon tutorial instruction--that is,
> Each One Teach One--to teach the world's illiterates?

This is a fundamental question in all countries where the majority of the people are still illiterate. The answer to that question determines whether the adults of those countries can be made literate in this century.

If it is necessary to have highly trained teachers and specially constructed schools, and to find time when the adults can be brought together between their working hours and sleep, the immense cost and the problem of finding a time are almost insurmountable. If, on the other hand, adult volunteers can be organized to teach their illiterate friends at home at any hour of the day--each one teaching one-- the cost is very small.

So . . . is Each One Teach One possible? Twenty-five years of experimentation all over the world say "YES!"

In the Philippines we discovered that an Each One Teach One campaign is not only possible, but also wonderfully successful and inspiring, if you have the proper lessons and skillful leadership. But ordinary lessons like those we use to teach our children to read are not successful with untrained teachers.

A special type of lesson is necessary which requires a minimum of skill in teaching. The past twenty-five years of work in 96 countries and in 274 languages* have been concentrated chiefly upon the preparation of the kind of lessons that are easy to teach, and upon the other factors necessary to make Each One Teach One successful.

As a result of this quarter of a century of experience, we now have a well-rounded plan for liquidating illiteracy in any country-- swiftly and completely.

* See Appendix D for lists of languages and countries.

The plans for making adults literate--and keeping them literate with adequate, suitable literature--we will explain in some detail in this book.

But first we must explain the reason for starting our teaching in other languages with phonetics--not by learning the ABC's, but by learning the values of the syllables. This is very difficult for teachers of children in English to comprehend, unless they have learned to read some phonetic language like Spanish.

What is nearly impossible in English, because of its chaotic spelling, is child's play in Spanish, or Italian, or Portuguese, or the Malay languages, or any language of Africa, because they have just one sound for each letter. We have an average of six sounds for each vowel in English. The letter "o" has fifteen sounds!

Each One Teach One is possible--except in English. English is different from ALL other languages in this one respect: it has far, far the worst spelling of all the living languages in the world.

You never know for sure how to spell an English word if you never saw it before. Let a foreigner try to read this:

"I should come though a tough cough and hiccough plough through me."

In that sentence are illustrated six ways to pronounce "ough," and the foreigner has to remember them all! If you try to spell that phonetically* it would be something like this:

"I shuud kum tho a tuf kawf and hikup plow throo me."

Or, take these words: "Were you women here or there today?" In that sentence "ere" is pronounced three ways. Let's spell that phonetically so that a foreigner could read it:

"Wer yoo wimun hir or thair tooday?"

If no is pronounced "no," then to should be pronounced like "toe." No other language in the world has one-tenth or one one-hundredth of the spelling troubles that we have in English. It is because of the crazy spelling that educators in England and America have great differences of opinion as to how much, if any, phonetics should be included in the teaching of reading English to children.

---

* Phonetic spelling (linguists use a more precise word, phonemic spelling) is a system in which each letter, or combination of letters, stands for one and only one sound in that language. Casual inspection of the pairs of sentences on this page shows how far English is from being phonetic. In our opinion, the further removed a language is from being phonetic, the "worse" it is spelled. The problems of teaching reading and writing in that language are compounded over and over.

Because of our spelling madness, English teachers are slow to realize what a great advantage it is to learn the phonetics in a perfectly or almost perfectly spelled language. As soon as you learn the sounds of the letters in Spanish, for instance, you can pronounce any new word without help.

Take also, for example, the Malay languages of the Philippines, Indonesia, Singapore and Malaya. They have an average of 16 to 20 letters. Here they are:

> a   always pronounced as in "father"
> e   as in "they"
> i   as in "it" or "unique"
> o   as in "old"
> u   as in "rule"
> b, d, g (as in "go"), h, k, m, n, p, r, s, t, v, w, ng (as in "sing"), and (rarely) f.

THE FIRST LANGUAGE: MARANAW

If a student learns half of these letters in one day, he should be able to learn the entire alphabet in two days--with the right system. We found how fantastically easy that is in Lanao, Mindanao, with the first literacy campaign in the Maranaw language of the Philippines.

Maranaw has sixteen sounds, for which we adopted a perfect alphabet, using one Roman letter for each sound--and only one sound for each letter. Contrast that with English, in which every vowel is overburdened with many different sounds. Here are a few examples:

Ten sounds for "o"	Nine sounds for "a"	Five sounds for "i"	Nine sounds for "e"
women	cat	fish	been
worry	altar	friend	red
come	was	bird	her
rob	ah	child	bee
hold	any	ski	eye
or	able		beau
who	aisle		beauty
sorrow	all		fete
off	are		the
wolf			

There are two sounds in English for "c," two sounds for "ch," three ways of pronouncing "th," three ways of pronouncing "ed," two ways for "wa," seven ways for "ough," two ways for "eight," two ways for "ow," and many more multiple pronunciations.

The examples shown here should prove that English pronunciation can be achieved only by memorizing every word. Nobody in the
whole world knows how to pronounce every word in English correctly
because there are no sure clues to pronouncing new words which are
found almost daily in reading English.

On the other hand, every student learning to read Maranaw can
pronounce <u>every</u> word in his language as soon as he knows the sound
of just sixteen letters. Those he can easily learn in two days.

It is almost impossible to exaggerate this stupendous difference.
Even after it is explained, English-speaking people do not realize
that it means two totally different methods of teaching people to read.
The quickest way to teach people to read English is to teach them the
words through stories. The phonetics may be taught at an early
stage in the lessons, to help the student learn "regular" sounds of
letters. This is done in our <u>Streamlined English</u> lessons, but even
then the student must learn many common words in English by sight.
In studying English, the student never knows how to pronounce many
new words until he has heard his teacher say it several times.

The quickest way to teach people to read the other great languages is to teach the phonetics as quickly as possible so the students
can pronounce every word without the aid of the teacher. When the
phonetics are perfect the student can make more progress in reading
in one day in such a language than he can in English in one month--
thirty times as fast! Yes, I'll stand by that statement.

I had this proven dramatically in Lanao. As a graduate of a
teachers' college, and with graduate work in Teachers' College, New
York, I began with the only method I knew--the story word method.
It was deadeningly slow with illiterates. I then ventured to teach the
phonetics and it was like getting wings! The illiterates soared where
they had before walked like cripples.

I had discovered something exciting. In a fever of zeal (which
has lasted over twenty-five years) I tried first one way, then another,
to teach the phonetics. I borrowed a set of handprinting letters and
made a new chart on wrapping paper every few days, as fast as new
ideas came to me. In a few weeks I found what I wanted: three "key
words" which used all the consonants in the Maranaw language:

ma la ba nga	(a town in Lanao)
ka ra ta sa	(paper
pa ga na da	(to learn)

There are only four vowels in Maranaw:

a (as in English "Ah!")	i (as in "pique")
o (as in "hole")	u (as in "rule")

By mixing the other vowels with the syllables in the three key words, we were able to derive the following words (and many others):

ma ma	a ma	ma la	la ma	a la	la ba	ba nga
(man)	(father)	(big)	(yard)	(God)	(to profit)	(island)

mi mi	a mi	li li	a li	li ma	li o	la ngi
(girl)	(our)	(a name)	(a name)	(hand)	(outside)	(to wait)

mo mo	a mo	lo lo	a lo	ma lo	o lo	bo nga
(chew)	(monkey)	(dull)	(hello)	(pretty)	(head)	(fruit)

bu la	lu nga	lu ngi	lu ma	lu mi	gu lu buk
(wide)	(many)	(allow)	(smooth)	(to flatten)	(to work)

From these words it was possible to make many phrases and sentences, like these:

> **mama laba a mala**   (the man makes a big profit)

> **ama laba a mala**   (father makes a big profit)

(We did not, of course, have the English translation in our book.)

The other two key words, ka ra ta sa, and pa ga na da, were treated in the same manner. In three lessons the illiterates of Lanao could pronounce every word in their language, even words they had never heard. This does not mean that they were good readers, for each new word made them stumble. But we had only the task of training swift reading. After a student had seen a word five or six times he never hesitated over it again. So we acquired speed by using words so often that they were instantly recognized and also by printing many songs, epic and lyric, with which the people were familiar, and which they would sing or repeat as swiftly as we talk.

After three days, the Maranaw student was independent of the teacher in pronouncing every new word. This is so different from the dilemma of American school children, that teachers in America cannot believe it possible. All of us who read English are dependent upon someone else or upon a dictionary to pronounce new words all our lives.

We called this the "key word method." It proved very easy to learn.

But the most important thing was that it proved very easy and very pleasant to teach. There was no difficulty in finding volunteers because people asked for lessons and volunteered to teach them at home. In a few months we had four hundred people teaching others.

We paid twenty directors, and no doubt the others hoped that some day they, too, would be paid. These volunteer teachers needed no long instruction before they were ready to teach. They were drilled for a half hour and could teach almost perfectly. In fact, we spent more time on how to be kind to an adult than on teaching procedure.

Thus began Each One Teach One.

THE GROWTH OF THE CAMPAIGN

A very important event took place in the spring of 1932. The new Governor-General of the Philippines, the late Theodore Roosevelt, Jr., visited Lanao and made a lasting impression upon the Moros and upon our school.

We went down to Iligan to meet him as he came in on the boat. Fine arches had been erected over the entrance to the dock, and the people of Iligan presented him with the "key to the city." He lived up to all their highest expectations for cordiality, making them feel that he was really glad to meet each person who came to shake hands with him. When he was given the key, he made a short, but telling, address.

The following day Colonel Roosevelt came to our school in Dansalan intending to stay only a few minutes, but he stayed half an hour. He showed deep interest and made some very helpful suggestions. He was enthusiastic about the eighteen Societies of Educated Youth that we had organized around Lake Lanao, and listened attentively while some of these young Moros told him that they were meeting every week to answer the question, "How can we help our town, our province, our country, and the world?"

"This is not mere theory," they told him. "We have found thirty needs in our province and we have set our shoulders with all our power to meet these needs. Each of us has charts in his home and has promised to teach as many people as he can. We are distributing seeds around the four parts of Lanao. We are showing people how to keep well. We are encouraging people to send their children to school. Hitherto we have thought the only use of education was to become a clerk or errand boy in a government office; but we have discovered so many ways to be useful to humanity that we are intoxicated with enthusiasm."

Their eyes flashed and their voices had a new ring. These boys were dreaming dreams far beyond the borders of Lanao. They were tingling with eagerness to do something for all the world. One day I had read to them from a book which had just come out: "Two out of three inhabitants of our globe have still to be taught to read and write. The United States is sending hundreds of teachers to the Philippines to make those islands a world model for educational progress, but there are a billion more who need this help."

"Boys," I had burst forth, "you and I are in the biggest under-taking we ever heard of. This book says that two-thirds of the people of the world cannot yet read. Let's start a world campaign! Tell the literacy teachers I'll have my eye on them and very likely some may be called to foreign countries to establish literacy campaigns like ours. Write to the datos (chiefs) and tell them that you believe that a world literacy movement is beginning in Lanao and you are on fire with the idea."

The boys had caught fire! We started at once to see what im-provements we could make in our chart and in our methods of teach-ing. When we finished, there was roaring in my ears the assurance that we were going to arouse the enthusiasm of many leaders in this literacy enterprise, and that it would sweep around the world.

At one of our meetings, called to enable the young men to ex-plain to the datos about our dream of helping the world, Kakai Daga-langit stood up and said, " If we are going to do that for the world, we will first have to change our name. People think that Moros do nothing but murder and steal and spit betel nut. But now we have stopped being foolish and are getting educated. Why, most of us can read already! Please go to Manila and ask Governor-General Roose-velt to change our names. Tell him to call us 'Islam,' for that means we are trying to do the will of God."

When we had the primer easy to read and easy to teach, hun-dreds and then thousands of people came to ask for lessons. We had a large abandoned military building crowded with students and

Frank Laubach

From thirty years ago: Each One Teach One in Lanao market place.

teachers all day long. We bought a printing press and started a newspaper called Lanao Progress. It contained articles about health, agriculture, home life. It contained a simple version of the most important laws. It contained epic lyric poems which the Moro people
themselves composed. It contained stories that were found both in
the Koran and the Bible. It contained world information, for the
Moros were fast becoming interested in the world.

We prepared signs made of the flat sides of empty gasoline cans.
On them was only this figure - 100% - which meant that everybody
in the houses on which the signs were tacked had learned to read.
We had Centers in every market where one of our teachers spent
the whole day teaching those who could not read and training those
who wanted to teach, and selling our newspaper and our booklets.
The entire province was caught in a wave of literacy madness. Wom-
en who were confined to their homes taught one another.

Since this was my first experience with mass hysteria, I was
wholly unprepared to keep a record of the people who were learning
to read. We just did not know. We had a large poster with a picture of a thermometer on it and each week we recorded how many
illiterates our volunteer teachers told us they had taught. The number went up 300, 500, or 1,000 a week until our thermometer showed
70,000 people, which was 70 per cent of the entire population.

The news of this astonishing phenomenon spread all over the
Philippine Islands. People came down to see what had happened. The
Moros had a reputation for being a bloody tribe of outlaws and all
the Philippines were caught between hope and incredulousness as
they heard what was going on.

Dr. Bewley, The Director General of Education for the Philippines,
gave me a letter of introduction and I went all over the Islands preparing similar lessons in 20 languages. The lessons were all easy
to make because they are all Malay languages, with only 17 to 20 letters. Every syllable ended with a vowel.

This so-called Philippine method became rather famous in Asia,
Africa, and Latin America. People wrote letters to me, or to the
Minister of Education, or to the Governor General, asking how we
were doing it. I was eager to explore other languages of the world
to discover whether they could be taught easily by the phonetic method, or whether they were hopelessly irregular in their spelling,
as English is. We made a big map of the world, and as letters came
from other countries to Lanao (which was in the center of our map)
we put a red silk thread from that country to Lanao, until we had a
big wheel with 500 silk threads converging upon Lanao. The Moros
clucked their tongues in delight and said, "Just see how important
we are getting in the world!"

The Moros' enthusiasm no doubt increased my own, and my
enthusiasm no doubt fanned theirs.

THE FIRST LITERACY TRIP

When in 1935 it was time for us to return on furlough to the United States, Mrs. Laubach and I went by way of Asia in response to a
dozen invitations from missionaries to help them with their literacy
problems. When we took the boat several thousand Moros came down
thirty miles to the seacoast to bid us farewell. They made speeches
till 10 p.m., two hours after the boat was scheduled to leave. Then
they asked the highest Mohammedan Priest to pray for us. They
kissed my hand and said, "We will pray for you in every Mosque in
Lanao." *

At Singapore we made lessons in Malay and found them just as
easy to make as they had been in the Philippines. They have been
used ever since. Our first experiment in India was at Nagpur, where
I attempted to make lessons in the Marathi language.

I took our charts over to Mahatma Gandhi, and I still remember
the interest and the doubt which he expressed. He said, "I will watch
you with great interest, but I doubt whether 'each one will teach one'
in India as they did in your country."

The next year, to my great delight, Mr. Gandhi published in his
newspaper, Harijan, that he was converted on the matter of literacy
--that, if "each one would teach one" in India, the whole country
could learn in five years. They could too. At that time only 8 per
cent of the people in India could read. If each one would teach one
a year, the next year 16 per cent would be literate, the third year
32 per cent, the fourth year 64 per cent, the fifth year 128 per cent--
and that would make up for the rising population.

I tried lessons also in Hindi, with the Mennonite Mission.   I
knew that these Indian languages were much harder than the Malay
languages to teach phonetically just because they had so many letters.
I knew that another approach would be necessary, but I also knew
that it could be done.

Our next stop was in Egypt. We came while they were holding
a conference of Near East missionaries. It happened that Miss Con-
stance Padwick had edited and printed some of the letters which I
had written to my father from Lanao, so all of the missionaries
treated me like an old friend. **

We attempted lessons in Arabic. I found that the difficulties
were even greater than those in the languages of India, but I still
felt confident that with enough effort, we could make lessons that
were easy to teach and to learn. I went to Jerusalem and tried Arabic again and again, and to Beirut where we tried it for the third

* My son Bob, co-author of this text, had just finished Lanao High School
   and went with us on this, his first literacy tour.
** These letters have since been published under the titles Letters of a
   Modern Mystic and Learning the Vocabulary of God.   See Appendix A.

time. Then we went to Turkey and, to my great delight, found that
the Turks had thrown out the Arabic alphabet and had adopted a beautifully phonetic Romanized alphabet. We made lessons like those in
Lanao in the Turkish language and had them mimeographed, but the
missionaries were not able to contact the Turkish government so our
experiment in Turkey never had a fair chance.

When I reached New York City, several business men whom I
had known caught the excitement that we had felt in Lanao and organized the World Literacy Committee (now the Committee on World
Literacy and Christian Literature, a functioning committee of the
National Council of the Churches of Christ of the U. S. A.). That
committee loyally supported our literacy experiments so that it was
possible for us to return to the Far East, India, and Africa every
year until the war spread around the world in 1941.

We were working on a very small budget, being entertained by
missionaries, and without money to pay for more than the experimental editions of lessons we made. In India we experimented in twenty
languages, gradually getting better and better, though they never
were as good as they needed to be in order for "each one to teach one."

During the war I traveled for the committee throughout South
America, and in recent years the committee has sent a number of
literacy teams into Africa and Asia.

THE CONSTANT SEARCH FOR THE BEST

One thing which I began in Lanao was to make a trial, learn by
that experience, try again the next day or the next week, and so "keep
on without hurry, without rest, lifting better up to best." In Lanao I
could do it because I was master of my own time and of my own printing press, but in other countries I could keep on experimenting only
by moving from one language area to another, while the missionaries
tested what we had made. This was my primary business for the first
fifteen years of my literacy experience.

I was in quest of something which I knew could be done as well
in other countries as it had been done in the Philippines, and I knew
that the most important thing I could do for the world of illiterates
was to discover that something. Each One Teach One is a possibility
only if the lessons are easy, swift, pleasant to learn, and easy for
any untrained person to teach.

So we have experimented in the last thirty years with 274 languages. I do not think any experiment was lost. In the last ten years
we have developed a new a pattern which fits the phonetic languages
of the world--superbly easy to teach and easy to learn.

Chapter 2

The Modern Lessons—Stage I

We are still making changes and additions to our method, but they are not drastic changes. The most important feature introduced in the past ten years is the association of the shape of the letter with an object, the name of which begins with that letter. For example, to teach the letter "k" we might use the word "kick" and show a man kicking one foot high in the air, or the letter "s" can be associated with the word "snake."

The method is as old as the Egyptians. Their hieroglyphics are pictures which first represented objects and then came to represent syllables. (The Chinese characters do not represent sounds at all, but represent ideas.) The first time I saw this association of shape and letters outside of China was in Bombay Presidency, India, where the mayor of Poona had a motion picture teaching the Hindi letters by associating them with a picture that looked like those letters. You could teach them all to a bright student in a half hour.

I suppose the reason they did not adopt this method earlier was because it requires great effort to discover common objects which look like the letters, and because it requires a great deal of skill on the part of the artist to draw the pictures. The lessons which have been adopted by the Ministry of Education of India in the Hindi language and which are now used in teaching illiterates in the Village Development projects are a perfect illustration of this latest method.

For several years the literacy committee enjoyed the talents of a gifted artist, Phil Gray, whose skill contributed immeasurably to the success of the recent charts.

First Chart In Hindi

पाठ १

	श्रा	श्राम श्रा ।	श्रा	श्रा
			त्र	त्र
	ब	बनिया ब	बा	बा
			ब	ब
	त	ताला ता	ता	ता
			त	त
	ज	जामुन जा	जा	जा
			ज	ज
	क	कान का	का	का
			क	क
	म	मकान म	मा	मा
			म	म

Illustrations by Phil Gray

First Reading Lesson In Hindi

पाठ १

आम है।
बनिया है।
ताला है।
जामुन है।
कान है।
मकान है।

बनिया ताला लाता है।
बाबा ताला लाता है।
काका ताला लाता है।
मामा ताला लाता है।

बनिया आम लाता है।
बाबा आम लाता है।
काका आम लाता है।
मामा आम लाता है।

बनिया जामुन लाता है।
बाबा जामुन लाता है।
काका जामुन लाता है।
मामा जामुन लाता है।

बनिये का कान है।
बाबा का कान है।
काका का कान है।
मामा का कान है।

बनिये का मकान है।
बाबा का मकान है।
काका का मकान है।
मामा का मकान है।

(For translation see page 15.)

FIRST LESSON IN HINDI

On the preceding two pages is printed the first Hindi lesson, which
is similar in principle and appearance to the other lessons appearing
in this book and to the latest version of primers in many languages.

All the lessons in the primer are similar to the first lesson
presented as a sample here. Thus if a teacher knows how to teach
the first lesson perfectly, he can teach all the other lessons as well.
We always try to print each lesson complete on facing pages of the
primer. The left page of each lesson is the picture chart. There are
four columns down the page. The first vertical column contains the
pictures, the second shows how the picture and the letter look alike,
the third has the name of the pictured object, and below it the first
letter of that name. The fourth column contains a review of the letter for practice.

Every letter is shown at least five times. We have adopted the
principle that William James laid down years ago, that to know a
thing one must hear or see it at least five times. We always try to
show each new letter and word at least five times in each lesson.

Let us look at the Hindi lesson closely.

On the left page is the chart, with pictures associating the beginning of the word with the object for which it stands. For example,
the first picture is of an am (mango). To the right of that is a picture
with the first part of the word am (in Hindi script) associated with
the shape of the object am. Then comes a square with the word am,
and under it a, the beginning of the word am. In the square at the
far right are repeated the syllable a and its component syllable uh.

The other words are bunia (merchant or shopkeeper), tala (padlock), jamun (an Indian fruit with no exact English equivalent; we'll
call it a cherry), kan (ear), and mukan (house).

The object of the chart is primarily to teach the syllables. In
this chart each syllable has two variations: -a (as in "hot") and -uh
(as in "hut"). The student, by the time he has read the first reading
lesson, also has learned by repetition the words. These, then, are
what the student learns from the first chart:

Words	Syllables	
am	a	uh
bunia	ba	buh
tala	ta	tuh
jamun	ja	juh
kan	ka	kuh
mukan	ma	muh

The method of teaching the chart to the illiterate will become clear after studying carefully the method of teaching the <u>Engliddish</u> lesson which follows shortly, and after reading the psychology of the adult in a later chapter.

On the right page of each lesson in the primer is a story. The story should contain not more than four new words; all the other words were on the left-hand page. There is much more care taken in story building than appears at first glance. It must be very, <u>very</u>, VERY easy, so that the illiterate will feel no sense of strain. We would make the stories even easier if we knew any possible way to do so. Every word which appears on this story page is employed at least five times as quickly as we can use it.

Here is a translation of the story, so that you may understand the pattern which it follows. The groups of sentences are arranged here just as they appear on the page of Hindi.

This is a mango
This is a shop keeper
This is a padlock
This is a cherry
This is an ear
This is a house

The shop keeper brings a padlock
Grandfather brings a padlock
Father's brother brings a padlock
Mother's brother brings a padlock

The shop keeper brings a mango
Grandfather brings a mango
Father's brother brings a mango
Mother's brother brings a mango

The shop keeper brings a cherry
Grandfather brings a cherry
Father's brother brings a cherry
Mother's brother brings a cherry

This is the shop keeper's ear
This is grandfather's ear
This is father's brother's ear
This is mother's brother's ear

This is the shop keeper's house
This is grandfather's house
This is father's brother's house
This is mother's brother's house

(In Hindi there is a word for "father's brother" and another for "mother's brother," a fine distinction which our English word "uncle" doesn't make.)

Let us see why we have made this lesson as we have. It grew out of twenty-five years of constant creative experimentation. We have the pictures and the words and letters on the left side facing the story on the right side, so that the student can find the word he wants with little or no help.

In the story we have four people doing identically the same thing. The teacher must tell him "the shop keeper has a lock," but after that the student can read the next three sentences. Thus the teacher needs to help the student with only one-fourth of the reading matter on each page. The student reads the other three-fourths without the aid of the teacher. By the time the student has read this page he has seen every word at least five times and is familiar with it. Little or no drill is needed to fix this word permanently in his mind.

The student seems to have covered a very large amount of material--he has read two whole pages--and yet he has had to learn only ten words because each word is repeated five or more times. It is not necessary to have four characters doing identically the same thing, although it is the best device we have found to carry a real story.

People who do not teach illiterates themselves sometimes criticize our stories for not being interesting enough. They ask why we do not have a plot. The answer is this: the one great objective of the student is to learn to read as quickly as he can. If he can read the page without help, he gets a tremendous thrill and he does not need any exciting story to add to that thrill. If, on the other hand, he finds the page difficult, his difficulty will destroy all sense of excitement. What a foolish thing it would be for our textbook writers for children to attempt to write an exciting story with a plot in the first lesson, instead of something as simple as this: "I have a cat. Sister has a cat. Brother has a cat."

Have you ever tried to read a joke in a foreign language which you knew imperfectly, as I have often done? Unless you understand exactly what the point of the joke is, you do not laugh; you feel cheated. The same thing is true of a story which is too difficult for you in a foreign language. You get no thrill when you find a thing difficult to read or when you do not understand what you are reading.

Therefore, principle number one, two and three, in making these lessons can be simply stated: Make it easy. Make it easy. Make it easy. Interest must never be attempted at the expense of simplicity. That is the voice of experience.

At what age are adults too old to learn? The answer is "not so long as they are mentally alert and can see." We have personally seen adults in every decade up to extreme old age learn. One lady in Guatemala claimed she was 102 years old. Her eyes were still good and she learned with ease.

Here is a simple test for the adult's vision: place several dots close together on a page of white paper like this:

:   :.   :   :.

Ask the student to count each cluster. If there is some doubt, try other combinations of dots, but not over eight in a cluster.

If the student can tell you each time how many dots there are, his eyes are keen enough to see the big charts. He should also be able to read the smaller letters in his own books. The letters in the books should be large, much larger than the type on this page. Even in large type, however, some parts of the letters may be tiny as dots.

YOU'RE ILLITERATE--NOW LEARN "ENGLIDDISH"

It is difficult for you to appreciate how the lessons work unless you first play the role of an illiterate yourself. Among the lessons which we have made are two using Hebrew letters--one in Yiddish, which is spoken mainly in Europe and in the United States, and the other in Hebrew, which was prepared for Israel.

While make these lessons we conceived the idea of preparing a set of lessons with Hebrew letters and English words--"Engliddish." We urge you to learn to read the first lesson in "Engliddish" because it will help you, better than any long discourse we could write, to understand the feelings and the problems of the illiterates as they begin their first literacy lesson.

Instructions For Teaching "Engliddish"

The "Engliddish" first chart and reading lesson appear on the following two pages. And it is reprinted on a large folded sheet in the back of this book, along with instructions for its use. *

Study this sheet carefully. You should be able to learn to read "Engliddish" by yourself. When you have learned to read it, try to teach another person--putting Each One Teach One into practice!

You may wonder why we bother with this chart in an alphabet which is not used to write English. There are two good answers:

1. The "Engliddish" chart is arranged in an almost identical way to most of the lessons listed in Appendix D.
   When you can teach this chart well, you can teach any
   of the other lessons, providing, of course, you can
   speak at least a few phrases in the language you teach.

2. Your "student" speaks the language in which you are
   "teaching" him to read. This conforms to the cardinal
   rule in adult literacy: <u>Always teach a person to read
   the language which he speaks</u>. (Many failures have resulted from trying to teach illiterates to read a language which they know imperfectly as a "second tongue.")

Instructions For Teaching English

On the reverse side of the supplementary sheet is the first chart and reading lesson in English. Practice teaching this also, for it is the first of the Reading Readiness lessons which precede <u>Streamlined English</u>, the literacy book used as a basis for classroom and televi-sion teaching of English-speaking illiterates. **

* For extra copies of this sheet (20¢ each), write Box 131, Syracuse 10, N.Y.
** For complete Reading Readiness charts, or for a movie about teaching by TV, write Foundation for World Literacy, Hickman Bldg., Memphis, Tenn.

First Reading Lesson In"Engliddish"

דהים יז אַנ יר

דהים יז אַ גרל

דהים יז אַ דאָג

דהים יז אַ נאָוז

דהים יז אַ מאָוטה

דהים יז אַ ליפ

דהים יז דהאַ גרלז יר

דהים יז דהאַ גרלז נאָוז

דהים יז דהאַ גרלז מאָוטה

דהים יז דהאַ גרלז ליפ

דהים יז דהאַ דאָגז יר

דהים יז דהאַ דאָגז נאָוז

דהים יז דהאַ דאָגז מאָוטה

דהים יז דהאַ דאָגז ליפ

First Chart In "Engliddish"

BRIEF BUT PRECISE TRAINING IS ESSENTIAL

When you have practiced teaching Engliddish--and have actually taught several persons to read it--you would be able to teach almost any other chart. You would need to know, of course, the language well enough to speak with the student. But you would already have a good grasp of the teaching method.

Experience shows that we can train anybody to teach the first lesson so that he is letter perfect at doing so in about an hour. We teach it in front of our class of volunteers and then let each one try while the rest of us watch to see whether he will deviate at all from the method we use. By the time that a class of a dozen or more volunteer teachers have tried to teach this first lesson in any language they all know it perfectly. After they have learned the first lesson they can teach any lesson in the book by using the same procedure and almost the same words because we have deliberately made every lesson as nearly alike as we can, except for the change in the vocabulary.

With these lessons a literate person can begin to teach after an hour's instruction. We have found that volunteer teachers love to teach when they find how easy it is and how swiftly their students progress. We have also found that illiterates are thrilled at these lessons when they are properly taught because they learn so easily and they learn so much in such a short time.

Of course, no lesson can be taught successfully if the teacher does not have the right attitude toward the student. In Chapter 4 we will go into details of the psychology of teaching adult illiterates. The right psychology is as important as the right lessons.

A LESSON IN THE ROMAN ALPHABET--SPANISH

By far the largest number of languages in which the Each One Teach One charts have been prepared are in the Roman alphabet. Illustrated on page 22 is the first chart of a Spanish primer.

We generally first teach the vowel "a" (pronounced in Spanish "ah"), because in many languages that is the most frequently used vowel. Here is how the first Spanish chart should be taught (in Spanish, of course, to a Spanish-speaking illiterate):

(Put your pencil on the first picture.) This man is saying ah.

(Point to the shaded picture next to it.) Here he is again, saying ah.
    See his open mouth and big chin. Say ah. (Wait for student's
    reply).

(Point to letter a.) Here is ah again. See how it looks like the open mouth and big chin. Say ah. (In each case, wait for student's reply).

(Point to a in third column.) Here it is again. Say it.

(Point to each a in fourth column.) What is this? What is this?

(Next picture down.) Here is a papá and his little boy.

(Picture to right.) Here is papá again. See his head and body. Say papá.

(Point to word.) Here is the word papá. Say it.

(Cover second part of papá with a finger, but don't obstruct student's view!) Papá begins with pa. This is pa. Say it.

(Point to pa below the word.) What is this?

(Point to each pa in third and fourth column.) What is this? This? This?

(Point back at each a in the fourth column above.) What is this? This?

(Point to next picture.) This is a mamá and her baby.

(Point to shaded picture.) Here is mamá again. Mamá begins with ma.

(Then point to word, tell the word, cover second part as before, point to each ma to be seen. Review the pa and the a by going back up the fourth column, asking for student's reply as before.)

(Point to next picture.) This is a dama (lady). See the feather in her hat. (Point to shaded picture, and proceed as before. Always review former syllables up the right column.)

(Next picture.) This is a vaca. This vaca has long horns. (Proceed to the shaded picture, the word, the syllables, and review up the fourth column.)

After teaching the first chart, it is well to give the student some "flash cards" with the syllables on them. The teacher and student can play a game: the teacher holds up each card and the student tries to name it. If he names it correctly he puts it in his pile.. They play the game until the student can "capture" all the cards every time. The words in the first chart may also be put on flash cards. Some primers have detachable flash cards printed in the center of the book. When the student knows the syllable and the words well he is ready for the reading lesson, usually taught also in the first class session.

(Point to papá on the chart.) What is this? (Point to papá in the reading lesson.) Here is papá again. Say it.

First Chart In Spanish

Lección 1

		a	a	a a
		papá pa	pa	pa pa
		mamá ma	ma	ma ma
		dama da	da	da da
		vaca va	va	va va

First Reading Lesson In Spanish

a   papá   mamá   dama   vaca

papá llama a la vaca
mamá llama a la vaca
la dama llama a la vaca

papá va a la vaca
mamá va a la vaca
la dama va a la vaca

papá da agua a la vaca
mamá da agua a la vaca
la dama da agua a la vaca

papá ama a mamá
mamá ama a papá
la dama ama a papá

papá va a mamá
mamá va a papá
la dama va a papá

(Point to <u>vaca</u> on the chart.) What is this? (Point to <u>la vaca</u> in reading lesson.) Here is <u>la vaca</u> again. Say it.

(Point under each word as you read.) This says "<u>papá</u> calls the cow." Now you read it. (Point under each word as student reads.)

(Point to <u>mamá</u> on chart.) Who is this? (Point to <u>mamá</u> in reading lesson.) This says "<u>mamá</u> calls the cow." Read it. (Wait for student to read it. Then tell student: Read it again faster.)

(Point to <u>dama</u> on chart.) This is <u>la dama</u>. (Point to <u>la dama</u> in reading lesson.) Here is <u>la dama</u> again. What is she doing? (Help student read the sentence if necessary.)

(Point to <u>papá</u> in second group of sentences.) Who is this? This says "<u>papá</u> goes to the cow." Read it.

(Proceed in similar fashion with <u>mamá</u> and <u>la dama.</u>)

(Point to <u>la vaca</u> in third group.) What is this? This says "<u>papá</u> gives water to the cow." (Proceed in similar fashion with other two sentences in the group.)

(Point to <u>mamá</u> in next sentence.) Who is this? This says "<u>mamá</u> gives water to the cow." Read it after me.

(Point to <u>la dama</u> in next sentence.) Who is this? Now read all of this. (Pointing with pencil under words as student reads, have him repeat it faster the second time.)

(In the fourth group, point to each word of first sentence as you say "<u>papá</u> likes <u>mamá.</u>") What does this say? (Point to each word as student reads.)

(Proceed in similar fashion with the other sentences in the group.)

(In the last group, point to each word of first sentence as you say "<u>papá</u> goes to <u>mamá.</u>") What does it say? (Point to each word as student reads.)

(In the next sentence point to each word as you say "<u>mamá</u> goes to <u>papá.</u>") What does this say? (Point to each word as student reads.)

(Proceed in similar fashion in the last sentence.)

(Review entire page, including the words at the top.)

THE FIRST LESSON IN ARABIC

Still another type of alphabet is illustrated on page 27 by the first chart in Arabic, prepared for the campaigns in Egypt. The Arabic-speaking person, who has studied how to teach the other lessons in

this chapter, will be able to teach this chart in a similar manner. So
it will not be necessary to include here complete teaching instructions.

The four words in the chart are these:

"arnap" (rabbit)   "bab" (door)
"nar"   (fire)   "taj" (crown)

In each frame at the left the word appears below the letter (a slight
variation from the usual procedure). The letters in Arabic have different forms, depending upon whether they occur alone, or at the beginning, middle or end of a word. Thus you see a full and an abbre-
viated form of the initial letter of each word in the frame, printed
above the word.

The translation of the story on page 26 is below.

This is a rabbit
This is a door
This is a crown
This is a fire

A rabbit in a house
A crown in a house
A door in a house
A fire in a house

This is a rabbit in a house
This is a crown in a house
This is a door in a house
This is a fire in a house

THE PRIMERS ARE STAGE I

How many lessons there are in a primer depends upon the length
of the alphabet. As a rule five or six syllables of the alphabet are
taught each day. In simple languages like the Polynesian languages
between Hawaii and New Zealand, there are only twelve letters. These
can be taught in one or two days. All of the Malay languages are almost as easy to teach. The languages of India require about fifteen
lessons. All of the languages using the Arabic alphabet require about
fifteen lessons. Spanish, Portuguese and Italian and many African
languages require about ten lessons. French requires eighteen. As
soon as the phonetics are well-known, the primer ends. The student
is given a certificate or diploma, indicating that he is finished with
the primer and is ready for the other readers in the series.

First Reading Lesson In Arabic

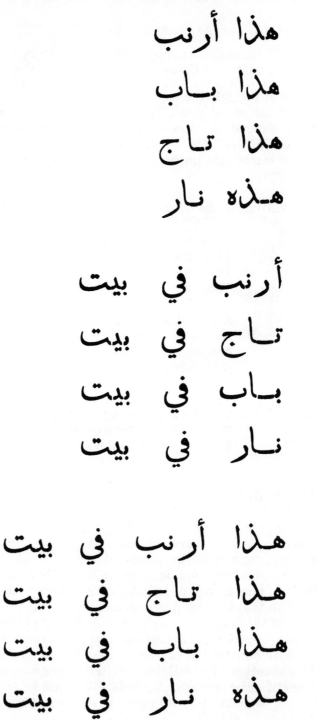

هذا أرنب

هذا بـاب

هذا تـاج

هـذه نـار

أرنب في بيت

تـاج في بيت

بـاب في بيت

نـار في بيت

هـذا أرنب في بيت

هـذا تـاج في بيت

هـذا بـاب في بيت

هـذه نـار في بيت

First Chart In Arabic

Streamlined English is a textbook which teaches the English phonetics in 30 lessons. Even after the student knows this book he will have trouble with many irregular English words. But in 95 per cent of the languages of the world the student can read every word without help from a teacher or a pronouncing dictionary. (For fascinating books on languages and alphabets, see Appendix A.)

Throughout this book we shall use the term Stage I to indicate the primers. A complete literacy and literature program must include one or two well-prepared graded readers, which we call Stage II (like the one described in Chapter 3) and an abundance of materials in Stage III and Stage IV (as described in "Writing For New Literates" --the second part of this book).

Robert Laubach

First to learn to read the Medlpa language was this New Guinea chief.

Chapter 3
Graded Readers—Stage II

How much graded material do illiterate adults need before they can read the ordinary newspapers and books? This cannot be answered in one sentence, because the difference between Asia and Africa, for example, is enormous. In Asia there are ancient written languages. The newspapers and books employ a written classical vocabulary in which many of the words are not used by the illiterate people. In these languages it is necessary to build up a new body of literature. In many cases the new literate adult will read nothing except the literature which we provide, all the rest of his life. Only the brighter adults will ever attain the level of the standard literature which the college graduate can read. In some respects this is an advantage because all the new literature provided for the newly literate adults can be carefully prepared with a view to meeting his greatest needs.

In Africa and Latin America the tribal languages of the Africans or of the American Indians employ the vocabulary known to all the literates. Once they know how to pronounce their syllables they can pronounce and understand every word that is printed. However, there is not much reading matter of any kind. So it is necessary to produce a larger quantity of reading matter on the Stage III level.

Even earlier, when the student has finished Stage I (the Primer), he needs a great deal of practice in reading. The graded readers of Stage II supply that, and at the same time give the reader vital material that meets his needs. There need not be many graded readers in each language. Once written and thoroughly tested, the Stage II graded readers may be as standardized as the primer in Stage I.

Two types of graded readers have been prepared to follow our primer:

1. Religious Materials

   Missions want religious material. For them we prepared a graded Story of Jesus based upon the Gospel accounts. This has been translated into about forty languages and printed in more than half of them.

2. Socio-economic Materials

Governments desire practical information that helps students
to increase the production of their land, to practice measures
of hygiene and sanitation, and to live a cleaner, healthier,
more prosperous life. For these countries there was prepared
a series of books which agricultural and health experts helped
to design.

The contents of these two courses, one for missions and one for
governments, follow the same pattern. The sentences are short; the
words are all familiar to the illiterate. Five to ten new words are
used in each lesson; each new word is repeated at least five times,
as soon as possible after being introduced, so that the student will
become familiar with it.

There are generally 90 lessons in the graded series of Stage II,
following the primer. The primer has the same principle in regard
to vocabulary--ten new words a day, and each word used five times.
By the time the student finishes the graded series of approximately
100 lessons he has a sight vocabulary of about 1,000 words, and also
the ability to pronounce every new word slowly.

The primer, as previously noted, may be taught either of two
ways: a teacher may have a class, or a volunteer may teach by the
tutorial system--Each One Teach One. If volunteers are organized
in a community, the tutorial method brings far larger and more sat-
isfying results. However, it must be supervised by someone trained
in organizing Each One Teach One campaigns.

We have found that the graded material after the primer may be
taught in classes although the tutorial method is also good for the
graded series.

ANAND, THE WISE MAN

The graded series prepared for the government of India Community Projects Administration is a good sample of the type of reading matter governments desire. The best available experts in agriculture and health were consulted. They were asked this question:
"What are you trying to teach the village people? What do you believe
they need to know most? You tell us in your vocabulary, and we will
translate it into their vocabulary." They gave us about 90 subjects
which they considered important.

These subjects were written in story form--the story of Anand
(or Akbar in Afghanistan, or U Sein in Burma, or Salah in Egypt,
etc.) and his wife Sevati. In each chapter there is some vital information, accurately and simply told. As the student reads the story
he identifies himself with Anand, who has many similar problems.

The information that helped Anand and Sevati will help the student.
By the time he has read 90 chapters, the student, like Anand, will
become wise indeed. The following are some of the chapter headings:

> Anand reads about about balanced diet
> Anand reads what vegetables to eat
> What a pregnant woman should eat
> Anand reads about itch
> Anand reads that flies carry dysentery
> Anand reads how to protect baby from flies
> Anand puts filth in a long narrow trench
> Anand makes a latrine
> Anand learns how to grow better crops
> Anand gets seeds from the government
> Anand buys an iron plough
> Anand learns how to have bigger oxen
> Anand learns how to sterilize his bulls
> Anand learns how to make a garden
> Anand makes a good garden
> Anand plants fruit trees
> Anand plants trees for fire-wood
> Anand reads that rain washes away his rupees
> The value of Mung Type I
> Anand reads how to make sore eyes well
> Importance of vaccination
> Anand learns to boil drinking water
> A beggar brought cholera to the well
> Anand reads about a safe well
> Anand teaches his wife to read
> Anand reads about malaria
> Anand reads how to kill mosquitoes
> Anand learns what to feed a baby
> Anand learns how to raise better chickens
> Anand learns to feed chickens vitamins
> Anand's neighbor has T. B.
> Anand's wife learns how to make potato chapati
> Sevati reads how to make tomato chatni
> Anand reads about leprosy
> Sevati's daughter has a new baby
> Anand gets rid of rats
> Anand reads about his government
> Anand learns about typhoid
> Anand learns about nitrogen
> Anand protects his paddy crops from Gundhi bugs
> Anand learns about Community Projects
> Mohan learns how to make soap in his home

Anand learns about locusts. . . and neighbors
Serindar builds a kitchen
Anand makes the primary school better
Anand digs a well
A woman is a helper
Improved seeds get better crops
Agriculture is the best work
Parents talk
A new hand pump
Building floors
Building the walls and the roof
The bad child
A tree is known by its fruit (grafting)
Good medicine

Here's the first chapter in the Anand Reader. You will notice that it uses ten new words, not found in the primer. Each word is employed five times. It is extremely difficult to construct such a lesson at the outset--like trying to walk with your legs tied, because you have no vocabulary to use from previous lessons.

Chapter 1

Anand Learned to Read

Anand learned to read.
    He learned to read.
Anand learned to read books.
    He learned to read books.

Anand learned to read good books.
    He learned to read good books.
Anand learned to read.

Anand was a good man.
    He was a good man.
Anand said to his wife
    I have learned to read.

Anand said to his wife
    I have learned to read good books.
    He said to his wife
    I have learned to read good books.

Cover
Illustration

Anand,
The Wise
Man

Phil Gray

Anand read to his wife.
  He read to his wife.
Anand read good books to his wife.
  He read good books to his wife.

Anand said to his wife
  These are good things in this book.
  He said to his wife
  These are good things in this book.

Anand said to his wife
  We will do these good things.
  He said to his wife
  We will do these good things.

Anand said to his wife
  We will do the good things in this book.
  He said to his wife
  We will do the good things in this book.

New Words
(Words Not Found in the Hindi Primer)

Anand	learned	read	books	good
said	have	these	things	wife

The English version of the complete <u>Anand, the Wise Man</u> has been mimeographed and is available to aid in the preparation of a similar graded reader in other languages. (See Appendix A.)

A graded reader in English, based on the 850 words of <u>Streamlined English,</u> is titled, <u>Making Everybody's World Safe.</u> It is particularly suited to people well educated in another language who are learning English.

The importance to the success of a literacy program of a good Stage II graded reader cannot be exaggerated. Stage I, as has been stressed, may be taught most successfully in an Each One Teach One, or in a small class situation. This should continue into Stage II reading, during which the student may gradually be placed more and more on his own in reading. Thus, when he is ready for Stage III materials, he will be almost completely an independent reader, with his reading skill well developed, and his reading habit well formed.

The reader--now truly a "new literate"--will be eager for the many varieties of subject matter offered in Stage III, and later, in Stage IV. The preparation of these materials will be discussed in Part II of this book.

Robert Laubach

Students of Marathi Primer, with letters on blackboard, Poona, India.

Chapter 4
How to Treat the Adult Illiterate

The untrained volunteer teacher who uses the lessons described in this book will as a rule get the best results if he confines himself to a class of from one to four pupils. (Do not mix adults and children!) Even if he has several pupils it is well to let one do all the reciting while the others are silent observers. This is called "tutoring." The tutor should sit as low as his pupils, not stand over him. The voice of the tutor should be as low as his pupil's, clear and just loud enough to be heard distinctly. The teacher must save his words, not saying one needless sentence.

Teachers trained in normal schools can handle larger classes; but they will do well to experiment with the plan of teaching one bright student while the class observes, and asking this student to teach another what he has just learned. Nothing more quickly lifts an adult out of his sense of inferiority than this proof of confidence. A trained teacher can have a roomful of adults all teaching one another.

The teacher of children confronts a wholly new situation if he tries to teach adults. He must reverse many of the practices to which he has long been accustomed. He must treat his adult student not like a child or an inferior, but as politely as he would treat a high official.

The slightest suggestion that the teacher feels superior will ruin the teaching, for the illiterate adult is extremely sensitive. He suffers from a sense of inferiority. Even when he boasts and swaggers, he is revealing an "inferiority complex"--which means that he tries by bombast to hide from himself and others his real feeling of insignificance.

It is exceedingly easy to discourage the illiterate. If we say "no" to him twice, he will probably refuse to recite the third time. For this reason the word "no" is crossed out of our vocabulary when teaching adults. We say "yes" when we mean "no." Unless his mistake is rather serious we ignore it. When it is necessary to correct him we do so in an indirect way. For example, if he should mispronounce "hat," calling it "hate," we could point to a hat and say, "Yes, what a pretty hat you have!" Give him a compliment instead of a correction!

Treat the student like a king! If you heard a king mispronounce English or any other language you would never say, "Your Majesty, you didn't pronounce that word correctly."

Many a teacher stands over his class with ear cocked to catch the first small error and pounce on the pupil like a hawk swoops down on a chicken with beak and claws. The class becomes a battle between teacher and pupils, who develop into implacable enemies; the recitation comes to resemble running a gauntlet more than cooperation for a common good. The three most pitiless "hawks" I ever met in my life were professors in a state teachers' college! I tremble at the memory of them yet, after forty years. Many children become poor students because such teaching frightens both memory and reason out of them; they are scared stupid.

The unhappy children have to remain in school even when they are suffering torture; for fear holds them. But if the illiterate adult is made unhappy for one minute he will get up and leave your class, and denounce literacy to everybody he meets. He can be kept studying only if he is happy and increasingly enthusiastic about his rapid progress. What everybody in this world loves most is somebody who will discover an unsuspected diamond in him. The illiterate, paralyzed with despair, if you tell him how bright he really is, tingles from head to foot. I have seen tears fill many eyes, tears of a new hope and love.

LOVE YOUR STUDENT

Never teach a man if you do not like him. The illiterate cannot read books but he does read human nature, and he knows in a second whether your smile reveals real brotherly interest. You must learn to love people, not for what they are now, but for what you know you can help them to become. Personally I try always to pray for my student, conjuring up the finest dream I can imagine for him, wondering what God would make out of this man if he had a perfect chance. "God," I keep saying silently, "help me to give this student the greatest hour of his life, and the beginning of all Thou dost hope for him."

Whether telepathy or some gentle smile on one's lips reaches the student I do not know, but whatever the cause, he responds with a new light in his eyes and a new ring of confidence in his voice. His shoulders go back, he laughs with delight at this, the profoundest stirring of his soul since he was born. To have felt this new awakening in hundreds of illiterates sitting by my side, has, I testify, been my greatest source of happiness. I do not recommend the teaching of illiterates primarily as the duty of educated people, but as the source of one of life's keenest joys.

One of the attractive aspects of this type of volunteer literacy

campaign is the joyous experience people derive from teaching as
well as from learning. The more people we persuade to help one another without pay, the nearer we approach a really blessed human
society. It is down this road of mutual aid and love that the hope of
the world lies. We cannot make the world over merely by lecturing
or preaching; we help people to engage in projects of loving helpful-
ness like Each One Teach One, or in cooperative societies, and they
learn love in action. This is one of the basic principles of modern
education--"learn by doing."

One of the faults which most teachers need to overcome is a mis-
use of fingers as pointers. The teacher's finger should not jump
about nervously seeking for the right word, for the student's eye follows it around and becomes confused. Be sure that you know where
you want the student's eye to follow. Then move your finger in a slow
curve so that the eye can follow easily. Graceful curves free from
jerks are beautiful.

Some people would teach better if they were handcuffed. They
are forever watching an opportunity to shoot a long shaky finger into
the lesson at the slightest pause, as though good teaching consisted
of proving how much quicker and brighter they are than the student.
This, of course, is all wrong. We are trying to convince the student
that he is bright, not to prove our superiority.

TOO MANY WORDS WASTE TIME

Another important bit of advice is this: Don't repeat a word after
the pupil. If he says "flower" correctly don't say "flower" after him.
It sounds patronizing and irritates adults. Besides it wastes time.
Nearly every teacher violates this advice without realizing it. Ask
somebody to remind you when you parrot your students, and you will
find your teaching speedier and happier when you have broken the
habit.

Don't waste a second or a word. The first fifteen minutes are
the most precious with illiterate adults. The lesson is best when it
is swiftest--when it is finished before the student realizes it has
more than begun. Then he leaves, exclaiming, "This is the easiest
thing I ever saw!" You reply, "Easy for you because you are so
bright!"

Resist the temptation to indulge in a speech before the lesson.
One minute rightly employed will persuade almost any illiterate to
study if his mind is not worried about other matters. The fascination
of the pictures and very rapid progress will carry him on. He will
be finished before he is tired or dreams of stopping.

Some teachers of children emphasize drill. But drill is disagreeable and, at times, painful. Drilling means going around and around

like a drill which a dentist uses to prepare a cavity in your tooth for
filling. Our lessons have no drilling, no going around in a circle, and
no pain! There is review. But this review should be done with patience and love. And the teacher should not insist that the student
learn every last detail of one chart or of one page before he goes on
to the next.

Adults want progress, the faster the better, so long as it is easy.
When a student covers a great amount in a short time with little effort, the exhilaration he derives will lure him back for the next lesson.

LET THE STUDENT SET HIS OWN PACE

Keep out of the adult's way. He will almost invariably learn faster than children learn, but how fast or in what way he will learn
best, one can never predict. Adults differ far more than children
in their knowledge and mental alertness; this is one reason why the
"one by one" method is preferable. Almost every illiterate recog-
nizes a few letters and some illiterates know all the letters without
being able to read words. You must neither hold the student back nor
push him faster than he wishes to go. Let him take the lead and go
at his habitual speed, for then he will be happiest and make the best
progress. Suit yourself to his character and background.

Don't tell the student what he already knows. On the other hand,
don't try to catch him by asking what you think he doesn't know. Bol-
ster up his confidence by testing him--if you must test--on what you
are sure he knows. Don't for a moment let him think that he is failing, for every failure will push him back into the slough of despond
from which you seek to help him pull himself. When he has taught
another, that will be his final examination!

Don't rush in to fill every momentary pause; but on the other
hand, don't allow the pauses to become embarrassing. What the student has forgotten, tell him with the least possible emphasis, with
no raising of eyebrows, or loud voice, or tone of disapproval. Never
ask a question like "Why have you forgotten?"

Never ask a question twice. Tell the student at once if he hesitates to answer. Never cause him to blush or feel uncomfortable for
a single moment. This requires courtesy and imagination.

Thousands of experiments prove than an average adult will learn
in less than one-fifth of the time required to teach a child. This is
because the adult has a large speaking vocabulary and needs only to
learn what old familiar words look like. The average child must
build up vocabulary from small beginnings.

The adult may not have quite such a keen memory as the child
(at forty-five the mind is about four-fifths as retentive) but he can
reason many times better than a child. When lessons and teaching

lean heavily on reasoning and lightly on memory, the progress of many adults is astounding.

If a student yawns, stop at once and ask him to write. It is fruitless to try to teach when a student is tired. If this happens more than a few times, it indicates that the lessons are uninteresting, or, more likely, that the teacher has talked too much.

Sixty per cent of the success in teaching adults lies in the manner of the teacher. Since the spirit of the teacher is so important he ought not to teach when tired. It is better to teach a few hours or even one hour radiantly than to teach many hours with signs of fatigue.

It is especially necessary for the director of a campaign to radiate confidence. There must be no bad days for him. If he has been out late or has a headache or indigestion or troubles, he should go into hiding until he can give his best. The manner of all the volunteer teachers is likely to be patterned after that of the director. For this reason infinite care should be exercised in the selection of a director with an overflowing heart and native-born courtesy. In a literacy campaign we need faith, hope, love--these three; and the greatest of these is love. It has no substitutes. When it fails, everything fails.

Robert Laubach

Teacher training session conducted in the interior of Liberia.

IN SUMMARY

Teachers, we regret to say, need to be warned that the process,
from start to finish, is not what they have learned in training colleges. These are the fundamental differences:

1. We teach one at a time.
2. We say just as little as possible; waste no seconds.
3. We do nothing excepting what appears on the page of
   the primers.
4. We finish in about fifteen minutes.
5. We have the students teach others after they finish
   the primer.
6. We do not have tedious drill.
7. We never say "no."
8. We don't enforce discipline.
9. We make our lessons easy fun.
10. We treat our students like kings.
11. We use trees, verandas, fences as classrooms; and
    any hour or minute is school time.
12. We encourage every literate person to teach without
    training. The chief business of the director is to
    encourage other people to teach.
13. New literates can teach others--and they like it.
    Let them do it!
14. The lessons should give him the greatest hours of
    his life. Everything should contribute towards that
    goal.

Many teachers reading this page will say, "I have had years of
experience and know how to teach. I know this is nonsense." Very
well, then teach another set of lessons the old way. Don't ruin these
lessons. For our lessons are built to be taught this way. Charts and
method fit like hand in glove.

The Seventy-Year-Old Beginner

Many illiterates over sixty years of age have learned to read.
The following story is typical:

An old man named Devia, a leader from the village of
Ghumen in Batala District of India, when first asked if he
would like to be able to read, merely laughed. The question was ridiculous! He was nearly seventy, his old eyes
were dimmed with many years of working in the fierce
brightness of the sun. One might as well ask him if he

would like the moon for a pocket watch.

But a book was brought forth, its large letters easily discernible even to his old eyes. With a sceptical shrug of his shoulders he bent down over the book and followed instructions.

In half an hour he was able to recognize certain signs and pick them out all over the page. He learned how they were pronounced and what they meant. Even then his doubts were not banished. He was absent the next day at class; so a messenger was sent. The old man came with a look of shame and fear in his eyes. We told him there was nothing to be afraid of. No one was going to laugh if he made a mistake or two. His honor was safe. So again for half an hour he sat and worked with the rest. He surprised himself! Before the end of the second half hour he was reading simple sentences!

By the third day old Devia was one of our most enthusiastic students, taking his book with him wherever he went, working away with his reading with determination and vigor. Devia became one of the most enthusiastic supporters of the adult education program, and taught others of his village to read.

Robert Laubach

In Angola: Some of 450 students receiving diplomas for finishing the Primer, while 300 teachers receive certificates of patriotic service.

Chapter 5

A Comprehensive Plan for Literacy

A great literacy campaign was conducted in India between 1935 and 1940, one of the greatest in modern times. It is described in India Shall be Literate. * Nobody knows how many people were taught to read, except from the census reports, which indicate that 30 million people passed the literacy tests who could not have passed it at the beginning of that period.

Why did this campaign dwindle and in many places come to a complete stop? The Second World War was primarily to blame, but there were also other factors. One was the lack of a good graded series to follow the first primer. The gap between that book and the standard literature was very great. There was also an almost complete lack of simple newspapers or magazines or books for the semi-literates to read. So many millions, perhaps twenty millions, learned a little and then lapsed into illiteracy again because they had nothing simple and interesting to read. A third reason was often, though not always, a lack of competent directors to keep campaigns going. A fourth reason was because many of the texts used were poor, and they were often taught badly. The texts which I helped make in twenty Indian languages between 1935 - 1940 were not nearly so good as those we have since learned to make.

From the mistakes and shortcomings of the early campaigns, we have learned to lay much more substantial foundations for modern national literacy campaigns.

During the past eight years (1952 - 1960) we have been preparing comprehensive plans for making countries literate, at the requests of a number of governments. The most elaborate of these plans was made for India while we were employed by the United States Government to help the Indian Government in its Community Projects Administration. The Indian Government has a gigantic plan to reach the village people of India, to teach them to employ more scientific agriculture, and to follow the laws of hygiene and sanitation more scientifically. It trained village workers in more than forty schools, which

* See Appendix A.

42

were provided for by the Ford Foundation.

Our literacy team was invited to prepare textbooks to teach the people of those villages to read, since 90 per cent of the village people were illiterate. We went from province to province and prepared, in eleven Indian languages, primers and graded readers like those which have already been described. Then we were asked to prepare a comprehensive plan for making India literate. This plan was presented to the Ministry of Education; and, in the words of the Director of Education, Mr. Humyan Kabir, it was adopted in principle as the working basis for making India literate. Part of this plan is suitable for any other country with a literacy problem. *

India, as we have said before, has been greatly concerned about literacy for thirty years. In this report we listed the types of organizations which have cooperated with the central government or have been working independently. They were:

1. Departments of Adult Education in state governments.
2. Other departments of government, like the Labor Department, requiring literacy of their employees.
3. Community Development Projects that include literacy.
4. Semi-governmental campaigns, like that in Bombay City.
5. Literacy organizations, like South India Adult Education Association.
6. Literacy campaigns of religious organizations.
7. Campaigns conducted by industries, like Tata Iron and Steel.
8. Campaigns of labor unions among their members.
9. Campaigns of women's organizations.
10. Youth organizations, like Boy Scouts and 4-H Clubs.
11. Campaigns conducted by students, especially during vacation.
12. All literate people, teaching at home, each one teaching one.
13. Local village campaigns, directed by school teachers and others.

In the light of the experience accumulated by these organizations, we can see some of the defects of the campaigns of 1935-40. We can also see great reason to be encouraged, if these defects are remedied. India may profit by the pilot experiments of the last two decades.

The first defect of the early campaigns was the lack of either control or effective stimulation from the central government. The British policy in her colonies was to subsidize private agencies and to effect some degree of censorship. There was in Delhi a Commis-

* How It Can Be Done, available from Laubach Literacy and Mission Fund, Box 131, Syracuse 10, N.Y.

sioner of Education. His chief function was to study the educational
programs going on in India, to evaluate them, and to report on which
were worthy of aid from the British government. There was little
leadership emanating from the central government, though there was
solid work in describing and evaluating what was going on. Mr. Arthur
Mayhew's volume on education in India was important, and thorough.
The famous Sargent Report still stands as a monumental study of Indian mass education and community development.

Under the new Indian Government, the central Ministry of Education has taken a much more active interest in literacy. Two other organizations have also taken an active interest. The first is the Plan-
ning Commission of the Community Development Projects; the other
is the Indian Council of Agricultural Research, which is producing
simple, attractive, well-illustrated matter about agriculture.

Lessons were printed after they were properly prepared and
tested. In eight languages they were paid for by the International Cooperation Administration of the United States Government. In three
languages they were paid for by state governments of India. In Hindi
they were paid for by the Central Indian Ministry of Education.

Program Summarized

The complete program which we recommended to India may be
summarized as follows:

1. Large picture-letter association charts (like the Hindi
    chart in Chapter 2, but much larger, about 3 feet high,
    and attractively printed in several colors), to be pasted
    on the walls* of villages two months before a campaign
    begins so that villagers may teach themselves the let-
    ters. Such charts are now for sale in Hindi and are be-
    ing made in nine other languages.

    With a very little assistance from a neighbor every
    villager can and will learn his alphabet in a few weeks.
    We recommend that he be required to learn the letters
    from the charts before he will be permitted to study the
    primer. There are from four to six charts in each Indian
    language, depending upon the number of important letters
    in each alphabet.

    If the illiterates learn their alphabet from the big
    charts, without any formal teaching, they will be able
    to read the primers which we provide in a very short
    time. In this way a village can be made literate quickly

---

* A problem has been to develop a smooth hard surface, a waterproof
  adhesive and a termite-proof and waterproof varnish for paper. The Dow
  Chemical Company, Midland, Michigan, has been working on these problems.

and at small expense.

2. Stage I--The Primer, built upon the vocabulary of the wall charts and carrying the student to a complete mastery of phonetics, teaching about 120 words, and enabling the student to read simple sentences.

3. Stage II--Second Reader, based upon the vocabulary of the Primer, introducing only ten new words a day, repeating each word at least five times. Each lesson contains at least one highly valuable fact the villager needs to know about raising better crops, avoiding malaria, leading a happier life. This Second Reader adds 1,000 new words to the reader's vocabulary in 100 chapters.

   The above charts and Primer and Second Reader constitute a scientifically graded series, each lesson carefully built on the preceding lesson with a strictly controlled vocabulary--the most modern method of building textbooks.

4. Diploma forms for all who graduate from Primer and Second Reader; also "certificates of patriotic service" for teachers of illiterates.

5. Training classes to drill teachers in the perfect way to teach this type of material. Poor teaching can spoil the best lessons. A stupendous waste of time, money and also of students comes from failure of teachers to fit their teaching to lessons. The Central Office needs a highly skillful staff of expert teacher trainers to travel from one class to another.

6. Schools teaching simple journalism, and workshop courses training writers to write plain, fascinating material. Also training in the art of interviewing experts in agriculture, health, children, home life, cooking, and government; and writing the wisdom of the experts in the language of the villager, weaving it into fascinating stories.

7. Women must be trained to write for women. There must be a Woman's Country Journal, and many women's booklets, by and for women.

8. Latest rotary presses to produce the lesson materials in color or in black by mass production, so as to reduce the cost.

9. A simple Farm Journal, based upon the previously learned vocabulary of 1,120 words, written in easy,

fascinating style, attractively illustrated.

10. Newspapers and wall newspapers to be printed and distributed to the villages. The wall newspapers might be pasted up beside the large charts; new ones could be pasted up every week or fortnight.

11. Booklets and pamphlets using a limited vocabulary, written fascinatingly, simply, with profuse, attractive illustrations, bearing on all themes most vitally interesting to the villagers.

12. Libraries in the villages. A room can be provided in a village where newspapers and library books are available, tables and chairs provided. On the wall of this room the charts may be placed. The librarian can help illiterates when they need help in understanding any picture. Or the librarian can read to the illiterates if he has time. Or, in villages where a room is not available, at least a "Tin Trunk Library" can be supplied. *

13. A central book depot where all lessons and simple literature of every language may be purchased.

14. An aggressive and efficient organization trained in publishing, selling and distributing all this literature.

We recommended that these materials and facilities be provided by the Central Government. The Central Ministry of Education was not to have authority to compel people to use this material. It could only say, "If you want the best results at the least cost, this is what we recommend."

The Central Literacy Office would be a part of the Ministry of Education. It would be in close touch with the Ministry of Health, Agriculture and in more or less close touch with the other Ministries of the Government, because the reading matter to be provided must make people more efficient in their jobs, healthier, better citizens.

The Goal

A five year plan for the war against illiteracy was proposed. This plan aimed to weld together the many separate campaigns into a mighty army, coordinated, equipped and trained to "Win The War Against Illiteracy--Enemy No. 1."

This army would lack one characteristic of an army in a "hot" war: it would not be able to issue orders from any one central com-

---

* See "Tin Trunk Libraries," in Chapter 15.

mand. For this reason it might be more accurately The People's Crusade.

In another respect, this crusade would be weaker than an ordinary army. An efficient army can discard the old-fashioned weapons and use the latest and best simply by issuing an order. But in this People's Crusade it is not possible, by issuing orders, to discard the old-fashioned weapons used in many areas. The textbooks and methods of teaching can be changed only if the people are willing. The use of the latest and best materials can be accomplished by persuasion, and by convincing demonstrations. This kind of demonstration is a function of the Central Literacy Office.

This is the sort of plan which has been recommended to several countries. If carried out faithfully, an entire country could be made literate in a few years.

Central Adult Education Committee

Poster from India, symbolizing literacy breaking chains of ignorance.

Chapter 6
How to Conduct a Campaign
in a Small Village

CHOOSING A VILLAGE CAMPAIGN MANAGER

The question as to who is qualified to become manager of a village campaign will depend more upon the personality of the man or woman than upon any other factor. He can be taught the technique from a book or at a conference, but a winsome personality is something that comes out of a kindly heart full of genuine love for one's fellowmen.

In some cases the village teacher will prove to be the best manager, but not always. If the teacher is doing his school work well he is very tired after school hours. A teacher acting as manager is likely unconsciously to treat the adults like children and to offend them by his patronizing, superior attitude. It is difficult to break down the habits of years, and to change from a "schoolmaster tone of voice" used with children to a "friend-to-friend voice" in dealing with adults. Schools are employing painful drills, and limping along at a rate that no illiterate adult will tolerate. Moreover, they are likely to consider their experience more valuable than new theories. Another handicap is that teachers supplement their written primers by endless lectures of their own. The new lessons for illiterate adults described in this book require no lectures whatever, but are taught with the fewest words possible.

Before a teacher is ready to act as campaign manager he must unlearn many of his habitual ways of teaching. He needs to attend a training class at least as long as other prospective managers. There is a subtle temptation to say, "He is a trained teacher and does not need instruction." If he is teachable, he ought to be the best choice; but if he thinks he knows all about it, without being trained, do NOT use him.

Our village manager may be a college student willing to devote his two months' vacation to this work. Students may go to neighboring villages each evening, taking turns, so as to relieve the burden of each student. This has been practiced successfully by Hislop College, Nagpur. (See "College Training Abroad," page 118.)

48

Managers may be found among supervisors of cooperative societies, constables, or other village officials. Nurses are excellent. Women can direct a campaign as well as men. In most of India it is necessary to have two campaigns going simultaneously, one for men, the other for women. Both Moslem and Hindu custom prevents men from teaching women outside their own immediate families.

The party leader may be the best village manager in leading the campaign of literacy. Where the village is largely of one religion, a kindly and public-spirited priest or other religious worker may be effective.

Many young men who have studied law have found little or nothing to do, and these men may be glad for the privilege of helping their countrymen. In many cases retired men or women as old as sixty or even seventy may be the best possible village managers. Age lends prestige to respect. It is better to use them than to allow their last and wisest years to be wasted. It makes no difference about the age or profession of the man or woman; what matters is the greatness of his love and understanding, and his ability to work with all classes without prejudice.

When the village manager has been selected, he must be given thorough instructions at training institutes. If he reads English, he should own this book for careful study and reference.

A MONTH BEFORE THE CAMPAIGN OPENS

Posters plastered on the village wall should contain reading matter of the greatest interest and value to the villagers. The most gifted, imaginative writer in the language area ought to be set aside to do his best work in discovering and answering these needs of the villagers: the latest prices of articles villagers desire to buy, where and how they can secure cheaper and improved plows and more productive seeds, how to get out and stay out of debt, etc. Posters would vary with the trade of the villagers. Helpful posters might emphasize one or more of these advantages of learning to read:

Why You Need to Read

1. So you can read letters from relatives and friends and write replies.
2. So you can sign your name instead of using a thumb mark.
3. So you can read documents and not be deceived by money-lenders, landlords, lawyers, or ticket agents at railway stations.
4. So you can get valuable knowledge about farming, raising livestock, where to get the best prices, how to get out and

stay out of debt, cooperative banks, child care, diet,
first aid, and ten thousand other secrets.
5. So you can get better wages.
6. So you can read stories, proverbs, laws, conundrums,
dramas, newspapers, and magazines.
7. So you can have more self-respect and a higher standing
in the community.
8. So you can become a teacher of others.
9. So you can vote intelligently.
10. So you can have a voice in the councils.
11. So you can catch up with world progress.
12. So you can better help your children by example and
training.

Distribute simple books full of valuable information in the language of the villagers to those who can read, and ask them to read
to others. All this should be done a month before the contemplated
campaign begins.

MAKING A SURVEY

To know how many of the needed lesson materials to order, it
is necessary to determine the number of illiterate men and women
in the village. It is not necessary to write down all the names or to
make a detailed census at the outset, as this would use up the time
and energy of those who ought to be teaching. Careful tabulations of
the illiterates have been done in some small villages before the campaign begins, as in villages of Egypt. But generally, a rough estimate
of the number of illiterates will suffice.

Ordering Supplies

After the survey has been made, order the following supplies:

1. One or two sets of the large picture-word charts to be fastened in conspicuous places in the village.
2. A supply of small duplicates of the large charts, sufficient
for all the illiterate adults in the village.
3. A supply of the primers, enough for the first few weeks
of the campaign.
4. A supply of report sheets like the one below, equal to
one-tenth of the village population.
5. A supply of diplomas, or certificates of promotion. Keep
an order for more of these well in advance of need.
6. A supply of certificates of service for the teachers in

Each One Teach One.

7. A supply of second stage readers; perhaps half as many as the order for primers. Be sure to order more of these well in advance if success attends the campaign, for nothing is more disheartening than the lack of readers after the primer is mastered.

8. Small notebooks for the directors and the literacy committee. Stationery for the campaign manager.

9. Slates or cheap paper tablets, slate pencils or lead pencils, equal to half the adult illiterates to be taught.

10. In the office for the campaign manager, a table, chairs, good-sized cupboard for all supplies.

A Simple Record Blank for Each Teacher in the Village

Name of Teacher _____   Teacher: Return filled-in
blank to campaign manager
Name of Village _____   at the end of each week.

Date	Student's Name	Lesson Number	Remarks

(Complete blank would fill a sheet about 9 by 12 inches.)

SEEKING AND TRAINING TEACHERS

The village manager must find and train teachers. He will, first of all, make a list of men and women who know how to read and write in his village. These will include those who once attended school but forgot all they ever knew. Everybody--men and women, old and young, officials and private citizens with much learning or with little--every reader is to become a member of the teaching staff of the "village university."

Having written a complete list of his "university staff" or "faculty," the manager will call these prospective teachers together and tell them how they may cooperate in teaching the village. The manager's first task is to train them to teach, by making a demonstration of actual teaching before them. We have already seen how this is done in Chapter 2.

The village manager must be sure to impress upon the teachers

the psychology of good teaching. Though already treated in detail in
Chapter 4, these principles bear repeating here:

Repeat no word after your student. For example, if he
says "crow," do not repeat it. Speak in a voice as low as
the student, so you can hear whether he is reciting with
you. Never raise your voice. Low, pleasant tones are
used by the best teachers, just loud enough for the student
to hear. Speak plainly and you will not need to be loud. Do
not drill. Do not go around in a circle.

Do not notice small mispronunciations. Try not to correct your student directly. Never say "no." If you say "no"
four times your student will be afraid to try the fifth time.
Say "yes" when you mean "no!" Look surprised and pleased
and say "fine" with rising enthusiasm as you go along. When
he is done with the lesson, say,

"You are very bright. You finished in only a few minutes!
You will make a fine teacher."

Never do for him what he can do without your help. If he
hesitates, join in quietly and drop out again when he is over
his trouble. Do not hurry to help if he is thinking, but do
not leave him in embarrassment.

Say "Splendid!" several times, and look greatly pleased.

The manager can demonstrate all these principles by teaching
an illiterate as an example to his teachers. If he has conducted the
demonstration properly, he will give the illiterate the greatest hour
of his life and be an inspiration to all the teachers.

The village manager may teach a few persons each day as an
example to his teachers. But his chief task is to promote the campaign in many ways, to encourage his teachers, and to give public
credit to the new literates. In the most conspicuous place in the village, for instance, the manager may post the names of the teachers
and all of their students. In other ways, some suggested in this text,
and others devised by an ingenious manager, he may keep the literacy
campaign continually a topic of village interest and conversation.

Indeed, a well conducted campaign may sweep through a village
of almost any size so that within a month or two practically all the
adults will have begun to study.

When illiterates are ready for graduation from the primer they
should be offered diplomas with much ceremony in the presence of
the whole village. It is well for each teacher to bring his own pupils
forward for the diploma. This diploma will say very simply, in
attractive print:

_____ has finished the Primer
and is ready for the second reader, <u>Anand</u>.

Signed,

_____   _____
(His teacher)   (Director, Mayor,
                                 or other official)

The students who have finished the primer will then be asked to
teach another group of students--Each One Teach One. Another graduation ceremony will take place within three or four months, or
sooner.

It is well to invite prominent persons to do the actual distribution
of the diplomas, as this will leave an indelible impression on the
minds of the students and encourage them to continue as students
and teachers.

The volunteer teachers should also receive certificates of patriotic service, signed by a prominent person, saying something like
this:

_____ has done a patriotic deed for
his country by teaching at least one person and
thus helping get rid of Enemy Number One to the
progress of our country.

Signed,

_____   _____
(Literacy Director)   (Mayor or other
                                 high official)

Villages will receive wholly different treatment under spcial circumstances. For example, the Training School at Gakhar in the Punjab conducts a campaign, utilizing the teachers of the schools as
teachers of illiterates, and holding classes in the large plaza. It
will frequently prove best to adapt this plan, especially where government officers are in a position to exert considerable influence
upon the illiterate villagers.

In many places in the world, town after town is thus made literate within a few months. While the primers are being taught by the
Each One Teach One method, the <u>Anand</u> graded reader may be taught
in classes like those we have in ordinary schools, each student reading some of the text.

The usual rule is Each One Teach One for Stage I (The Primer)
and classes for Stage II (the <u>Anand</u> graded reader). In some places

Example of Teacher's Certificate in Hindi
(With English Translation)

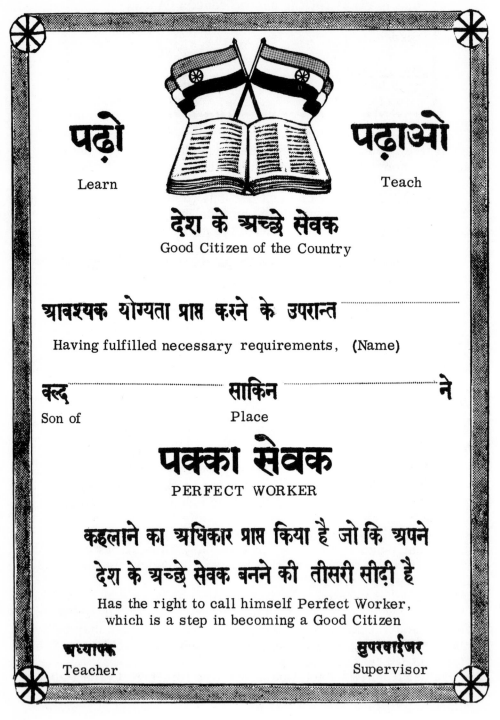

पढ़ो   पढ़ाओ

Learn   Teach

देश के अच्छे सेवक

Good Citizen of the Country

आवश्यक योग्यता प्राप्त करने के उपरान्त

Having fulfilled necessary requirements,   (Name)

वल्द   साकिन   ने

Son of   Place

पक्का सेवक

PERFECT WORKER

कहलाने का अधिकार प्राप्त किया है जो कि अपने

देश के अच्छे सेवक बनने की तीसरी सीढ़ी है

Has the right to call himself Perfect Worker,
which is a step in becoming a Good Citizen

अध्यापक   सुपरवाईजर

Teacher   Supervisor

Aids to Encourage Teachers

Left: Chief of a Uganda village holds plaque for winning inter-village literacy contest. Every teacher wears a literacy button (above) showing literacy lesson.

Indian poster shows literacy dispeling ignorance and superstition.

campaign directors prefer to continue Each One Teach One to the end
of the graded courses in both Stage I and Stage II.

EXAMPLES OF VILLAGE LITERACY CAMPAIGNS IN EGYPT

Excellent examples of campaigns in small villages are to be
found in the current literacy work of the Evangelical Church in Egypt.
In the village of Hirz, during five months of 1952-53, 400 of the total
population of 1,000 were taught to read. The campaign was under the
general direction of Miss Davida Finney and Miss Marjorie Dye of
the United Presbyterian mission. Miss Finney is convinced that the
first reason for the success of the campaign was that the pastor, the
Rev. Menis Abdul Noor, pledged five months of his time to supervise
the campaign. And the Mayor of Hirz was strongly back of the campaign.

First, a training session was held in the right way to teach the
primer. The pastor, a field director and three Bible women were
trained at the start of the campaign. They in turn trained another
100 to teach. Four men and one woman were chosen as supervisors.

A census of the village of Hirz was made. There are ten streets
in the village. On each door a house number was painted. Every man
and woman was recorded in each house as to whether he could read
and, if so, whether he would teach.

The five supervisors divided up the town, and watched and helped
the teachers under them until they had finished the primer with their
students.

Then a graduation ceremony was held. The Mayor came, and
each of the 29 graduates read before him. Then he awarded them
their diplomas. There have been several periodic graduations since.

The people became so enthusiastic that they bought books and
went around asking, "What is this, what is this?" while they taught
one another and themselves.

In a few months the Hirz church started a campaign in the adjoin-
ing village of Jaweer, which is 80 per cent Moslem. There they
trained six supervisors, of whom four were Moslem. The Christians
taught in the church, while the Moslems taught in a room which the
mission rented at a cost of $1.50 a month. By November, 1954, di-
plomas had been awarded to 194.

The people of Hirz started a campaign in still another village
named Diab, where they have taught the church members, but not
yet the rest of the town. They propose in time to make four more
villages literate.

Here are some of the results of the Hirz campaign:

1. They opened a day school.

2. They built a community room with a library.

3. The Mayor bought a fine Jersey cow. Assiut College became interested and gave a Jersey bull. The live-stock is rapidly improving.

4. The U.S. Technical Cooperation Mission gave the town chickens, which are improving the quality of their own chickens. A beautifully printed and simply written booklet on the care of chickens has also been distributed by TCM.

5. The villagers repaired both the Protestant and the Coptic churches.

6. An elder in the church bought a taxi, and thus began the first contact with the outer world that village ever had. The road was terrible, as they are in all the villages, and the villagers began to improve it.

In the Village of Manhari

The pastor and session of another village, Manhari, asked for a campaign. This request, in writing, fulfilled the first condition upon which the mission will start a campaign; for the desire of the village is essential to the campaign's success.

The church agreed that all its members would take an active part. This type of general enthusiasm is the second requirement of a successful campaign. In December, 1954, the official opening of the campaign was announced from the pulpit. The next evening both men and women came to the church to a demonstration of the method of teaching. For a week the women came in the daytime for teacher training, and the men at night, for the crowd was too large to handle all at once.

A committee was formed, made up of the pastor, two elders and five deacons, along with leading church members. Early in the campaign a grouping system was adopted for closer supervision of teachers and their students. Soon there were six groups of men teachers and their students, and six groups of women teachers and students. About 260 men enrolled and about 100 women, including both teachers and students.

As soon as possible, supervision of the teaching was put in the hands of two of the best teachers from each of the twelve groups. These village supervisors now do teaching, they check on the teaching in their own groups, and they are responsible for bringing in new teachers and students. New life has come into the campaign by thus firmly rooting it in the village of Manhari itself.

A diploma-awarding ceremony was held in January, 1955, and

another in February. The village Mayor awarded the diplomas. The Laubach literacy team was present for the second occasion and caused a great deal of excitement.

When the Christian new literates complete the primer, they are given the twelve-book series of The Story of Jesus. When they have read the entire series, they are enrolled in a Bible study class with the pastor, studying Mark.

After the students have read the third book in The Story of Jesus, they are ready to begin reading the monthly magazine for new literates, El Nur (The Light). They can subscribe to this publication for about 18 cents a year.

From the continuing experience of village work, these principles for conducting a thriving literacy campaign might be set forth:

1. Stir up initial enthusiasm for the campaign. Get prominent village leaders interested.

2. If possible, the village itself, through its leaders, should request the campaign.

3. Conduct thorough training sessions in the right way to use the charts and primers.

4. Provide for close supervision of the campaign, dividing up the large group into smaller groups, each with its supervisors.

5. As soon as possible, pick local men and women to supervisory posts, thus making the villagers feel the campaign is really their own.

6. Hold diploma-awarding ceremonies at frequent intervals. Invite some prominent person, such as the Mayor, to make a speech and give diplomas.

7. Order an adequate supply of Stage II and Stage III reading materials which are suited to the religion, culture and economic needs of the people. There should be included a regularly published periodical for new literates.

8. Employ numerous promotional devices, such as buttons for lapels, diplomas, house markers, literacy "thermometers, " etc., to keep enthusiasm high.

9. Be aware of the villagers' expressed desire to extend their campaign to other villages, and help them in this. Nothing so stimulates a campaign as the villagers" feeling that, as they are becoming literate,

they can help others along the same path.

There follows a complete and definitive description of the on-going campaign at Manhari. It well serves as a model for a small village campaign in any part of the world.

CARRYING ON THE LITERACY CAMPAIGN AT MANHARI, EGYPT

By Davida M. Finney, Campaign Director
Halana Mikhail, Field Director
Marjorie Dye, Literacy Worker

The Goals

The goals before us in our work in literacy:

1. To help people to read sufficiently well so that they will continue reading after they finish the prescribed course of study during a campaign, both for pleasure and to their own profit.
2. With Christians, we want to form in new literates the habit of daily Bible study and worship, so that they will increasingly understand more about God's loving Holy Spirit and want to please Him.
3. By forming in them the habit of reading, we want to help them enter new fields of knowledge in better ways of living: in health, agriculture, means of improving their economic condition, an understanding of true patriotism, and in a recognition and appreciation of spiritual truths.
4. We want, too, by encouraging each to teach another, to encourage a friendly spirit toward all, so that a real community spirit will emerge which will lead to the development of village betterment projects.

The Personnel At Work In The Campaign

1. The Sponsoring Church or Village Committee of Management

2. The General Campaign Director

3. The Field Director

4. The General Supervisors

5. The Village Supervisors

6. The Village Teachers

7. The Pupils

The Local Committee

The Pastor and Church Committee, or leaders representing the group.

1. The Local Committee is the body which arranges for a campaign in any village or town. It is this Committee which complies with two conditions:
   (a) It submits an official request to the Campaign Committee asking for a campaign; this request is to be signed by each member of the Local Committee.
   (b) It pledges the support of every member of the group asking for a campaign.
2. The Local Committee provides the housing for any members of the Campaign Committee who come to carry on the campaign. With the housing, it also provides what essential furniture is needed and which the Campaign Committee cannot easily provide.
3. The Local Committee is the host of the Campaign Committee, and is responsible for the safety of the Campaign Committee. It represents the Campaign Committee in the village or town and secures the support and cooperation of the local inhabitants in the work of the Campaign.
4. The Church Committee and Pastor pledge that the pastor will give the major part of his time for a period of three months in active participation in the work of the campaign. After the first three months, the Pastor gives whatever time is needed in promoting the work of the campaign until it comes to an end.
5. The Local Committee pledges that one or more of its members shall be present at all group meetings.
6. The Committee is responsible for the good order at group and public meetings.
7. It is responsible for providing more teachers and pupils as the campaign expands.
8. Each member of the Local Committee sponsors one of the groups into which the enrollment is divided. He shares in the work of his group.
9. (a) The Pastor begins a Bible class as soon as new literates have finished reading the series of the Life of Christ.
   (b) The Committee members help the new literates in studying the Daily Devotional booklet. They lead this study in the group which they sponsor or they delegate this responsibility to some suitable person.
10. The Committee visits from time to time all members of the church or community who should be sharing in the Campaign.
11. The Committee promises to pray each day for the success of the Campaign.

The Campaign Director

1. The Campaign Director is responsible for the promotion, expansion and general supervision of the campaign, and also for the production and use of the Primer, readers, and follow-up literature used in the campaign.
2. He promotes the campaign among those interested in literacy work in the United States and Britain, and among missions, churches, and the public in Egypt.
3. He maintains a close supervision of the work carried on and, together with the Field Director, plans for its administration and expansion.
4. He accounts for all funds used in the campaign and reports regularly to the Committee on World Literacy and Christian Literature in New York. He submits his accounts once a year for auditing to the American Auditing Committee.
5. He makes a constant effort to expand the work of the campaign among all those in Egypt interested in literacy work.
6. He is responsible for the correctness and efficiency of the teaching.
7. Together with the Field Director, he is responsible for the employment and dismissal of all those employed by the Campaign Committee in the work of the campaign. He signs all contracts with such employees.
8. He plans with the Writers Fellowship for the writing of Stages II and III of campaign literature and is responsible for the publishing of these books and pamphlets.
9. He is responsible for the ordering of books for village libraries, and for their efficient use. The village Committee of Management pays for the books and has the direct supervision of the library room and of the library books.
10. He is responsible for the financing and the publication of the newspaper El Nur.
11. He promotes and helps to put into effect village betterment projects.
12. He is responsible for the effectiveness of the general campaign, for the spirit of all employees, and for the development of the good spirit of those in the community sharing in the campaign.

The Field Director

1. With the Campaign Director, the Field Director is responsible for the promotion, expansion and general supervision of the campaign, and also for the production and use of the Primer, readers, and follow-up literature used in the campaign.
2. He is responsible for the carrying out of the plans made for the

campaign.
3. He is responsible to the Campaign Director for the efficient work
   of the General Supervisors.
4. His chief duty is to judge carefully the correctness of the teaching
   done under general supervision of the General Supervisors.
5. He is responsible for the personal conduct of the General Supervisors.
6. He is responsible for the good spirit among all employees, and
   for their attitude toward those with whom they work.
7.. He keeps careful records of the work done and gives these to the
   Campaign Director.
8. He keeps the accounts of money used and reports to the Campaign
   Director.
9. He cooperates with the Campaign Director in all the work of the
   Writers Fellowship.

General Supervisors (Qadis)

1. Each General Supervisor will be present at all teaching sessions
   under his supervision. He will be responsible for the teaching,
   not only in these sessions, but also for the teaching of individuals
   during the day.
2. As the campaign increases in numbers, he divides those enrolled
   into smaller groups of teachers and pupils.
3. He chooses from among the able teachers in each group two to
   serve as group supervisors. These share with him in developing
   the work of the group.
4. He must never forget that his primary task is the training of the
   group supervisors:
   (a) He must be sure that they know the correct method of teaching.
   (b) He and the group supervisors then train the teachers at an
       agreed time. They do this by taking not more than six teach-
       ers at a time, and by having an illiterate present.
   (c) When the teachers are trained, the group supervisors super-
       vise the teaching in the group. At the beginning they limit
       themselves to two or three teachers in order to be sure that
       each is correct in his work. After these teachers teach cor-
       rectly, they then help two or three more, and so on until all
       in their group are adequately trained.
   (d) If a group supervisor is unable to do the work of supervision,
       the General Supervisor will replace him with someone else.
5. The General Supervisor visits the members of his group with the
   group supervisors:
   (a) to ask about absentees
   (b) to secure more teachers and pupils
   (c) to arrange for teaching anyone who cannot come at night.

6. He will enroll as teachers all those who finish the course in reading.
7. He will see that no pupil is advanced from one reader to another until he has been examined in the book he has just finished.
8. See No. 8 under Village Supervisors.
9. When the pupil finishes the course of reading, he makes sure that he begins Stage III reading.
10. In keeping the daily group record, he notes the advance of each pupil. This will enable him to know when exams are due, and also will reveal to him the work of teachers, especially with weak pupils.

Village Supervisors

1. Each Village Supervisor will always be present at the teaching sessions in his village, and he shares heartily in the work.
2. He will maintain order and quietness in his group.
3. He will visit the teachers and pupils of his group in their houses to ask about absentees. He will also do his best to secure new teachers and pupils for his group.
4. In his work of supervising teaching, he will make sure that the teacher does not advance the pupil from one lesson to another until the pupil is able to read the lesson correctly and comprehends what he reads.
5. The supervisor will arrange with the General Supervisor of his group for the examination of a pupil when he has read through any book in the course. This means that he will be examined when he has finished reading the Primer, each book in the Life of Christ, or each of the four "Selected Readings."
6. He will choose those pupils who read well and with comprehension to become teachers.
7. He will train new teachers in the correct method of teaching and supervise their teaching.
8. Together with the General Supervisor of his group, he will enroll those who finish the 12 books of the Life of Christ in the Bible Study class taught by the pastor, and will enroll as soon as possible those who read sufficiently well in the study of the "Daily Devotions" conducted by the sponsor of his group.
9. When observing a teacher at work with a pupil, he must be careful not to correct the pupil, but to help the teacher to be correct in his teaching.
10. He helps the teacher to encourage the pupil to observe and correct his own mistakes. If the pupil does not yet know the sound of a letter, he returns him to the primer and gives him again the basic instruction of letters, vowels, etc. The teacher must never tell the pupil; the pupil helps himself under the guidance of the teacher.

11. He must honestly honor and respect every teacher and pupil in his group, and he should make each feel his importance in the work of the group.
12. The importance of writing must be very clear to him. Each teacher must start the pupil writing letters, then words, then sentences, beginning from the first lesson.
13. The Village Supervisor takes over full responsibility of the group during the absence of the General Supervisor.

Teachers

1. Each teacher will always encourage his pupils and be cheerful and happy in his teaching.
2. He will give his full attention to his teaching for the time of the teaching period, and this he does heartily.
3. He must understand that the correct teaching of the Primer is the secret of his pupil's success in learning to read. He must therefore be sure that the pupil comprehends each step taken in the Primer. For instance, he must be sure that the pupil knows beyond any doubt the sound of the letters before he is given the lessons on the vowels, etc.
4. When the pupil reads any word, the teacher must be sure that he has pronounced it correctly. Then he makes sure that the student understands the meaning of the word.
5. The teacher must be sure that the pupil reads correctly all preceding lessons before advancing him to a new lesson.
6. He must be sure that the pupil comprehends what he reads.
7. If a pupil makes many mistakes in his reading in a book following the Primer, the teacher should return to the Primer and review the points at issue.
8. In the lessons on the vowels (the "shedada," the "secun," etc. -- vowel signs in Arabic), the teacher must be sure that the pupil understands these thoroughly before passing on to a subsequent lesson.
9. The teacher must be exact in teaching by the method of Laubach, according to the instructions given him.
10. The teacher will present his pupil to the examining committee when he has finished any one book.
11. A certificate of merit will be given to each teacher when he proves himself faithful and correct in his teaching.

The Pupil

Let us never forget that the pupil is the most important person in the campaign.

1. Our one desire is that he will learn to read sufficiently well so

that he will not relapse again into illiteracy. By this standard all our work is judged, both by the village itself and by outsiders.
2. We must manage to share this conviction with the pastor, village committee and the supervisors, or we shall never reach our goal.
3. The first step to take in reaching this goal is to win the personal friendship and affection of the pupil. He must find in us a very deep respect for all that concerns him.

Other Projects Essential To The Success Of A Literacy Campaign

Publicity At The Church Services

1. Talk from the pulpit
   Each Sabbath there should be a short talk from the pulpit about the advance of the campaign, or about some phase of it. This talk should usually be given by the "Qadi" (General Supervisor) but he may sometimes profitably ask someone else to speak. It is expected that the pastor will always add a few words confirming what the Qadi says.
2. The Qadi will exhibit, at the church, charts or diagrams illustrating:
   (a) The advance of the campaign, or
   (b) The names of those taking part in it, or
   (c) Any information which will interest the church members about work being carried on.
3. It is hoped that the Qadi will use his own initiative about informing and enthusing the church and community.

The Library

1. The Qadi will try to persuade the church or village committee to set aside a room as Library and Community Room. It should be furnished with a club lamp, table and chairs, and a cupboard for books.
2. Two people should be appointed to be responsible for the library and room. In a church campaign these two should be the pastor and one lay-member; in a village campaign a village notable with a layman.
3. There must be a record of books in the library. Whenever new books are bought or donated, these too must be recorded.
4. There must be a book for recording the withdrawal and return of books. These can be had from the Literature Office in Cairo.
5. The layman responsible for the library will open the library at fixed hours during the week. He must always be present at these times to keep records, maintain order, etc.

6. The librarian will give to the Field Director a monthly report on withdrawals of books, etc. Forms are provided for these reports.
7. The sum of 8 pounds is available for each library which conforms to the above regulations. The books bought with this sum will be kept in the container furnished for them. After six months, this lot of books will be sent to another village or town, and will receive another lot of books from that village or town.
8. The Qadi will give general supervision to the use of the Library and help pastor and librarian to understand it.

The Newspaper

1. The Committee expects every new literate to become a subscriber to the newspaper El Nur. The Qadi will secure the help of the pastor and church committee in getting every newly literate man and woman enrolled as subscribers. The Qadi will evolve various ways by which he will interest the new literate in the newspaper.

Daily Devotions And Bible Classes

1. The Qadi will daily make note in his Group Record Book of any pupil or pupils who are able to read and understand the "Daily Devotions." These pupils he will place in the class conducted in each group by a member of the Church Committee. The chief purpose in holding this daily class is to help church members to use this booklet daily with their families.
2. The Qadi will at once enroll in the pastor's Bible study class each pupil who finishes the entire series of the Life of Christ. Non-Christians he will enroll in the library and see that they read follow-up literature.

Follow-up Literature

1. All those who finish the course of reading in the campaign should be enrolled as members in the library. Here they will be helped to choose follow-up literature which they will read under the supervision of the Qadi.

Talks And Bulletins From The General Supervisor

1. It is hoped that the Qadi will contribute what he can to the development of better living in the community. In addition to sharing what he knows with the villager, he will, if he feels able, speak on specialized subjects or write bulletins for the study of the villager.
2. He will give lantern and flannelgraph talks, sharing this equipment

with other General Supervisors.

3. The Qadi will work out a six-months' program, with the Field and General Supervisor and the Church or Community Committee of Management, to be given by out-of-town specialists. These talks will cover the areas of health, family life, agriculture, community living, etc.

Use Of Each One Teach One

Literates, both church members and those not of the church membership, have joined quite spontaneously in the work of teaching. It is true to say, therefore, that the method, Each One Teach One, appeals to many in the community. This general enthusiasm is a demonstration of the true spirit of our work; we come to help any and all who wish to learn and are willing to help. It is expected that the Qadi will take advantage of this fact, and do his best to draw into cooperation with us as many as wish to come. The Qadi should be careful, however, to keep developing a sufficient number of village supervisors to train teachers and supervise the work, so that good order and good teaching will be maintained.

Committee on World Literacy & Christian Literature

Miss Halana Mikhail (right) teaching ladies in an Egyptian village.

Chapter 7

How Literacy Campaigns Are Conducted in Urban Communities

EXAMPLE OF BOMBAY

Bombay has furnished more experience in starting campaigns than any other great Indian city. It is blessed with an unusual number of public-spirited leaders.

In April, 1939, Shri B. G. Kher, the Premier of Bombay, acting as chairman of a new organization called "The Bombay Literacy Campaign Committee," started a new high-pressure campaign more far-reaching than any Bombay had ever tried before. Publicity was pushed with great vigor. Posters were plastered on automobiles, tram cars, and busses, announcing the coming campaign. Flyers were dropped from airplanes. Men and women of all ages were urged to undertake to teach twenty each!

During the months of March and April, Miss Godavari Gokhale of the Servants of India Society was responsible for the finding and train-ing of 2,000 volunteer teachers. Young people responded with great enthusiasm. The Hindustan Scout's Association, the Bombay National Guards, the Bombay City Ambulance Corps, the Independent Labor Party, the Students' Union, and the Swastika League, * as well as schools, colleges, debating societies, and women's organizations, volunteered their services.

Lessons employing the picture-word-syllable method were pre-pared by Miss Rustomjee and Miss Khandvala, but teachers were allowed to follow the methods to which they were accustomed. On April 4, the "terrific campaign," as they called it, opened with mass meetings addressed by the governor, premier, and many prominent men.

On May first the actual teaching began at 520 centers, in Marathi, Gujerati, Urdu, Hindi, and Kanarese. They had "expected about 20 students to enroll in each center, but the people had been so stirred by literacy propaganda that there was an unexpected rush to enroll. Consequently, 120 more centers had to be opened; but even that

---

* The "swastika" is an ancient symbol of the Orient, which the Nazis adopted. There was, of course, no connection between the Bombay group and the Nazis.

addition has not met the demand." Adults enrolled numbered 10,773, of whom 9,679 were men and 1,094 were women.

Newspapers gave the campaign front page publicity. The Illustrated Weekly of India said:

"Bombay Trade Union organizations are whole-heartedly supporting this move, and, being in constant touch with the workers, they are going to play a very important part in the drive.

"About 2,000 volunteers are participating in the campaign. Five hundred university and high school students, 200 women and 400 men municipal teachers will do the teaching and supervising part of the job. Most of the workers are giving their services free; only a few are being paid.

"The classes naturally were held near the residences of the students. College and school buildings, also municipal, government and private premises were at the disposal of the Committee. Most of the classes were held in verandahs, or in rooms or in open spaces between chawls. Naturally the workers attend in greater numbers at their own doors. . . .

"The classes were held between 7 and 10 p.m. Each class consisted of about 20 pupils. They attended the classes at any time convenient to them, for one hour. Writing materials were supplied free of charge. Every class had two or three teachers and the work was supervised by experts. The pupils were expected to read, write and count up to 100 within a month. . .

"The Bombay Government decided not to employ any illiterate and to eliminate illiterates from the ranks of those already employed...."

The Bombay Collection Committee, during the months of March, April and May, tried to secure funds in five ways:

1. By approaching individuals.
2. Writing letters to trusts.
3. Publishing appeals for funds.
4. Making box collections from house to house.
5. Requesting adults to promise to teach one or pay 2 rupees.

At the end of the first twenty days of this May campaign the Bombay Committee issued this statement:

"The opinion of Organizers, Superintendents, Supervisors, teachers, and, above all, of students, as ascertained by some written reports and in talks, is not only definitely in favor of continuing the work, but it is felt by all that there will be a keen disappointment, especially on the part of the students, if the work is not continued at least on the present scale. In organizing the work on a permanent basis, amalgamation of some of the classes is practicable. The bulk of opinion is in favor of employing paid teachers though some honorary help may be available in superintending and supervising the classes if some conveyance allowance is provided.

"If illiteracy is to be wiped out completely within a very short period, not only must the effort be on a large scale and vigorous, but it must be planned in detail with a complete survey of the number of the illiterate population divided according to wards, languages and communities, with an estimate of the resources in men and money required."

By August 1939, 5,000 were made literate, and 15,000 by February, 1940, at a total cost of 48,000 rupees.

Brief Description of the Bombay Scheme

Each literacy course in the city extended over a period of four months and consisted of instruction which gave the pupils just the ability to read simple books especially prepared for them and write their names and short easy sentences. The literacy classes were held for an hour or so daily for six days of the week at times suitable to the learners, either by day or night. Each teacher, who was not necessarily a professional man, handled about 15 to 20 pupils and a supervisor was appointed to supervise about 10 to 15 classes. Guidance to teachers regarding the methods of teaching was given by arranging demonstrations by experienced teachers in municipal or secondary schools at some central places.

At the end of each course a literacy test was held and literacy certificates were awarded to those who satisfied the test. With a view to enabling the new literates to keep up the reading habits acquired in the literacy classes, and to prevent them from falling into illiteracy again, the Adult Education Committee had a plan of supplying them with post-literacy reading booklets for about a year after they left the classes. At the end of the last session, which closed on February 29, 1940, a specially written booklet was given to those adults who had achieved literacy.

The adult pupils (generally between the ages of 15 to 50) were supplied with books, slates and other equipment free of charge. The municipal and secondary school buildings, the Bombay Development Department, and the Bombay Post Trust and the municipal buildings were allowed by the authorities concerned to be used free of rent for accommodating these classes.

EXAMPLE OF POONA

Professor Bhagwat, City Administrator of Poona, organized what he called "The Students' League for the Campaign Against Illiteracy." Hundreds of boys and girls of high school and college age joined the League. It had the following rules:

1. Any boy or girl below 21 years of age can be a member of the League provided that he or she signs a pledge to teach reading to at least ten illiterates among his or her neighbors.

2. Every member shall send, with his application for membership, a list of literate and illiterate residents of the house in which he resides.

3. Every member shall be entitled to training in the easy methods of teaching and will receive a set of books for his use.

4. Every member of the League shall submit a weekly report to the leader of his group.

5. There will be a weekly meeting of the group members and a monthly meeting of all the members of the League in Poona City for receiving reports about progress made by each member and the difficulties met by him, and for chalking out a program for future work.

The campaign began in June, 1939. The ambitious plan was outlined by Professor Bhagwat: "By July 1, we are trying to have some classes in 30,000 families. By October 22, we shall have made at least 30,000 new literates at a cost not exceeding 6,000 rupees.

TELEVISION'S RAY OF HOPE FOR THE WORLD'S ILLITERATES

The scene now shifts 12,000 miles and it is 20 years later, just before eight o'clock in late September 1959. A group of a dozen or so adults--men and women--are seated on both sides of a long table pointing towards the stand which supports a square box with familiar "rabbit ears" protruding.

Promptly at eight the cheery music of a tinkling xylophone comes from the box, and the words STREAMLINED READING march across the screen. A moment later a friendly face appears on the screen.

"Hello!" says Mrs. Helen Brown, the television teacher. "I'm glad you've come to improve your reading. Before we begin today's lesson, I want to introduce the man who wrote the book we are going to use. Here is Dr. Frank C. Laubach."

Dr. Laubach appears on the screen, and in a short talk congratulates the listeners for taking this great step forward. He points to the large, inflatable globe he carries with him everywhere, and tells how people all over the world are also taking this giant step of learning how to read. His enthusiasm radiates from the screen. The listeners, now members of the new TV class, can hardly wait for it to begin.

The teacher returns to the screen. "Today," she says, "we are going to learn the names and the sounds of some of the letters." She then begins teaching from a large chart (similar to the one on the supplement sheet in the back of this text). The lesson seems to go swiftly, even though enough review is provided so that the students can keep up. In a total of about 28 minutes, the first of 98 filmed lessons (called kinescopes) is finished. *

While the TV teacher has been giving her lesson, an assistant teacher right in the classroom has been going from one student to another, helping only when asked. Now, with the TV lesson over, the students and the assistant teacher stay perhaps a half hour. The students practice writing the letters b, c, d, f, g, and h, which the lesson had taught, while the assistant teacher quietly helps with any problems which may come up. Then the class is dismissed, with a cheery reminder to come back early for the next TV lesson.

The TV Classroom--Its Numbers Are Unlimited

Where is the classroom just described? It might be in a room of a church, a library, a community center, a school, in a civic organization, or in someone's home in or near Memphis, Tennessee. Here the program is telecast from WKNO, the community-owned educational station where the Streamlined Reading programs started.

Or, this class might be in the cafeteria of a large factory in Charlotte, North Carolina, watching the program over WBT, a large commercial station. In this case the time would be 6:30 to 7 in the morning, the only time commerical stations can afford to give without a sponsor. Even at this early hour more than 700 registered students were learning to read within the range of WBT in the spring of 1959.

One factory we visited, the Radiator Specialty Company, provided its reading class with free coffee and doughnuts after the lesson, before the workers started the eight-o'clock shift!

The possibilities, as demonstrated in the three years of Streamlined TV Reading, are virtually endless, for attacking illiteracy both in the United States and abroad. In the 'sixties we shall see a great development of TV literacy, even in countries which as of now do not have telecasting or receiving equipment.

WKNO–Memphis Shows The Way

In the spring of 1956, Dr. Laubach, on one of his perpetual tours of the United States, spoke in Memphis. In the audience were two persons who caught a vision of a new literacy service. Keith Nighbert was director of a brand-new educational television station owned by the city of Memphis. Mrs. Pauline Hord was a reading teacher with

---

* A film, Ray of Hope, demonstrates the method and tells about the program. Order from Foundation for World Literacy, Hickman Bldg., Memphis 3, Tenn.

HIS RAY OF HOPE

CAL ALLEY, THE COMMERCIAL APPEAL

years of experience. Mr. Nighbert saw literacy as a "natural" for
the new educational station. He and Mrs. Hord formed a team whose
contagious zeal soon had many other persons in the city interested.

Mrs. Hord spoke to church and civic groups, educational organ-
izations--anyone and everyone. The Chamber of Commerce adopted
the TV teaching project; the newspapers, especially the Commercial
Appeal, gave every meeting and every announcement full play.

The Memphis Section of the National Council of Jewish Women
contributed money, and have, all throughout the programs, donated
thousands of "woman-hours" of assistant teaching or record keeping.
Many groups contributed classroom space. Television dealers and
individuals contributed or loaned television sets for use in the classrooms (Elvis Presley, the Memphis boy of rock-'n-roll fame, gave
one of the sets).

In these months of getting ready, a team was preparing the
teaching materials and the pilot programs. Betty Mooney, formerly
of Literacy House, India, came to help. She had been on the team
which helped develop the first edition of Streamlined English, which

was to be the basis for the TV teaching. Miss Ruth Knowlton was
the first teacher on the screen, to be followed by Mrs. Helen Brown
the next year on kinescopes. A number of volunteers with training at
Koinonia Foundation served from a few weeks to many months helping
prepare the materials to accompany Streamlined English. The complete set, for a two-year course, is:

Course I	Reading Readiness charts (like the sample provided as supplement to this text)
	Streamlined English, by Frank Laubach
	Writing Exercise Book, by Pauline Hord
Course II	A Door Opens, by Betty Mooney
	Workbook for A Door Opens
	Going Forward
	Workbook for Going Forward

The student pays only for the cost of the materials, about $3.
There are no tuition or other fees for him. While the writing team
was working, others were out scouting for illiterates. A sociology
class in a Memphis college conducted an area survey to determine
just who the illiterates were, and what their jobs and educational
background were like. In our country an illiterate does everything he
can to hide his illiteracy from others. The very word "illiterate" is
taboo; persons are urged to come and "improve their reading. "

The First Year's Course Is Carefully Evaluated

Finally, the time for the opening of the first course arrived.
The mayor of Memphis proclaimed a "Literacy Day," and on a September day in 1956 the three-times-a-week TV course began.

A grant was received from the National Educational Radio and
Television Center, Ann Arbor, Michigan, to enable a careful evaluation study of the literacy program to be made. Three series of tests
were given to the students to determine progress, and 150 students
were interviewed by trained persons to find environmental factors to
be considered in the study. A detailed, voluminous report was sent
to Ann Arbor at the conclusion of the first year.

In February 1957 the first graduation ceremony was held. Some
200 students, who had successfully finished Course I, were awarded
diplomas by Dr. Laubach, visiting Memphis for the occasion.

In the spring of 1957 Course I was repeated, and Course II begun in the following half hour, thus making a whole hour of TV literacy three nights a week over WKNO.

The following year, from the experience of the first year, the
beginning Course I was stretched into two semesters, and the series
of 98 kinescopes prepared. A lease-or-sale arrangement was set up
for distributing the films to other communities.

Nadia Photo

TV teacher Ruth Knowlton, with Mrs. Pauline Hord and Betty Mooney.

The Foundation For World Literacy Is Organized

TV teaching in Memphis soon gained national attention: a special Sylvania educational television award, an article in Life and others in educational journals. Queries and requests for help started coming from every major city in the country. * Educators from almost 30 countries visited Memphis during the first three years. A pilot film for the teaching of Arabic was made by Dr. Laubach in Egypt, and one in Hindi was made at Memphis by George Prasad of India, on a visit from his studies at Syracuse University School of Journalism.

Clearly, the demand for TV literacy in other communities, combined with television's enormous potential, called for an organization to meet the challenge. The citizens of Memphis again rose to meet this challenge, and in August 1958 the Foundation For World Literacy was begun with a meeting attended by top educators of the nation.

The originators of the Foundation envision an educational center in Memphis, to which persons from around the world will come for training, and where films and videotapes may be made in many languages. A prominent citizen gave office space for the Foundation's first headquarters. As this text is published, sources of funds to turn this vision into action are being sought.

Two schemes for the promotion of literacy have been proposed: a national plan, drawn up by the noted educator William S. Gray and committee, and an international plan, formulated by a committee headed by Richard Cortright, of Baylor University Literacy Center.

* For an information kit on how your community can start a TV literacy campaign, write Foundation for World Literacy, Hickman Bldg., Memphis, Tenn.

AN URBAN UNIVERSITY REACHES OUT TO AN ENTIRE STATE

The Story of Baylor Literacy Center

By Robert C. Likins

A permanent university center for teaching literacy specialists and for aiding the development of literacy programs was established at Baylor University, Waco, Texas, in 1957.

The Baylor Literacy Center is directed by Prof. Richard W. Cortright, a member of several Laubach literacy teams, and a partner in the founding of Literacy House at Allahabad, India.

Success of the Baylor Literacy Center is due largely to the careful coordination among its staff, American and foreign students studying literacy at the university, and volunteer teachers from Waco and other communities in Texas and nearby states. The Center has developed a combination program of classroom theory and practical field work, as preparation of literacy technicians for community and world service.

Enrollment preference is given to: 1. students from abroad who expect to return to their homelands to serve as officers in literacy programs, and 2. American students who desire to serve in literacy programs in the United States or abroad, in programs sponsored by governments, missions, foundations or other organizations.

Curriculum Includes Basic and Advanced Studies

Literacy studies may be pursued as an undergraduate major, or as a minor on the undergraduate or graduate level. Besides Americans, students from Argentina, Hong Kong, Spain, Peru, Brazil, United Arab Republic, Lebanon, Indonesia and Italy have enrolled.

The following basic courses are offered: Basic literacy studies, a survey course in which literacy primers are examined, and new ones prepared. Introduction to linguistics, covering the essentials of descriptive linguistics. Writing for new literates. The first and the third of these is also available by correspondence.

Advanced courses include: Advanced literacy studies, including teaching by television, and setting up of literacy programs in the United States. Advanced linguistics, with emphasis on linguistic techniques in learning a second language. Senior literacy studies, concerned with responsibilities of directing a regional literacy program. In addition, an international internship is being arranged, providing field work experience in the United States and in Mexico.

The Baylor literacy training rounds out its theory courses with practical field experience, which may include teaching of illiterates, writing for new readers and helping to conduct literacy workshops,

Windy Drum

Billboards, handbills, radio and television ads bring in the students.

Baylor Reaches Out In Community Literacy Workshops

The Center has found that the best way to begin a literacy pro-gram in a community is to hold a Literacy Workshop, because:

> 1. The Workshop trains persons in the best way
> to use the literacy materials.

> 2. It stimulates further interest in the community
> to carry on a successful literacy program.

Successful Literacy Workshops have been held in 17 large and small communities of Texas, and almost that many in New Mexico, Oklahoma, California and Colorado combined. One of the primary goals of each Literacy Workshop is to help organize a local Literacy Council. By leaving a community with an organized Literacy Council, systematic literacy outreach can be multiplied effectively.

Excerpts from the Waco Literacy Council Charter, which has been used as a model in other communities, indicate the stable plat-form on which an ongoing literacy campaign may be based:

Purposes and Activities of the Waco Literacy Council

1. The purpose of the Council is to find and teach illiterates in the Waco area to read and write in English and/or Spanish.

2. The officers of the Council are a Chairman, to be elected annually, a Vice-Chairman for training of teachers, a Vice-Chairman for continual survey of the areas literacy needs, a Secretary-Treasurer.

These officers comprise the Council's Board and set its policy.

3. The Council meets the first Tuesday of each month.

4. The Council holds training sessions for new teachers in September and October, and throughout the year upon request.

5. The Council's Literacy Center at Baylor University is open from 7 to 8:30 p.m. Mondays through Thursdays to train teachers and teach illiterates.

6. The Council invites all interested citizens in the Waco area to take part in its work. Persons who subscribe to the purposes of the Council and take part in its program thereby become members.

7. The Council invites prominent citizens of the Waco area to become members of its advisory board.

8. The Council and its work in the Literacy Center is financed by voluntary contributions.

In its outreach to other communities, the Council is prepared to help a small core of persons in a community to solicit the interest of other key persons. Keen interest on the part of church groups, civic organizations and educational institutions in a community is a "must" before the start of a local campaign. The Waco Literacy Council will send one or more of its staff members to a community to aid in this preliminary work.

The basic information needed to help stir up community interest is contained in this condensation of a leaflet the Council sends ahead:

Getting My Town Started On A Literacy Campaign

Why Hold A Literacy Workshop? Ten million adult Americans are functional illiterates. Texas has nearly 800,000. Next year we will probably have more. Our state government can't wholly meet the need. Individuals and groups can help--you can help, your group can help.

Who Should Come To The Workshop? Every literate in your town should be invited. This is Each One Teach One. But it is more than that. It is one person making a new friend of another. It is a community witness for everyone.

How Do We Hold A Workshop? You need a nucleus organization to sponsor the Workshop--your church, your club, or a civic organization. This group may call the Workshop in its name, but it will invite other groups to attend. It will publicize the coming Workshop, and invite the press, radio and TV. It will pay the transportation and expense of the Workshop leader from Baylor.

Windy Drum

One or more classes are held every evening at the Literacy Center.

When Do We Hold A Workshop?   Within a month of starting
your literacy teaching.   It doesn't take long to train a
literacy teacher.   A common procedure is to begin in the
evening at 7:30 and run until about 9.   Then begin again the
next morning at 9 and run until noon.

What Is Done In A Workshop?   The Workshop's leader will:
    Show everyone exactly how to teach the lessons.
    Show you how to find illiterates in your community.
    Explain   how to present a literacy program on TV.
    Show how to write simple stories for new literates.
    Show in movies and filmstrips how literacy is being
        carried on in other communities.

Who Will Help Us Organize A Literacy Council? The leader
of the Workshop will help you and other interested citizens
of your community to organize the permanent Council.

Baylor Experiments With TV And Teaching By Mail

For seven months in 1958 a local, live TV program taught new
readers to read and write English.   Tapes have been made for the
teaching of reading in English and in Spanish by radio.
Now the literacy and the writing courses are taught by mail--
the first correspondence courses for credit in these fields. Recently
organized is the Western Writer's Guild to encourage writers for
new readers. All of these enlarge Baylor's local and world outreach.

Chapter 8

How Provincial and State Governments Have Organized Campaigns

Literacy campaigns in India fall under two general classes: those directed by governments, and those under private control. The dividing line between the two often was not sharp. Several which were called "unofficial" were conducted by government officials with government money. For example, the "unofficial" campaign in Aundh state was led by the Rajkumar himself.

EXAMPLE OF BIHAR

The most impressive government campaign conducted in India in modern times was in Bihar Province. The government made a grant of 80,000 rupees. Four types of schools were started:

1. Several score of adult schools, unaided by the government, were established by the Tata Iron and Steel Company at Jamshedpur. Others of the same type were established by sugar mills and by collieries.

2. Missions and other organizations with more willingness than money were aided by being given free blackboards, pencils, chalk, charts and primers, and a small amount of money each month for oil.

3. Colleges and high schools in which teachers or students were willing to teach as extra-curricular work were given free primers.

4. Teachers of day schools were given 5 rupees per month for teaching in regular adult schools at night, if the classes contained 25 students.

The last three received help from the government. The industries were supposed to be able to pay their own expenses. The sugar mills were pressed to open fifty school centers each and were told about how much they should spend--6,000 rupees. Other industries were urged to open centers which they were to support.

Every part of the Province was attacked at once, but not everywhere with the same energy. Seventeen areas were selected for intensive work, with the aim of making every man (not every woman) literate within six months! Whether any of the seventeen areas succeeded fully in this aim is doubtful, though many of them did exceedingly well.

The prevailing languages in Bihar are Hindi and Urdu. The primers used in Bihar were in large clear type. They combined short sentences with phonetic drill. They used no pictures because of their cost. The method was a compromise, having been prepared by a committee, some of whom were trained in the latest western story methods, and some of whom believed in the old Indian way of teaching the letters.

Each teacher was expected to teach this primer by his own favorite method and, as the committee said, "the real work depends upon the intelligence and ingenuity of the teacher." The primer was not adapted to the needs of the untrained volunteer teachers, because it required too much ability, though it proved satisfactory for well-trained teachers.

There was a great deal of excellent propaganda in Bihar. The motto, "Each One Teach Ten," could be seen in the adult education centers and schools. Young boys went to towns and villages singing rousing songs about the value of being literate, ending each verse with the refrain, "Each One Teach Ten!"

In three months the illiterate was supposed to be able to read and to know a little arithmetic. A test was given each three months by the sub-inspector of schools. If the student passed, he graduated into the "post-literate course," consisting of lectures on hygiene, agriculture, household and bazaar accounts, poems and stories, geography, history, local self-government, duties to the family, cattle diseases, weights and measures, money, communal relations, and other practical information that the teacher might desire to give. Lantern slides were used for some of these lectures. There were three readers provided for the post-literate course so that the student would not forget how to read. He was also given Roshni, a fortnightly magazine published for semi-literates by the Bihar government.

An enrollment form was filled out by the teacher, to be sent to the central headquarters. This form asked how many Hindus, Moslems, and Christians were taught (men and women separated); how many Hindus studied Urdu, how many Harijans* studied, how many

---

* Translation: "Children of God," a term promoted by Gandhi and still widely used to refer to the lower classes.

Moslems studied Nagri letters; and how many educated people volunteered to help teach.

There were three kinds of committees filling the stages between the teacher and the Minister of Education in the government organization:

1. A Center or School Committee (the center meaning the school), which helps and supervises the teachers.

2. A Sub-divisional Committee, with the Sub-divisional Officer acting as President.

3. A District Committee, of which the President is the Tax Collector (a very important official); and with him are all the important district officials.

4. At the top was the Minister, heading the Provincial Committee.

After Bihar Province had seen twelve months of intensive literacy teaching, a celebration was held in May 1939. The Minister of Education announced that four and one half lakhs of people had been made literate (a lakh is 100,000). It was encouraging to find that the number of students being taught was rising each quarter, the last quarter showing 139,867. One village in Shahabad reported that every man was literate. Every chowkidar* and policeman in the whole province had become literate or lost his job by government edict. The police had six months' warning.

A study of Bihar's statistics revealed the enormous difficulty of making India literate. If Bihar continued as she was doing, teaching five lakhs a year, it would require fifty years for her to make those literate who were now living. But meanwhile in fifty years the population would have increased fifteen millions. Besides this, two-thirds of the adults now living would be dead and a new batch of illiterates would need to be taught. Bihar had far and away the finest record thus far in India, but it was not enough even to hold her own.

So we face a sobering fact, as witnessed in Bihar. In large cities of large countries, though the number of illiterates taught may sound impressive on paper, the birth rate exceeds the literacy rate. The birth rate, moreover, is constantly accelerating. The prospects for a future literate population under such circumstances looks bleak indeed--unless all-out concerted efforts are made within the next few years by private groups and local, provincial and national governments.

---

* A term referring to the host of minor employees in government and business, such as messengers, servants, guards, etc.

Chapter 9

The Challenge to Teach Women

The census reports that only one Indian woman in fifty can read. In many of the other countries of the East and of Africa that percentage may vary from about four per cent down to one-tenth of one per cent. The peculiar problems associated with teaching women in many of these countries make particular emphasis or even special campaigns for women essential. This brief chapter deals with a few of the problems of teaching women.

Women usually find it inconvenient to attend classes because they have children to look after at home. Hence, wherever adult classes are organized, it will be necessary to have women volunteers to arrange for the collective care of small children while their mothers are receiving instruction. The problem of the education of women who have to supplement the family income by work outside the home, particularly that of women employees in factories, is beset with great difficulties. The lot of these women is very hard, for they not only have to perform their duties in the industrial establishments, but also have to work at home, both before they leave their house and when they return. Under these circumstances, it is futile to expect them to attend a night school or benefit by its instruction.

The only hope that can be entertained with regard to the education of such women is to hold classes for them on the premises of the industrial establishment where they are engaged. An appeal should be made to the industrialists to regard the eradication of illiteracy among their laborers as a social and moral duty and arrange classes for them in the company premises during working hours.

It is comparatively easier to launch an attack upon the illiteracy of the urban women than on that of rural women. In the rural areas, the paucity of educated women who can teach the adults is the greatest handicap. And it is difficult to get women teachers from the towns, as they find it unsafe to go and live in the villages alone. There are two methods by which women teachers from the towns can be secured for rural work:

1. Establish a center in the villages, where a teacher,

a health-visitor and a midwife might work together.

2. Send married couples with the necessary training for
   rural work, so that both the husband and the wife may
   serve in the educational program.

As matters stand for women's classes, though women teachers
are always to be preferred, in most cases the adult women will have
to attend the men's classes because no women teachers are available.

In the adult schools for women, sewing classes or the teaching
of some simple cottage industry should precede the actual classes,
as these would attract the women and induce them to attend regularly.
Music and other recreation should always be provided. In the old
days in many countries, knowledge used to be imparted to the people
through music and song and through the narration of stories. No wonder it attracted the rustic minds.

Mere literacy should not be the goal of the adult education program. The women's range of information should be widened by talks
and magic lantern lectures, and wherever possible, by the cinema
and the radio, which have proved of immense value in eradicating
illiteracy. The minds of the voters should be released from the cage
of ignorance in which they are imprisoned, so that they may be ena-
bled to discharge creditably the responsibilities and duties with which
they are invested. At the general talks and lantern lectures, women
who are already literate should also be invited.

Happily, there is nothing in any of the great religions of the
world which prohibits women from receiving an education. It is true
that the purdah system isolates many Moslem women from men and
confines them largely to their homes. This makes education more
difficult, but by no means impossible. With the Each One Teach One
home study method, purdah need not be a very serious impediment
to literacy. Many of the great Moslem women leaders of India manage to work effectively from behind their veils.

When the Premier of Bombay wanted to be sure of a great success for the literacy campaign in May 1939, in the City of Bombay,
he threw the burden upon Miss G. Gokhale, an immensely competent
woman, because no man in Bombay could have done so well. Two
other competent women, Miss Rustomjee and Miss Khandavala, wrote
the primers. Miss R. Dongre's lesson primers and her successful
classes in Bombay are also notable. These she started as sewing
classes. Friends were asked for cast-off clothes. The women could
take them home when they were properly repaired. While the sewing
went on, stories were read to the women until they themselves wanted
to learn to read.

Yet, splendid as the ability and enthusiasm of women are, the
unhappy fact remains that they are as yet not organized against

Robert Laubach

Women in Delhi practice writing their lessons on slates.

illiteracy and are making far slower progress than the men. All in
all it seems well within the truth to say that ten men are learning at
the present time for every woman--and yet seven women are illiterate for every man!

There is too much tendency on the part of the educated women
to depend upon government and upon the leadership of public-spirited
men. The men as a whole will disappoint the women, not so much
because they mean to do so, as because it is difficult to divorce themselves completely from their deeply entrenched habits of thought.

When women realize that they must depend wholly upon themselves, and organize as fully as though men did not exist, their drive
against illiteracy will get on faster. They will get far more from the
men if they assume the initiative and appeal for help. To insist upon
merely following men's leadership is to condemn their sex to perpetual ignorance.

The problem of literacy especially for women has long been recognized, as evidenced by this resolution. (All too often, unfortunately, little action has followed the most promising of resolutions.) It
was adopted by the India Adult Education Association:

This Conference, while recognizing with regret that adult
education among women is lagging behind that among men,
owing to the difficulty of gathering pupils into teaching
centers and to the wide-spread lack of trained leadership,
would stress the fact that women must be given an educational and cultural opportunity equivalent to that of men
if the ideals of enriched living are to be achieved. It is
self-evident that a different curriculum and different methods must be developed for this work. This Conference
urges that experiments be made in a triple approach to
courses of study:

1. Courses designed to equip women for their primary
   task of homemaking: child welfare and child psychology, hygiene and first aid, nutrition, needle craft, etc.

2. Courses for the developing of the cultural life, such
   as literature, music, civics, history and other courses
   which make literacy a prerequisite.

3. Training in the various cottage industries whereby a
   woman in the home may help to raise its economic
   level.

Women will need to be taught at home more often than men. The
time of teaching will be between 12:00 and 3:00 p. m. , since women
as a rule must care for their husbands and children in the evening.
The contents of the lessons, to be most interesting to women, ought
to deal with their household activities. Indeed, there is everything
to gain by making the teaching of women a specialized work, gathering suggestions from the experiences of men, but not attempting to
imitate men's campaigns.
A great new day of hope is dawning for the men, but will it include the women? Not unless the women include themselves--not by
demanding things of the men but by doing the work themselves. They
must--and they can.

Chapter 10

How to Hold a Literacy Conference

"How long should an ideal conference be held?" The answer to that question leads to another question: "What kind of conference do you mean?" There are at least seven varieties:

1. A conference to organize a district literacy drive. There might best be a series of meetings, each an hour and a half in length, and perhaps a week or a month apart. For large cities where prominent men with crowded programs participate, the time must sometimes be cut to one evening.

2. A conference to pool experiences. This is very desirable after a campaign has been conducted. For example, if college students have taught illiterates during vacation months, they should meet at the opening of the new school term to report and exchange ideas, for they will have the most valuable kind of knowledge-- that born of experience. Their findings should be duplicated or printed for distribution.

3. A conference to inspire, lecture, and instruct the community. Seldom can such a meeting exceed one evening session or perhaps one evening a week. One type might be a symposium where several speakers considered various problems of adult education.

4. A conference to learn from a campaign specialist. How long the conference should be depends upon the wishes of the specialist and the interest of the people. In our own case we find that four days with morning, afternoon, and evening sessions, will enable us to cover the most vital points in a literacy campaign. Ordinarily it is difficult to keep unpaid people longer than this.

5. A conference during the Director's visit to a village. The first organizing visit to start the village campaign will often need to be a week in length. Return visits of a half day to a day should be made every three months.

6. A special conference to train teachers for an intensive campaign. Such conferences vary greatly in length. Students of Madras University studied for four days just before their vacation campaigns. Much better, however, is a conference of twenty days if it can be arranged. Miss Laura F. Austin describes one such conference:

"A training class for teachers was held in Kosamba, India, for three weeks. The first two days were given largely to preparatory lectures concerning the work of carrying on campaigns for literacy. On the morning of the second day the method of teaching the first lesson was given to the teachers. That evening the whole group, about seventy strong, went to the villages. We found a few learners, but not nearly enough to provide one learner each for our 66 registered teachers. On the second night there were more learners, for they were looking for us. On the third night there were still more, and soon we had more learners than there were teachers! Nor did the enthusiasm die down.

"By the time we were ready to close the summer's work, about 120 persons including twenty mission teachers, had taken the work in method and some ninety illiterates had had the benefit of the practice teaching.

"At the closing program four new literates rose in the presence of the large audience and read a page out of a book of easy reading which they had not previously seen. The first read his page without a mistake and in a smooth-running style. The others also did well. A good many more of the others could have done the same. This was after thirteen days of being taught. Writing was also taught, with creditable results.

"A badge, to be given to the new learner when he satisfactorily finishes the prescribed work, was designed by this teacher group. It consists of a white India on a black background over which a rising sun shines. Around the edge is inscribed 'Learned After Becoming Adult.'

"Another practical task undertaken by the students of the summer school was the selection of words from the dictionary which they think are in common use in the illiterate villager's vocabulary.

"Besides this training, teachers had the privilege of the other courses in Cottage Industries, Physical Culture, and Scouting which the school was carrying on."

7. Lesson-building conferences as a rule require a longer period. To a very great extent the success of a conference depends upon what goes before it and what follows it. Questions like these should be worked out in advance: who are to be present, what officers to have, who are to be the officers, who are to do the speaking, the agenda, and the committees to be appointed. This can be done by a small committee, meeting at least five times in advance, one

member of the committee in particular spending at least forty
hours of hard thinking, writing, and interviewing.

The Secretary, who should continue to act after the conference,
must be the most interested, practical, and efficient person available.
If he can take stenographic notes he will get fuller minutes. It is
essential for him to use a typewriter well. The permanent value of
a conference depends largely upon how well these notes are written
and given publicity.

MAKING THE CONFERENCE A SUCCESS

Decide what the conference is for; what changes in thought and
action will result from it, if successful.

Make a list of all who should be present. The letters sent to persons or organizations whose attendance is sought need not be long;
they ought to be definite.

The important lesson to be emphasized, at the risk of being rep-
etitious, is that every last detail of a conference ought to be worked
out well in advance and with complete detail. Generally speaking, the
better a conference is thought out, the better will be the results.

Not only must program and schedule be worked out with great
care, but many other details as well. Among these are the lodging
and boarding of delegates and the assurance of a hall in which they
will not be disturbed.

The table of literature for sale or free distribution requires a
good committee of its own. This committee must have four months'
notice so that it can get its material from publishers. Somebody
must be at the table to explain and sell or give away what is on exhibition. Distribution by sale or gift of an abundant supply of lessons
is always an important part of a conference.

If at all possible, tear all delegates away from their own environment and take them to some secluded retreat where they cannot
carry on their usual tasks, or (what is even more important) be
bothered by the usual interruptions. It is precisely those who will
be most useful for a literacy campaign who are most frequently disturbed by telephone calls, visitors and letters. Generally speaking,
large cities are the poorest places for conferences because there are
too many disturbances, distractions, and attractions! It is not good
for the morale of a conference for some of the leading delegates to
drop in once in a while from other duties. If the conference desires
to take a half day of recreation let all of them recreate together.

In Appendix E is a long list of aids to a literacy conference, including topics for discussion. A committee preparing for a conference will find many of these ideas of value.

Chapter 11
Literacy Directors and Their Duties

For an effective literacy campaign, a full time provincial director and several district directors are necessary. Although the actual
teaching of illiterates can be done by all types of people, there is no
hope of large success unless a campaign is well directed by trained
men and women who stimulate, instruct, correct, organize, and
appeal.

The director must have no other work, and he must have abundant energy as well as consummate tact. He must possess a tremendous passion for this task, realizing that it is at once one of the most
difficult and one of the most vital tasks confronting the new India.
He must possess a great love of people, a love that yearns and prays
for the emancipation of the masses, and rejoices when they are released from bondage of mind and body. He must carry into this work
a religious fervor and sacrificial spirit. He must have a dogged per-
severance that will never say "Impossible." Few are the men and
women who possess all the qualities that combine to make a really
great director.

Since everybody does not possess these qualities, in what way
shall we discover the right persons? There are just two things we
can do: find them and train them.

First, observe high school and college students who are teaching
illiterates, and offer scholarships to those who show special qualities
of character, leadership, and teaching ability. Second, offer special
courses in the training schools, so that those who demonstrate their
ability may secure the best possible training as directors. General
high schools, colleges and training schools must cooperate in the quest
for hopeful young men and women.

It is not in theoretical classes but in actual teaching of illiterates
that we shall find men and women with the rare gifts necessary for
this work. It is highly important for governments and private organizations to keep promising students under their eye.

A great danger lies in appointing people for reasons of their high
standing and influence. Always (almost) such men lose interest when
work is uncomfortable, and thus they spoil the campaign. Men and

90

women from the villages and from lower walks of life are very likely
to succeed. They will feel passionately eager to help the people from
whom they sprung; and for this reason, other things being equal, they
should prove superior to those who have never experienced the pains
and heartaches of the underprivileged illiterates. People from villages also understand the psychology of their kindred and are likely
to be practical, whereas many city-bred men are impractical vision-
aries when dealing with village problems.

A director should observe how campaigns are successfully carried on in other regions. He will do well to visit regions carrying on
the most successful campaigns and participate in them for at least
two months. He ought to read the literature of adult literacy and keep
up to date with the progress of literacy in his country and other countries.

The director must know his own district and formulate a plan
that will fit its needs in the light of the resources he has at hand. He
must have imagination to prepare an original program to meet this
situation.

Every director of literacy will be eager to exchange experiences
with every other. The body of new knowledge is accumulating so rapidly and so fruitfully that a wise director will be in touch with every
place where experiments are being tried. Other parts of the world
will offer fruitful suggestions also; but conditions abroad are so different that all foreign ideas should be regarded as suggestive and
not conclusive.

The district director is first and last a traveling man. He has a
little correspondence with the central office, but his chief service is
to visit as many villages in his district as often as possible. It would
be ideal if a man and wife without children could be directors together;
for the women's campaign needs even greater effort than that of the
men.

In opening a new village, he will need to stay longer than upon
later visits. Just how to begin such village work is described in detail in other chapters.

Mr. Sundaram of Dornakal remained from three to four days in
one center. A typical paragraph from his report says: "During the
month of July, conferences were held in five centers with 205 mission
workers and 295 village Christians from nearby villages. We spent
three to four days in each village and sold over a thousand charts."

Where the field to be covered is very large, a great deal can be
accomplished in a one-day conference, leaving the day before and
after the conferences for visits, organization, and interviews. Such
conferences of village leaders should be held in a central place,
accessible with little or no cost to the delegates, many of whom will
walk. If possible, food should be supplied free. The forenoon may
be devoted to discussions on theoretical considerations and the after-

noon to practical experimentations with illiterates and teacher training. The evening should be devoted to lantern slides where these are provided, or to lectures on the burning problems connected with literacy, such as (1) reasons why literacy is necessary, (2) adult education, (3) relation of literacy to social reconstruction, (4) democracy.

In Bombay the response of the illiterate population to such propaganda exceeded all earlier expectations. Because of the right propaganda, illiterates came in such numbers that the 400 centers which had been provided proved inadequate, and 120 more were opened at once.

What hours of the day to devote to conferences depends very much upon the season. In the hot months there is no use in trying to keep enthusiastic with the thermometer standing above 100 F. The meetings can then be early and late. Many of our conferences have run from 8-10:30 a. m., 3-5:30 and 7:30-9:00 p. m. It is well to have a recess of five minutes at the end of each hour.

Just how many villages can be covered by one director? This is a question that has no final answer as yet. Each director has his own opinion. Thus far the workers have been so few and the regions so great that nobody has dared to suggest a maximum limit. They have often been placed in fields entirely too large for anybody. They have done intensive work in a small part of the region, hoping that later they may reach the other districts, or that their example may be followed far beyond their actual reach. But the question as to the correct area for a director can be answered only by experience.

June Dohse

Writers' conference in India considers farm topics for new literates.

Under very favorable circumstances it should be possible to hold two conferences each week, if each is a day in length. This would mean eight a month, or twenty-four each three months. The director ought to be able to make a round trip every three months. If we estimate how many villages can be represented at each conference, we are able to arrive at a judgment as to how many villages the director can cover.

Conferences may be small or large, with only ten in attendance or with 300, though the best work is done by most directors with not less than 20 and not over 100. If a director has 24 conferences a quarter, and averages 100 villages represented in a conference, he might conceivably "cover" 2400 villages. But this is a very heavy program, even under the most favorable circumstances. He could not visit these villages and would need an assistant to go ahead of him to set up the conferences. Much would depend upon the organization existing when the campaign began. In Dornakal, with 1500 teachers under good control, Mr. Sundaram could reach farther than the average director.

Ordinarily, it would be better to hold only one conference a week and to devote the remainder of the six days to intensive visitation of villages, gaining first hand experience, and stimulating and strengthening and correcting local campaigns. It is neither necessary nor desirable for the director to visit every village four times a year, but he ought to visit it at least once. He can visit one, two or three villages in a day, seldom more. A live-wire director should average five villages visited a week or 60 every three months, or 240 a year. That seems to be the limit of what he can do well.

Professor Bhagwat, with his fine engineer's imagination, constructed the following set-up for sixteen millions of people in Bombay Presidency. At the top is the director of adult education. Under him are 25 supervisors, each supervisor in control of 20 organizers; 500 organizers, each one covering 150 to 200 square miles; and 18,636 village workers. In order to fill gaps and provide for expansion, he would have 37,272 apprentices serving with the village workers.

Mr. Bhagwat says the chief function of the supervisor would be to "supervise training of village workers and organizers," arrange for recruiting them, and transferring them when necessary. He wants his supervisors to be forty years of age and to have had five years experience as an organizer.

In summary, the district or provincial director should know, both by theory and by experience, all of the following things:

1. How to deal with governments.
2. How to teach the lessons; how to train other people
to teach them.

3. How to make a village survey of literate and illiterate people.
4. How to mobilize a literacy army.
5. How to test the results of teaching.
6. How to hold special literacy graduations and festivities.
7. How to prepare lesson materials and follow-up literature.
8. How to train others to write these.
9. How to print an attractive book.
10. How to publish a newspaper for new literates.
11. How to translate and to guide translators from English to other languages, or from any one language to another.
12. How to discover native folk-lore and poems and other interesting materials.
13. How to appraise the value and readability of books that are already in existence.
14. How to classify these books according to their readability and according to their themes.
15. How to organize reading rooms, and install libraries and put these under safe supervision.
16. How to distribute books, magazines, pamphlets, and newspapers in the villages.

Robert Laubach

First literacy lessons for stone-age men of New Guinea.

Chapter 12

How Private Organizations Conduct Literacy Campaigns

WHAT INDUSTRY CAN DO FOR LITERACY

One of the most remarkable illustrations of cooperation between industry and government in the elimination of illiteracy was the campaign of the Tata Iron and Steel Company in Jamshedpur, as a part of the great Bihar literacy drive.

The Company initiated its campaign on July 4, 1938. With thoroughness such as we might expect of the greatest steel mills in the British Empire, a Committee of Fifty-one, headed by Mr. J. J. Ghandy, General Manager of the Company, was appointed. Each member visited a school center at least twice a week and submitted a report. A small central committee of four examined these reports and took action on them, recommending lines of action to the President. Mr. Ghandy responded with the following message:

An Appeal To All Workers

The Honorable Minister for Education's scheme
will not only teach the illiterate adult to read and write,
but will widen his mental outlook; it will impart to him
a knowledge of the rights and responsibilities of citizen-
ship, and transform him into an intelligent patriot; it
will banish the shadow of crime, disease and poverty
from his life; it will eradicate the evil of indebtedness;
and it will convert him into a literate, efficient member
of society.

The Mass Literacy Campaign, originally launched
during the last summer vacation purely as a temporary
and voluntary measure, has already met with vast success all over the province, and is now due to enter its
second phase, when it will be placed on a permanent
and partly paid basis, and will comprise village libraries,
cinema and radio talks and regular instruction in reading
and writing throughout the year.

I have known of numerous instances in which your
ignorance has been exploited by unscrupulous money-
lenders and you have been prevailed upon to sign prom-
issory notes for amounts far in excess of what you
actually borrowed, and of instances in which ignorance
has led to serious accidents in the plant and on the road
outside. I have also known of numerous occasions on
which you have been led astray by false promises held
out to you by irresponsible self-seekers. It is only with
the growth of literacy amongst you that you will be able
to minimize the evil of indebtedness, add to the general
security of life through a better understanding of 'Safety
Principles' and realize that the Company's prosperity
is your prosperity. Unless there is perfect peace and
harmony between the two, production will fall and profits dwindle, and there will be no possibility of the Steel
Company paying you any bonus, as it has done during the
last four years.

I am aware that some of you possess the skill required in the Works for higher paid posts than you oc-
cupy at present, but the one great barrier to your progress is illiteracy. If only you decide to overcome this
obstacle, I see no reason why any one of you should not
be able to rise to posts of responsibility by dint of loyal
and hard work.

This movement is being run entirely by funds contributed by public-spirited citizens and deserves the
whole-hearted cooperation of you all. I would therefore
appeal to every one of you, man or woman, with all the
emphasis at my power, to make full use of these mass
literacy centers, and convert yourself into literate,
efficient workers, capable of promoting not only your
own interests, but also those of the Steel Company.

>   J. J. Ghandy, General Manager
>   The Tata Iron & Steel Co., Limited

Mr. Ghandy was awarded the Lady Hallett Gold Medal by the
Ministry of Bihar in recognition of his distinctive work in connection
with adult literacy.

WHAT UNIVERSITIES AND OTHER SCHOOLS CAN DO

Sketched in here are a few of the many fine examples of how
colleges and secondary schools have undergirded the literacy

campaign in their areas. These experiences are presented not so much as blueprints as for their inspiration to schools everywhere to design service outlets to meet the needs and opportunities in their own countries.

Colleges

At Hislop College in Nagpur, Professor D. G. Moses organized the "Social Service Society" in 1932. It held several night schools-- one in a college building where college students taught illiterates to read and write in Marathi, Hindi, or English and gave them the rudiments of arithmetic. The enrollment from year to year was about 150, the average attendance 100.

About 300 new literates attended these classes, and 136 students took turns in teaching or in doing some other form of social service at one time or another.

Professor H. A. Dharmaraj in reporting on this work writes: "When we began five years ago we had hardly twenty students, but today there are over 130 with whom social service is a passion. The students are doing all the work; theirs is the inspirations, theirs is the credit."

Such is the spirit of college students in many parts of India. They are, as a rule, far more eager to lift India out of illiteracy by hard personal effort than older people are to give their resources to finance campaigns. One gets the impression that here is immense idealism and boundless surplus energy chafing to come to grips with social need.

One morning I reached Baroda at the impossible hour of 1:30 a.m., expecting to spread my bed roll in the station until daybreak, as I had done many times before. What was my amazement when five college students, all total strangers, stepped forward, each throwing a garland of roses over my head, and begged me to attend their youths' literacy organization. This at 1:30 a.m.!

A very successful literacy school was conducted in Jubbulpore on the verandah of the Leonard Theological Seminary under a large electric light. Under the supervision of Professor Habib Yusufji the classes were taught by theological students. Illiterates learned Hindi or Urdu, while the literate students who desired to continue their studies further were taught English. The method of using new literates to teach others was practiced with fine results.

At Jubbulpore are at least two other thrilling student adventures. From Robertson College there went a dozen to twenty college men under the leadership of Professor Jwala Prasad to teach a village three miles distant and to bring about its social reconstruction. The Hawabagh Girls' Training School in the same city has taken under its wing a village a half mile distant.

In Madras University a group of young students banded themselves together for war on illiteracy and spent several weeks in Jaya Mansions, Madras, listening to lectures and learning the methods of teaching, in preparation for a summer of reconstruction and literacy work.

Students of Forman Christian College and of other colleges in Lahore and Amritsar, and students of Moga Dayanand Mathradas Intermediate College, all trained by Miss E. J. Smith, spent the summer vacation teaching in their homes and elsewhere. Representatives of Kinnaird College taught during their holiday in Kashmir.

The students of Lahore, full of burning zeal, organized what they called The Anti-Illiteracy War Council, which represented, they said, a large proportion of the students of the city. Students in the Council represented: Sengal Private College for Women, Mahila Women's College, Central Training College, Islamia College, Hailey College, D. A. V. College, Sikh National College, Kinnaird College, Forman Christian College, Rang Mahal, Law College, and Government College. They began in April with fifteen days of propaganda, including posters, radio, handbills, leaflets and processions. This was followed by a drive for pledges that each educated person would teach one illiterate. Then during the month of May, voluntary workers were to teach with all their might.

Twenty young men and women from the University Settlement in Bombay went to a village in the Surat region and, in about three weeks, taught 300 people to read. They boarded with the people, paying their board. They taught anybody anywhere in their homes, not in classes but one by one. They were standing ready to teach whenever there was anybody with a few moments to learn. The people, suffering under terrible land taxes, and eager for emancipation, saw hope in education and were eager to learn. In Poona, each member of The Student's League Against Illiteracy promised to undertake to teach reading and writing to at least ten illiterates during 1939-40.

Mr. T. J. Kedar, Vice Chancellor of Nagpur University, made the suggestion that the usual four-year course in college be cut to three years and that the other year be devoted to training and practice in rural and general social service, of which adult education would be an important part.

In our observation, college students do not need compulsory measures. They are willing, as a rule, to go further than their teachers. Here, for example, is one student's proposal:

"Require every student preparing for a Bachelor's Degree to make 100 literates without any cost to the state. The degree Doctor of Letters would be conferred upon anybody making a thousand people literate." (The degrees earned this way would thus benefit thousands.)

High Schools And Primary Schools

The primary teachers were the cornerstone of the Bihar campaign, and almost, if not wholly, the cornerstone of most of the other campaigns of prewar and postwar India. They were expected to teach adults at night after they had taught children by day. Thousands of school teachers were at work teaching adults after school hours.

School teachers must be careful not to sap their energy teaching both day and night. By enlisting the help of their school students, the teaching may be greatly multiplied. The students may teach at home evenings and during holidays. This can be stimulated by offering rewards, or by requiring the teaching of one adult for promotion.

Robert Laubach

Afghanistan school teacher (right) teaches illiterate army draftee.

Clearly it is inherently wrong to expect these teachers either to be efficient when working double time, or to help India by abandoning the primary room to do adult teaching. As a rule they leave what they can do better to attempt what they can do less well. There are places, perhaps tens of thousands of them, where the responsibility for the education of the adult must fall upon the primary teachers, but in those places he needs to be trained in the art of so managing his task that others take the burden off his back.

Mr. Bhanot, seeking the reasons why the great Punjab campaign of 1921 gradually died out, a campaign which depended upon the primary teachers doing extra work, found the following weaknesses in the campaign, which he regarded as fatal:

1. Fictitious enrollment, "not unoften paper schools."
2. Not as popular as the statistics indicated--only 10 per cent of the enrollment received certificates.
3. A colossal waste of time, labor and money.
4. Something radically wrong in the whole system and method.
5. Adults taught as though they were children.
6. Teachers unpleasant and unpopular.
7. Adults and young boys often taught together.
8. Teachers tired by hard day's toil.
9. Lack of suitable textbooks and well-defined course of study.
10. Non-existence of suitable continuation literature or follow-up magazine.
11. Lack of sufficient suitable propaganda to arouse public opinion, resulting in apathy.
12. Lack of devoted volunteers.

It is precisely these weaknesses, every one of them, that the primary teacher needs to face in a training school or special conference before he be allowed to teach adults.

WHAT UNOFFICIAL SECULAR ORGANIZATIONS CAN DO

Unofficial and semi-official organizations of all kinds are springing up throughout India, which have as their primary or sometimes their secondary objective the abolition of illiteracy. Indeed, there seems to be such an organization in almost every town and city of any size. Some of them are famous; some are not known even in their own city. Some of them are led by the people who have the power to make a large success. Some of them are more or less temporary clubs, debating as to whether illiterates need to be literate in order to advance. Some of them are led by eager young students who have little or no influence but much surplus energy and a great deal of zeal to do something. Those which seem ineffectual may turn out to be very useful. Many of them need encouragement and good advice.

Bombay has for a number of years had two organizations, one called The Bombay City Literacy Association, organized by ex-Mayor K. F. Nariman; the other, The Bombay Adult Education Association.

The former of these organizations taught adult laboring men, often in shops and factories. They employed the children's primers used in the Bombay Schools. Miss Shanta Bhalerao of the Servants of India Society taught women in their homes or in hallways or at a social settlement house under supervision. Miss R. Dongre prepared a fine primer as a result of her experiments with illiterate women, while Miss G. Gokhale acquired the invaluable experience and reputation which fitted her later to assume the responsibility for the great Bombay drive of May 1939.

In Bengal the All-Bengal Literacy Campaign had the support of the Vice-Chancellor and other officials. Likewise in Indore, Nagpur, Raipur, Lucknow, Allahabad, and Lahore, government officials took leading parts, though in an unofficial capacity.

The Coordinating Committee for all these literacy movements was the All India Adult Education Committee at Delhi, although it had no real authority except to call conferences. The First All India Adult Education Conference, which was held in March 1938, applied itself chiefly to the study of what ought to be done.

The All India Women's Conference has placed "a literate India" at the top of the list of their objectives--including all women. Their problem is very much more difficult. There is widespread indifference among men, and in some quarters active opposition, to women becoming literate.

Mr. G. T. J. Thaddeus, General Secretary of the India Boy Scouts, initiated a movement for the Boy Scouts to take up literacy. This is one of the most useful ways of doing a good turn for somebody every day. The Boy Scouts can be of tremendous aid, not alone by teaching but also by aiding publicity, acting as salesmen of newspapers for semi-literates, doing secretarial work, and running errands.

WHAT RELIGIOUS ORGANIZATIONS CAN DO

Almost every religious group can find basis in its holy writings supporting the teaching of its people to read. In many instances the clergy of several religions have also become fervent teachers and literacy supervisors. In some Buddhist countries most of the literates have learned to read in the temples. Hindus, Moslems and

Christians teach their own kind and reach out to teach neighbors of
another religion. Early in the Koran, Moslems are urged to teach
all their members to read. Christians are motivated by the desire
to have all men read the Word of God for themselves.

The "Servants of Omdoa," a group of wonderfully devoted Hindus, are employing every opportunity to promote literacy as a part
of their social service program. They are active in Bombay, Poona,
Allahabad, Calcutta and other cities.

Congregations of churches need to be stirred and directed towards concerted action. Pastors and leading church members should
take an active part in the direction of a church-centered campaign.
Here are some of the ways in which they can get the church members
to teach:

1. Make the members of the Church alert to this good
   cause. Talk to people about the subject and point out
   the need for literacy. Tell them that it is the duty of
   Christian people to help their fellow brothers who are
   illiterate.

2. Have special prayer long before the campaign begins.

3. Preach to the people from the pulpit on "Adult Literacy and the Congregation."

4. Challenge Sunday schools, high schools, colleges,
   hospitals, young boys' clubs, girls' clubs, etc., to
   teach.

5. Train church members to teach the primer before the
   campaign starts.

6. Conduct classes whenever and wherever possible.
   Each One Teach One.

7. Open a library. Let the people come to read. Have
   enough interesting materials for reading, etc.

8. Be writers. Write for new literates. Write booklets
   and pamphlets and interesting, fascinating articles.

9. Encourage church members to advertise and sell
   follow-up literature.

10. After the students finish the Primer, have a gradu-
    ation ceremony.

11. Give them the second book, The Story of Jesus. Let
    them read this book for two weeks.

12. Tell them why you are teaching them:

Tell them the Story of Jesus and the Resurrection. Jesus is still here. He said, "Lo, I am with you always." He is trying to help you to join His Father's family. We must speak to Jesus to offer our lives. Prayer is speaking with Him.
Tell the story of the Prodigal Son. Tell them that it is good for the followers of Jesus to join the church so that everyone can help one another. Tell them if they will join the church you will be glad to have them.

How To Do Literacy Work In A Christian Village

In villages in which there is an active church and many of the villagers are members, the literacy campaign may aim to teach as many of the villagers as possible, both Christian and nonChristian. The literacy director, if he is from another area, may show the local leaders how to use the following techniques:

1. Hang posters and pictures on the walls of the church or on the walls of the houses of Christians in the village. Cut pictures from newspapers or magazines.

2. Create an interest for learning by personal talks, by public lectures.

Committee on World Literacy & Christian Literature

Christian villagers, having finished the Primer, get New Testament.

3. Live right in the village, if possible, and have close contact with the people.

4. Organize an evening worship program for two weeks. Give part of the worship to those who are literate. Let them tell a Bible story, sing, or read a passage from the Gospel before the congregation. That will motivate the others.

5. Now you are ready to start day or night classes. If there are difficulties, try to teach people in their homes, in the farmyard, on the way to the well, in the field.

6. Find out those homes where at least one member is literate. Help them to carry on the family worship.

7. Put a picture of a "ladder of literacy" in the homes where people are learning to read. As each member of the family learns to read, color in another rung of the ladder. This way you create a sense of pride and achievement.

8. When a person finishes the first five lessons in the Primer, give him a picture of Jesus.

9. If a person has taught 5 lessons to his friend or neighbor, give him a picture also.

10. Give a badge or a certificate when a person finishes the Primer; then give him the Story of Jesus to read.

11. Plan a Christian Literacy Festival--Easter or Christmas week is a good time. Make a condition for admission--he who has finished the Primer will be allowed to come to the Festival.

12. Have contests in the Festival--public lectures, films, a literacy booth, games, recitations, singing, acting, etc.

13. Start a lending library in the church or school.

14. Have a graduation. Invite a government official to present diplomas.

15. Collect photos of people learning to read and keep them in your library.

Chapter 13
Training for Directors, Teachers and Writers

PERMANENT LITERACY CENTERS ABROAD

LITERACY HOUSE, INDIA
By Elizabeth Mooney

Literacy House, which started at Allahabad, India, is a practical and growing demonstration of a way to help a country tackle its problem of illiteracy. Literacy House has evolved a pattern which may be of help to other countries interested in a nation-wide literacy program. As mentioned previously, many literacy campaigns and projects have gone on in India since 1935. Plans and methods were worked out by various agencies and individuals. But there was no center to integrate work, to give systematic training in literacy methods, to produce and supply materials. There was no one place where government, churches and private organizations could send candidates to become experts in literacy techniques.

Literacy House did not start out being all of these things. It began as a pilot experiment conducted at the invitation of the Extension Department of the Allahabad Agricultural Institute. The first training course was held there from February 17 to March 18, 1953, under the leadership of Dr. Frank Laubach, then Literacy Consultant to the Indian Government under TCA (the United States Technical Cooperation Administration). Dr. Welthy Fisher served as administrator of the project and has continued in that capacity. Miss Elizabeth Mooney and Mr. Richard Cortright assisted as teachers and supervisors. George Prasad became full-time teacher-supervisor.

Forty students representing eighteen states and all the major language areas came for this first course. They ranged in educational qualifications from high school graduates to those with M. A. degrees. Among them were teachers, journalists, clergymen, and social workers. Some were sent by state ministers of education, some by directors of community projects, some by churches, and others came on their own initiative.

Literacy House has held 19 short courses to date (June, 1955),

each four weeks long, thus sending out about 500 well-trained teachers. But in addition to this, there has been an opportunity for the
staff to give training in the basic principles of literacy teaching to
other groups. These include groups of social education organizers
and teachers who come to the Institute for a six-month training period, groups of agricultural extension workers who come for short
courses at the Institute, Home Economics extension workers, and
also regular students at the Institute who are taking extension methods.   Probably a thousand people have been reached this way and
have gone out with the additional tool of literacy techniques to help
them with their work. The staff has also taught students in the Basic
Education Training College in Allahabad.

From the beginning an effort has been made to keep the training
as practical as possible. "Learn to do by doing" has been one of the
basic principles. Workshop techniques are emphasized in place of
lectures. Dr. T. A. Koshy, head of the Extension Department and
Director of the Social Education Training Program at the Institute,
assisted in providing opportunities for practical work in the nearby
villages. He also made it possible for trainees to meet with village
workers of the extension project to discuss problems in connection
with literacy work. Trainees also had an opportunity to interview
Institute staff members who were specialists in agriculture, animal
husbandry and public health in order to obtain accurate information
for their writing projects.

Work In The Villages

Each evening the trainees went to a village to teach illiterates
to read and to try out materials written in class as a test for interest and vocabulary. It was there in the village that the trainees really learned what it means to teach an illiterate. It would be difficult
to say who learned the most in that month--the trainees or the villagers.   A college president had his first experience of sitting on the
ground around a lantern with a group of illiterate farmers. He had
to forget his dignity, his degrees, his theories of education; but he
came out of it with a new understanding of his fellow man and a deeper dedication to service. Teachers had to learn to keep quiet and
let their students talk. Preachers had to let their deeds speak and
not their words. Journalists had to forget their flowery phrases.
Men of high caste had to learn to sit with those of low caste. The
thrill of teaching and the thrill of learning broke down many barriers
which could not have been broken down in months of lecturing and
moralizing.

When this course was evaluated by the trainees, two words were
repeated over and over--"fellowship" and "inspiration." "I have
learned here," said one trainee, "what it means to live as a family."

Many another said, "I have been inspired to do something of real service for my fellow man." Similar expressions have been made in each of the following eighteen courses. Literacy House started with the purpose of training people in methods of adult literacy. It found itself fulfilling another purpose--training in group living, which is important in any type of social service.

These feelings of "inspiration" and "fellowship" are probably due to certain policies which have become fundamental at Literacy House. One is the continuing policy of taking representatives from different agencies and sections of the country and with different educational backgrounds. Sometimes it has been suggested that separate courses be held for college graduates and high school graduates. But these two groups have much to learn from each other, and having both in the same class keeps the staff on its toes. Each course is tailored to meet the needs of the particular group. This prevents "mass production," which can easily result from courses repeated over and over.

Morning meditations help to bring the group into harmony and offer inspiration. These meditations are not compulsory but are almost always regularly attended by all. Here inspiring words and ideas from different religions are brought to the group. Members meditate and pray together. They begin to see how they can give themselves in literacy work. One trainee commented, "I have learned how to forget myself and love others." They begin to feel the challenge of bringing light to those who have not been able to read. A Chinese proverb, "It is better to light a candle than to curse the darkness," has become a motto for Literacy House. A candle-lighting ceremony at the close of the course, when certificates are given to the trainees, has grown out of this and has proved inspiring.

Simplicity and informality of living have also helped the group become a family. Trainees sit on the floor for their classes. They eat in a common mess. They feel free to discuss problems with staff members. Literacy House is an open house. It opens its doors to visitors who come from all parts of the world. Trainees have an opportunity to meet outstanding journalists, educators, statesmen and technicians. Trainees share their own experiences with each other. In fact, they learn as much from one another as they do in their classes. Informal teas, excursions and recreational activities are part of the program. The trainee puts in many intensive hours of work during his month's stay but he also has a chance to broaden his horizons and uplift his vision.

Practical work in the village continues to be the most important part of the training program. It is the basis for all classwork and discussions. No trainee receives a certificate unless he has demonstrated his ability to approach the villager in a friendly way and has successfully taught at least five adults to read during the month of

किसान सुधारपत्र

Betty Mooney

Teacher George Prasad (right) helps trainees make wall newspaper.

his training. Some trainees have come with the idea of being supervisors and watching other people do the work. But only those who
have had day-by-day teaching experience can understand the method
and know the joy of the illiterate when his eyes are opened to the
printed word. Only the person who has taught can train and inspire
other teachers.

So, six days a week, trainees go out from Literacy House to a
nearby village to sit with their village friends and conduct their
classes by lantern light. Groups sit under a tree, on a porch, in a
house--wherever convenient--and with no special arrangements for
the teacher. Visitors often have difficulty distinguishing the teacher
from the students. And that may be considered a compliment. Wom-
en trainees go out to the village in the heat of noon because that
is the time they can find the women of the village free. Even then
the women must read with nursing babies in their arms or small
children playing around them. The lessons are constantly interrupted
by household duties.

Practical work includes making a village literacy survey at the
beginning of the course, organizing classes, and cooperating with
the villagers in a literacy mela (festival) at the close of the course.
In this literacy mela villagers are given an opportunity to contribute
their talents to the program, express their ideas and make it their
mela as much as possible. Usually it is presided over by the village

headman.

Literacy House believes in giving the trainees as much practical work as possible. But it also believes that the villager is not to be used as a guinea pig. One village may provide practical work for two or three groups of trainees but there will come a time when there are not enough illiterates to give the trainees the experience which they need. Literacy House then places a full-time literacy worker in the village to assume responsibility for continuing work--to train volunteer teachers, establish reading rooms, and do all possible to make the new readers independent. There are now twelve such workers under the supervision of a Literacy House staff member. So Literacy House fulfills another purpose. It has become a demonstration center of the process of making a village literate.

In addition to the hour and a half in the village each day, trainees spend about five more hours in discussion and workshops on matters pertaining to their practical work. Each trainee must be as nearly perfect as possible in the method of teaching. He learns not only how to teach his students to read but also how to teach them to write and do simple accounts. He learns how to meet individual needs and how to let each student progress at his own speed. He learns adult psychology, both in theory and in practice. He learns the techniques of village approach and gradually obtains an understanding of the whole pattern of village life. The trainee learns what is meant by functional literacy and how to know when a man is literate.

Training in Audio-Visual Aids

The trainee makes use of certain audio-visual aids to arouse and maintain the interest of the villagers. He finds that music is an effective medium for breaking down barriers between the educated and the illiterate. Trainees and villagers often sit together around some drums or a harmonium and share their feeling in music. Trainees may teach the villagers some literacy songs and villagers in turn sing some of their folk songs. Some songs they sing together.

Trainees learn how to make and use a flannelgraph, or "kuddar" graph,* as it is called in India. This is a useful and simple aid to arouse interest in literacy. Trainees write original stories based on actual situations in the village, showing how literacy can help to solve problems. As the story is told, pictures are placed on the flannel board. Flannel on the back of the picture makes it stick to the flannel on the board. But to the villager it looks like magic and he watches spell-bound.

---

* "Kuddar" is a type of home-spun cotton, which may be applied to the board and to the back of individual pictures. The pictures will then stick to the board as they do with the more expensive flannel board.

Puppet shows have proved to be a popular audio-visual aid. Trainees prepare simple hand puppets, write the script which includes music, dances, and humor, and present the finished show at the literacy mela. Men, women and children enjoy the antics of "these little people" and at the same time learn a lesson.

Trainees learn how to run a kerosene projector to show film strips in the village. They learn how to correlate the film strips with reading lessons so that the new literate will have a more vivid idea of what he is reading. Flash cards with outline pictures are also used for the same purpose. Trainees also learn how to demonstrate some of the improvements discussed in the Anand readers, such as making a compost pit, smokeless chula or bore-hole latrine. Workshops in the afternoon give trainees an opportunity to master the techniques of these audio-visual aids.

Learning How To Write

Learning how to write for the new literate is another part of the training course. In the first course held at Literacy House, Dr. Laubach was interested in completing a series of vocabulary-controlled readers for adults. So under his direction, trainees learned the art of using simple words, short sentences and repetition. They gathered information from experts, made it as interesting and simple as possible and tried it out in the villages. This work was continued in the following course under the direction of Miss Margaret Lee Runbeck, a well-known American writer. * She helped to arrange the stories into booklets and carried a plot through each book to add suspense and interest. These books were later published by Literacy House. So again Literacy House took on another job which it had not originally anticipated--the production of reading materials for new literates. Ram Telang, a graduate of the Hislop College Department of Journalism, was taken on the staff as editor, and Alfred Moses as artist, so that this work could be carried on.

After the Anand series were completed, trainees took part in other writing projects. Each trainee learns to make a wall newspaper to use in his village. He writes material which can be used in a magazine for new literates, such as Ujala, published by Literacy House. A new series of "how-to-do-it" books is now being produced and much of the material has come from the trainees.

---

* The untimely death of Miss Runbeck came suddenly in the fall of 1956. For several years she had given generously of her time and talents to the cause of world literacy. Readers may recall her charming books of some years ago, Time for Miss Boo, The Great Answer, Answer Without Ceasing, and more recently, The Year of Love. The latter, a novel set in modern India, was written during her India visit mentioned above, and was purchased by a major film company.

Trainees spend at least an hour a day in some writing project. This discipline not only helps them become writers but it helps them discard some of their misconceived ideas of what it means to be educated. Much pride is discarded along with big words.

Literacy House held a writer's workshop in April 1955, under the direction of Rudolf Flesch, a master in the art of simple writing, plain talk and clear thinking. He found that one of the greatest needs for the would-be writer for new literates is the ability to be specific. And in order to be specific he must know the needs and interests of the new literates. That is why teaching and writing go along well together.

Ujala, a fortnightly magazine started by Literacy House, grew out of a demand from former trainees for some follow-up material for new literates. Kastoorchand Gupta, a trainee of the second course and a man with wide journalistic experience, became editor. There are now 600 subscriptions and each copy is read by many new literates.

Evaluation Of Literature

This demand for more follow-up material also led Literacy House into another activity. In the last few years many books written in Hindi for new literates have been placed on the market. Some of these are very good. Some are not worth the paper on which they

Hugh G. S. Bivar

A literacy drama helps promote interest for teachers and students.

are printed. Some go through one edition and are not reprinted because no way has been found to get them to the new literates. Literacy House has undertaken to examine and evaluate all books written
in Hindi for the new adult reader with the idea of selecting the best
of these for distribution to the villages through libraries.

These books are analyzed and evaluated on the basis of subject
matter, accuracy of information, format, ease of reading and human
interest. The formula developed by Dr. Flesch for testing the readability and human interest of writing in English has been found helpful. Other factors such as size of type, number of pages and use of
color are also important in choosing books for new literates.

In the past two years some 800 books have been evaluated, and
from these 400 have been selected to go into tin trunk libraries. So
far, eight different sets of 50 books each have been compiled. Each
set contains books on various subjects and in different stages of difficulty so that every new reader in the villages will find a book to
meet his particular interest and reading ability. These libraries
are circulated in the villages where Literacy House is working and
about 100 additional sets have been sold to other agencies working
in the Hindi-speaking area.

Trainees have an opportunity to examine these books and learn
the techniques of book analysis. Some trainees from other language
areas are now examining the material in their languages to compile
similar libraries. Trainees visit libraries in the village and learn
how they are set up. This training in how to provide follow-up material will help to make literacy campaigns a success.

Help After The Courses Are Finished

To cover all that a literacy worker needs to know in the brief
period of four weeks is a problem. It is impossible to go into everything in detail. The course is streamlined as much as possible. The
major emphasis is on the techniques of teaching and starting a program. Trainees know that if they need further help when they are in
the field the services of Literacy House are available. Orders come
in constantly for materials. Hardly had the first group of trainees
arrived back at their centers before requests for materials began to
come in. Literacy House did not expect to be a distributing center
for materials. The books and charts were being published elsewhere.
But people wanted one place where they could write for everything.
Thus began the sales and distributing department of Literacy House.

Trainees also wanted to share their experiences in the field and
get new ideas. They wanted to keep up with what Literacy House was
doing. To fulfill this need, a newsletter, Literacy House Highlights,
was started. It goes out four or six times a year to ex-trainees and
others interested in literacy. Trainees come back to visit Literacy

World Education, Inc.

A few of the materials for new literates published by Literacy House.

House when they can. Plans are now under way for refresher courses. Staff members visit centers of ex-trainees when possible. Dr.
and Mrs. Paul Means, who joined the staff in 1954, have visited several centers and have begun to form alumni groups in various areas.
Mrs. Means sent out a questionnaire to all ex-trainees to find out
what progress is being made.

Mr. A. R. Siddiqi, teacher of literacy methods and supervisor
of practical work, has often helped village workers examine new literates to see if they are functionally literate. He has also given
three-day training courses to village teachers. Mr. Leslie Jacob,
of the audio-visual department, has given help in meals and farmers'
fairs. Literacy work is a thrilling adventure but often a lonely task.
So all of these contacts help to maintain inspiration and make trainees feel a part of a mighty army combating illiteracy.

Requests for help were influential in beginning Literacy House's
series of books to help the teacher. Two of these which are proving
very helpful are A Handbook for Social Education Material Writers
and a book called Puppets. Literacy House also designed certificates
which can be used for the new literates.

Then there has been some extension training. Literacy House
tries to meet the request of any organization for help in carrying on
a literacy training program. Teams have gone from Literacy House
to help mission groups in four areas. This summer a team has gone

to Himachal Pradesh to conduct five two-week training courses at the
invitation of the state government. Invitations are coming from other
state governments and will be accepted as soon as possible. Literacy
exhibits and demonstrations are in demand by community projects,
extension workers and others.

Literacy House Expands Into Literacy Village

The staff of Literacy House was enlarged to meet the expanding
program. At one time it consisted of twelve Indians and four Americans. Mr. Comfort Shah, M. A. from Delhi School of Social Work,
served as administrator while Mrs. Fisher continued as director.
Others on the staff included specialists in village approach, teaching
techniques, audio-visual aids, book analysis, simple writing, library science and art. They were not all specialists before they came,
but experience on the job and in service training helped them become
so. Opportunities were given to the staff to attend special conferences, to hold discussions and to meet other experts so that they
would grow in the whole field of adult education and rural uplift. The
artist on the staff took leave to study audio-visual aids, radio and
television in the United States. Continuous training of personnel is
part of the job of setting up a Literacy House.

Literacy House was located at the Allahabad Agricultural Institute for a year and a half. The advice and help of experienced Indians
there started it in the right direction. But its expanded program demanded larger quarters and an opportunity to grow, without depen-
dence on another institution.

On September 13th, 1956, ground was broken for the first buildings on the ten-acre campus outside Lucknow, India, to be known as
Literacy Village.* The Village includes an administration building,
with offices, classrooms, library, visual aid workshops. Dormitories and a cafeteria, several staff houses and servants' quarters
of simple design have also been built. An open-air theatre and a
House of Prayer for All Peoples is a part of this most unusual functional design.

In the summer of 1957 Ford Foundation provided a grant of money for a School of Writing for New Literates which is being erected
on the Campus of Literacy Village.

Mrs. Welthy Fisher is Founder and continues to be General
Director of Literacy Village. Dr. T. A. Koshy, one of the outstanding Christians of India, is Executive Director.

The center will have the departments it always has had, such as
publications, sales, audio-visual, library, classrooms, administra-

* By publication date of this text, the major portion of the building of
Literacy Village has been completed. Supporting its construction and
program is World Education, Inc., 45 East 65 Street, New York, N. Y.

tion offices, exhibits, storage of supplies. Groups of villagers can also be brought into the center to be trained as teachers after they learn to read. The staff will live in simple houses on the grounds. Through their way of living they can demonstrate to the villagers many of the things which are in the Anand books and prove an incentive to village improvement.

Literacy Village will rest on the basic principles which have helped Literacy House expand:

Flexibility
Help people help themselves
Help all communities where there is need
Keep the illiterate and his needs central in the program

Any Literacy House which rests on these four pillars will be sure to make a lasting contribution.

LITERACY HOUSE, EGYPT

In February 1955, a Literacy House was dedicated at Minia, Egypt, during the visit of the Laubach literacy team.* The establishing of a central training center seemed essential after the success of the village campaigns, several of which were described in Chapter 6.

Some of the functions of Literacy House might be listed as:

1. To train village literacy supervisors.

2. To train teachers to use the charts and primers.

3. To act as distributing center for the Primers and for Stage II reading materials.

4. To encourage and train writers for new literates.

5. To serve as a center for surveys of the needs of the nearby communities, and to develop reading materials to meet the needs.

6. To serve as a library and reading room, and to extend its services through portable lending libraries of the "tin trunk" variety.

7. To act as distribution center for the monthly magazine for new literates, El Nur. Eventually, Literacy House may become a publishing center also, though

* Literacy House, Minia, Egypt, is largely supported through the Committee on World Literacy and Christian Literature, National Council of Churches, 475 Riverside Drive, New York 27, N.Y.

it is more convenient and practical to publish in Cairo
at the present time.

Literacy House is under the general direction of Miss Marjorie
Dye, Miss Halana Mikhail, and staff. Dr. Davida Finney, guiding
light in literacy for many years, retired in 1958. The Reverend Samuel Habib, editor of El Nur, returned to his writing and editorial duties in 1955 after a year of study at the School of Journalism, Syracuse University.

The services of Literacy House are open to Christians and Moslems alike. There is a remarkable community spirit and feeling of
unity in the villages in which literacy campaigns have been conducted.
The presence of Literacy House is a permanent witness to the concern for village need. The people respond with cooperation and enthusiasm.

The "Literacy House" as a permanent institution in strategic
places has long been a dream of all who have worked with the illiterates. With the first two now in operation, one in India and one in
Egypt, the dream has now become a plan to open more Literacy
Houses, as funds allow, in many parts of the world.

Development Of Other Centers

East Pakistan. The East Pakistan Adult Education Center, at
Dacca, is spurred forward by a remarkable team: a retired British
Judge, Hugh G. S. Bivar, and an energetic Pakistani lady, Sarojini.
During the past several years their work has grown steadily. More
than 10,000 illiterates have been taught. In training sessions for
teachers, by 1959 about 1,000 men and 250 women teachers had completed training at the Center. Emphasis is placed on teaching women.

Calcutta, India. The West Bengal Adult Education Association
was formed twenty-two years ago. It has played host to several literacy teams in its area, and has served in growing measure the pop-
ulous Bengali language area. In 1959, in an announcement by President Kalidas Nag and Secretary Bilas C. Mukerji, a bold plan was
begun to start a new center at Habra, 30 miles from Calcutta. It will
serve as a training center, with facilities for 50 trainees at a time.

Valle de Bravo, Mexico. Several years ago an adventuresome
Californian went to this picturesque but largely illiterate valley three
hours' drive from Mexico City. There W.S. Thomas started teaching
illiterates. Now a Casa de Alfabetización is established, to which
persons from Koinonia Foundation and the Memphis literacy center
go for on-the-field training. Baylor University is exploring possibilities of granting credit for field work done at "The Valley."

LITERACY AND WRITING CENTER, EAST AFRICA

In the summer of 1959, a two months' workshop for African writers marked the opening of the Literacy and Writing Center at Kitwe, Northern Rhodesia. The Center has been established in response to requests from many Christian groups and individuals in Africa, a venture of faith for all concerned. It will be a service agency for the missions and churches in Africa, as they plan an all-out attack on illiteracy, and look ahead to a time of greatly increased production of Christian literature.

When the plan was first presented to the All-Africa Church Conference at Ibadan in January, 1958, the response was to "...warmly welcome the proposal," and express "...hope that the Center may be established with all possible speed." A year and a half later, the staff was at Kitwe to open the first workshop.

The most important question was that of leadership. Dr. and Mrs. Wesley Sadler were ideally suited to direct the Kitwe Center. Representatives of the United Lutheran Church in America, they have had long experience in literacy and literature work in Liberia. Additional missionary staff members will be assigned by American and British mission boards, and an African staff will be gathered.

A location was needed. From half a dozen countries came invitations. The Christian Conference and Study Center of the Copperbelt Christian Service Council in Northern Rhodesia provided a splendid answer. Located in Mindola, a section of the city of Kitwe, the Council built dormitories, classrooms and dining facilities to provide for the Center's needs. Quarters have been rented on a three- to five-year basis, so that funds can be invested in people, not buildings.

The Africa Literacy and Writing Center will have two basic emphases. Each year, some of the staff will move out into the field, visiting countries south of the Sahara to organize literacy campaigns and to train workers for continuing programs. Early in 1959, this is the kind of work Dr. Sadler was doing in Liberia, the Ivory Coast and Togoland.

But for at least nine months of the year, the Center will draw in groups of potential authors, who will come for workshops lasting three to six months. The purpose of the Center is clear: to find, train and encourage African authors to write for African readers in Africa. They will be selected by the churches and missions, and will return to direct programs of Christian literature across all of Africa.

At the 1958 annual meeting of the Committee on World Literacy and Christian Literature, Dr. Sadler said:

"The primary purpose of this Writing Center will be to teach Africans to write. There will be general writing

courses, and courses for editors of magazines and those
who are writing literature for use in Sunday school.

"Closely related to this, we hope to have instruction
in conducting literacy campaigns... showing how a campaign becomes a permanent part of the community, and
a permanent part of the activities of the church.

"The Center may help with language analysis. Many
new readers give up beyond the primer stage because, as
one African said, "it doesn't respond... it doesn't speak
to me.' This means the language hasn't been properly,
scientifically analyzed. Sometimes serious language problems can be ironed out in a few hours.

"The present plan is to bring in thirty Africans at a
time for a period of three months. Most of them will be
leaders from their own communities. All will have had a
fair amount of education. There will be the spiritual contact, the personal, friendly social contact we will have
with them, as well as what we teach.

"I ask you simply to put your imagination into high
gear and consider what it is going to mean to the whole
Lit-Lit program throughout Africa to have this long and
intimate contact with ninety African leaders each year.

"I want to say that we picked this assignment with
a great feeling of aliveness, a great feeling of thankful-
ness. We have been working with the Loma people in
interior Liberia--25 or 30 thousand people. We hated
to leave, in a way. But now we have before us a field,
not of 25 or 30 thousand, but of 25 or 30 million--and
many times that number of people to whom the printed
page will carry the Good News."

COLLEGE TRAINING ABROAD

In the fall of 1952, the first department of journalism in a col-
lege in India was started at Hislop College, Nagpur. Prof. Roland
E. Wolseley, on leave from the School of Journalism at Syracuse
University, was the director of the new department. Prof. Harold
A. Ehrensperger, formerly editor of motive, a magazine for youth
in America, was also on the staff, along with several Indian lecturers.

For several months preceding the start of the term at Hislop,
Dr. Wolseley visited several score of editors and journalists in all
the sections of India, gathering information about the procedures of
the Indian press and interesting the editors in the new college training in journalism. From this first real study of the Indian press
there came a book edited by Dr. Wolseley, Journalism in Modern

India.

As with every department of journalism, the main emphasis has been to train writers and editors for work in the general press of the country. A special course, called Writing Social Education Materials, was developed under Professor Ehrensperger's direction. For some years, as noted earlier, students of Hislop College had been going into the villages to teach illiterates. Now, students in this course carried on their visits to the villages, and returned to the classroom to practice writing articles to meet the needs of the villagers. From the experience and guidance of the course the first year, a Handbook for Social Education Material Writers was prepared. This was later published by Allahabad Literacy House.

The department of journalism at Hislop was staffed in 1954-56 by Prof. Everton Conger, head, William A. Dudde and Sam Krishniah, graduates of Syracuse University's School of Journalism, and colleagues. In 1958 another Syracuse graduate, K. Eapen Eapen, joined the Hislop journalism staff.

A department of journalism has been started at Osmania University in Hyderabad. Other colleges may shortly develop similar departments, thus attracting many students who at the present time go to the United States for journalism training. For the purpose of training writers to meet village needs, the closer the colleges are to the people with whom their students will work, the better.

It is to be hoped that departments of journalism in colleges in other countries may include courses in the kind of teaching and writing that this book is all about. Some colleges have offered courses in journalism at intervals. Ewha College in Seoul, Korea, for example began courses in journalism in 1952 under the direction of Miss Kathleen Crane. Others are encouraged to make it part of their curriculum.

PERMANENT TRAINING CENTERS IN THE UNITED STATES

The study of linguistics as preparation to learning a foreign language, and of phonetic analysis as an aid to reducing a spoken language to writing have been taught for a number of years. The Wycliffe School of Linguistics in Oklahoma, the University of Michigan, the University of Pennsylvania, Yale University and Hartford Seminary Foundation are but a few of the centers where linguistics and phonetics have been developed into a science.

Hartford Seminary Foundation

Training people to teach Each One Teach One and to write for the new literates are two distinctly different problems. There are

Syracuse "literacy journalism" class considers types of publications.

but a few centers for training in these fields. Hartford Seminary
Foundation, Hartford, Connecticut, gives training leading to an M.A.
or a Ph.D. in linguistics and the teaching of illiterates, plus some
instruction in the techniques of writing simple materials. The faculty
is composed of Dr. Henry A. Gleason, linguistics professor and
author of An Introduction to Descriptive Linguistics, and Dr. J.
Maurice Hohlfeld, literacy professor who has traveled in Africa and
the Near East as literacy consultant. Dr. William Walzer, of the
National Council of Churches, is visiting lecturer in journalism.
Other visiting teachers with experience in the field have included
Miss Norma Bloomquist, Dr. Wesley Sadler and Miss Margaret
Miller, all from Liberia; and Mr. Richard Cortright, an associate
with the Laubach literacy team.

School of Journalism, Syracuse University

At Syracuse University's School of Journalism, Syracuse, New
York, the student may become well grounded in all aspects of writing, editing and publishing--plus receiving training in writing follow-
up materials for literacy campaigns. Degrees offered are the B.A.,
M.A. and Ph.D.
The faculty includes Prof. Roland E. Wolseley, prolific and
authoritative writer and editor on journalism (i.e. Exploring Journal-

ism, Writing for the Religious Market, Journalism in Modern India);
Associate Professor Robert W. Root, formerly executive editor of
Worldover Press and correspondent in Europe and Asia, author of
Better Writing for Better Living and How to Make Friends Abroad;
and Robert S. Laubach, lecturer in journalism.

Summer courses have been offered since 1954 at Chautauqua
Institution, Chautauqua, New York, under the auspices of the School
of Journalism. This has proved to be an ideal time and place to
reach many students who cannot spare a year of study. The summer
courses are meant to give only the highlights in literacy and writing.
To become qualified for full-time work abroad in either field, a minimum of a year's training is necessary: literacy-linguistics at Hartford, or journalism for new literates at Syracuse.

By agreement between the two schools, a student may begin a
two-year course at Hartford, receiving training in linguistics and
literacy there, and go to Syracuse for the second year of journalism
and writing for new literates. He may then receive his M.A. from
either institution. Such a comprehensive course of study is recommended for men and women who will be directors of a literacy campaign and of the accompanying literature program.

Scarritt College

After several summer courses in linguistics and literacy, Scarritt College, Nashville, Tennessee, now includes training in these
areas in its winter curriculum. Mr. James Carty, with a background
of newspaper journalism and teaching, has conducted courses. Mr.
Earl Stevick taught literacy courses at Scarritt, and during his leave
for work in Africa in 1956-57, Miss Vivian Morter conducted the
courses.

Carver School of Missions

In the summer of 1956, Carver School of Missions in Louisville,
Kentucky, introduced credit courses in literacy-literature. Mr.
Richard Cortright taught courses in linguistics, literacy techniques,
teaching English as a foreign language, and writing for new literates.
Robert Laubach was guest lecturer in the last course. Mr. Cortright
and Dr. Frank Laubach taught the courses in the summer of 1957,
and Mr. Cortright continued the Carver summer courses in 1958
and 1959.

Koinonia Foundation

At Koinonia Foundation, Baltimore 8, Maryland, a Literacy
Center was established in 1956, and has been directed from its start

by Miss Nell Peerson. The Koinonia Literacy Center offers two four-month terms during the winter months, in literacy and writing for new literates. Short summer courses are offered, in addition to occasional one-week or two-week workshops. Practical experiences for the trainees is gained by teaching illiterates in Baltimore, both foreign and native-born. A small but versatile print shop at Koinonia helps produce reading materials for the new literates.

Literacy Center, Baylor University

Baylor University, Waco, Texas, in the fall of 1957 began its university Literacy Center, inviting Mr. Richard Cortright as professor and chairman of the Center. Baylor offers a B.A. degree with a literacy major, including studies in literacy techniques, linguistics, and the teaching of English as a foreign language. The student may also take courses in the foreign service studies curriculum.

The Baylor Literacy Center, in addition to the training for its college students, conducts classes the year around for the illiterates of the city. As discussed in detail in Chapter 7, the Center offers consultation services for the establishing of literacy campaigns in the many communities of the southwestern United States.

In 1959 the Baylor Literacy Center began a correspondence course in literacy and writing for new literates, available to persons throughout the world.

Other institutions are beginning to offer comparable training. Some professors, before starting such courses, are getting the opportunity to train at Hartford, Syracuse or Koinonia. Asbury College, Wilmore, Kentucky, for example, sent Miss Ruth Fess for first-hand training, and began a literacy and writing course there.

Wheaton College

Wheaton College, Wheaton, Illinois, began in the fall of 1958 to offer a writing major, which will be of special interest to many evangelical missionaries on furlough, and to young people preparing for the mission field. This step was heartily endorsed by Evangelical Literature Overseas, the recognized literature bureau of many evangelical mission boards.

SHORT COURSES IN THE UNITED STATES

A great number of missionaries, government personnel and workers with private institutions are going abroad each year without any training in literacy skills. They will invariably find themselves in contact with people in rural situations, where even a smat-

tering of know-how in literacy would help. In order to reach these
people, Dr. Laubach, during one summer, traveled to over twenty
missionary conferences and summer schools in the United States,
giving in one or two days a "Four Hour Course" in literacy, and con-
sulting on an individual basis with as many as possible. During another summer this endeavor was carried on by Mr. Alfred D. Moore,
executive secretary emeritus of the Committee on World Literacy
and Christian Literature.

Mrs. Amy Cowing, with the Extension Service of the United
States Department of Agriculture, for several summers has taught
groups of missionaries principles of writing technical materials in
an easy and interesting manner.

For several summers a short course in literacy was given by
Dr. J. Maurice Hohlfeld to a group of missionaries gathered by the
National Council of Churches for pre-sailing orientation at Meadville,
Pennsylvania. Dr. Hohlfeld has taught groups of missionaries at
Montreat, North Carolina, in successive summers. He has also
trained workers with migrants, under the auspices of the Home Mis-
sions Council of the National Council of Churches.

In the summer of 1958, courses were conducted in a number of
colleges, including Fort Wayne Bible College, Fort Wayne, Indiana;
The Community College of Denver University, Denver, Colorado;
Upland College, Upland, California; Berkeley Baptist Divinity School,
Berkeley, California; Carver School of Missions, Louisville, Kentucky; and Emory and Henry College, Emory, Virginia (sponsored
by the Council of the Southern Mountains).

In July 1959 the Council of the Southern Mountains sponsored a
literacy writers' workshop at Red Bird Mission, Beverly, Kentucky.
Mr. Richard Cortright of Baylor and Mr. Richard Creedon of Koin-
onia Foundation were instructors in the course. Mr. Robert Connor,
editor of Mountain Life & Work, the magazine of the Council of the
Southern Mountains, was a resource person for the workshop. Dr.
Edgar Dale, Director of the Educational Research Bureau of Ohio
State University, served as a consultant.

In addition there have been workshops at Koinonia Foundation,
at Burlington, North Carolina, and at Memphis, Tennessee. The
last was sponsored by WKNO-TV, which has pioneered in literacy
teaching by television, and was offered in conjunction with the first
large conference on television literacy teaching, called by Memphis.

The courses in literacy and writing for new literates at Chautauqua Institution, New York, sponsored by the School of Journalism
of Syracuse University, were held for the sixth successive summer
in 1959. Graduates of these courses are now working in more than
25 countries.

There is no doubt but that the training of personnel is one of the
greatest problems confronting us. Many types of institutions can

help in the training: the literacy house, the university and college, the school of journalism, and private and government agencies. Two types of courses are needed: regular degree courses to develop career persons in literacy-literature, and short courses of various kinds to add teaching and writing techniques to persons trained in other fields.

Personnel by the thousands are needed: some trained to teach, others to direct or manage campaigns, still others to write for new literates. Part II of this book deals with the training in the latter.

Edwin Carlson

Variety on a newsstand in Khartoum: movie starlet and picture of Christ. Literature for new literates must hold its own with these.

Part II

WRITING FOR NEW LITERATES

Chapter 14
How to Discover Writing Genius

WHO WILL DO THE WRITING?

The reading matter which is easy enough for new literates is largely meant for children. But illiterate men are no more interested in reading only children's books than educated men are. Adult illiterates are mature men and women, with burning life problems and adult points of view. Nothing else so forces one to face life soberly as does suffering, and the illiterates have suffered pain and hunger more than most of us have. Educated people constantly express surprise at the good judgment and intelligence of illiterate men and women.

People who have recently been illiterate must be provided with helpful books and papers, or they see no value in reading at all. They require literature written in their spoken language, just as mature and sensible as the papers and books we read. They especially appreciate answers to burning questions which they would go to any pains to have answered.

Unfortunately, nearly all writers have thought that this kind of writing was beneath them, that it would spoil their "style" and their reputation. There are a few exceptions to this rule, the foremost of whom is Rabindranath Tagore. He is far and away the most famous Indian poet, read throughout the world, because he discovered a secret in words. This is his secret:

THE SIMPLE WORDS MAKE US LAUGH OR WEEP

None of us ever weeps or laughs much over words that we read in books but never use in conversation. The words which bring with them a flood of emotions are the words which we have heard since childhood. It is the adroit use of these that makes us angry or sad or glad. Tagore is great because he knew the secret of weaving common words into phrases of great beauty and playing upon our heart strings.

127

Tagore's English has amazing force. If you open one of his volumes you see there the same words you have used since childhood. But he weaves those words into simple, profound poetry and philosophy that strikes like a sword into the depths of your soul. The world needs ten thousand Rabindranath Tagores who can create a new literature for the millions who are joining the ranks of literacy. This is not a pious wish; it is absolutely necessary. And since this is so, we <u>must</u> discover how and by whom this literature is to be written.

Since we need, not only a half dozen writers, but many thousands of them, ranging in ability from ordinary skill and talent to genius, we must search for them constantly.

The great literacy campaigns which Dr. James Yen began in China 35 years ago resulted in five millions learning to read. The Chinese were then forced to face this same problem, for the Mandarin classical literature was wholly beyond the illiterates. They have found the following methods bring results:

1. Offer remuneration.
2. Promote projects to enlist enthusiasm among possible writers.
3. Cultivate friendship between young writers and give them a chance.
4. Do nothing to restrict the freedom and initiative of writers.

In India, the chief hope of providing an adequate supply of literature lies in the schools. Diamonds are sought by examing tons of soil. Genius is as rare as diamonds and must be discovered by examining all promising "raw material." In one respect, genius is not so much like a diamond as it is like a rare mutation in plant life; the young bud is very easily killed unless it is properly nourished.

Nor can genius be discovered by giving students a written examination and selecting those with the highest marks. It is not only precocious ability, but also an unusual power of concentration, and a zeal which carries on after others are tired, the "capacity to take infinite pains."

Two persons may dash off a rough draft equally well. One may stop then, while the other writes and rewrites, improving with each rewriting until the good is transformed into the perfect. We cannot predict which of a thousand young people will develop this power to see it through to perfection, and therefore we must give every one of that thousand a full opportunity to prove his <u>ability</u> and his <u>will</u> to persevere.

Genius is likely to reveal itself at puberty, when the self-centeredness of childhood widens into passionate interest in other people and in social causes. It must, therefore, be sought and encouraged between the ages of ten and eighteen. Pupils of this age should be instructed in writing simple articles, within the compass of a limited word list. The best way is for the class to write one article on the blackboard so the students will understand how much hard work is involved. The article should be short, not covering over a half page, with short paragraphs, short sentences, the most familiar possible words, and packed with facts: NEW facts, INTERESTING facts, VITAL, USEFUL facts, answers to questions the villagers have always asked but never were able to answer.

To measure up to this standard of excellence in writing is a very high art and has secrets of its own. The chief secret is much <u>hard work</u>. Perhaps a half dozen books and magazines will have to be read, and fifteen or twenty persons interviewed to glean exactly the material you need. This material must then be organized into a preliminary outline. Then comes the process of writing once, then rewriting, reducing, improving, making each sentence stronger, until every sentence hits the bull's eye.

Tell the students: "If you ever get paid for a magazine article you will probably first rewrite it twenty times!" This is the high standard of excellence we must set before students.

Betty Mooney

Books well written sell fast, as this salesman's empty case testifies.

PUT HIGH SCHOOL THEMES IN PRINT--
NOT IN THE PAPER BASKET

Every school ought to have its own paper, published perhaps on
a duplicating machine. The students will be encouraged to write well
enough to have their articles published. A faculty committee will
choose what is worthy of publication.

The finest of all these essays should be sent by the editorial
committee to the principal, who in turn should send them to the director of education. His editorial committee should then select and print
the most useful of these articles in the provincial magazine to be distributed among all new literates. Every article published should bear
the author's name, and he should be paid a modest sum.

This recognition and payment will give young people the thrill
and the stimulus that will stir up their latent abilities and help them
to discover their own hidden possibilities. Many thousands of people
never know what they can do in this direction until the sleeping members are stirred and the will bent to writing. It is a matter that demands outside stimulus because it is hard work.

Those students who reveal literary ability while in high school
or college should be offered scholarships in a school of journalism.
There ought to be many such scholarships and they ought to be large
enough so that students could pursue their studies even though they
could get no help from home. It is the children of the poorest who
are usually best able to write with insight and passion to reach the
hearts of the illiterate masses. The reason there are so few writers
from the masses today is partly because some follow their father's
occupations, and partly because our educational system has not provided the financial resources for such students to continue their studies; thus they are lost to the "cause." Hitherto, writing has been
for, of and by the educated classes. But with the rising need of literature for the new literates, we must have writers from every class.

One of the fine aspects of this production of literature by students is the fact that it is one thing they can do for their country
while they are still in school. Some of the best essays many people
ever wrote were written while they were still under twenty. William
Cullen Bryant's "Thanatopsis" was written when he was eighteen
years of age. Perhaps you who read this will acknowledge that the
best essay or oration you ever produced was in your school days.

Young people are usually told: "You are to go out and help your
country when your education is completed." To say that is to violate
one of the fundamental principles of modern education, that knowledge
must be used almost at once or it will be lost. Literature is losing a
priceless contribution when we fail to utilize the vision and passion
which bursts forth in adolescence, to capture it and direct and encourage it before the fire dies down and the vision fades.

Chapter 15

How Shall Literature Reach the People?

Probably the weakest of all the many weak links in the literacy chain is our failure in putting literature into the hands of the illiterates and getting it read. One teacher reported that "we have an abundance of printed matter, but it is not being used by the people for whom it was intended." The trouble with this "abundance" of literature is that only a little of it is within the comprehension of new literates. Worse still, it is true that what is in existence too frequently fails to reach the villager. The whole situation is chaotic.

NEEDED: SALESMEN AND SALESWOMEN

Books and magazines as a rule reveal their true value on the cover less than almost anything else offered for sale. They must be sold by skillful salesmen, who know what people want and can tell them just where to find the answers to their wants. Men and women with a gift for salesmanship ought to be given the best training available in selling books and magazines, and then placed in centers to organize the distribution of literature.

In the United States and Europe, where book salesmanship has been brought to a high stage of perfection, men are given long periods of training in how to secure a proper introduction, how they should select their customers, how to get into homes, how to catch the attention of the customers, and just what to say in order to secure orders.

Nowhere, perhaps, have students as yet been utilized to sell books to villagers. Ultimately, with proper methods, a way will be found to sell literature so that salesmen can make a profit from their commissions. Until they do this, they will have to be paid salaries.

A young man desiring to enter a wholly undeveloped and a highly needed field may well step into book salesmanship at this juncture. It will ultimately prove enormously profitable for those who have ability and experience to take the lead. But the less the young man who enters this profession thinks of gain and the more he is possessed with a passion to help his country, the better he will succeed. He

131

may well tell himself a thousand times a day, "I am pioneering at
the most undeveloped point in my country's tremendous need. Whether she shall become an enlightened country depends upon my selling enlightenment to the ignorant. I am on the real battle ground of
the great war against ignorance." For all this is true. No conven-
iences of modern invention would have made progress without salesmen to convince people to use them. As Alexander Hamilton said,
"The salesman is the apostle who spreads the gospel of good things.
...If you want a true sign of prosperity, see whether the salesman
is abroad in the land."

We sometimes imagine that this vast accumulation of new things
(whether they are good or a nuisance does not now matter for our
argument) is due to invention. But the truth is that it is as much due
to the genius of sellers who, in one year, can sell to the public as
much as was formerly sold in thirty years.

If we read the selling directions of a successful book on salesmanship organization, we will find that they tell their salesman exactly what words to employ, just how to begin, just how to attract
attention to his goods, just how rapidly to talk, just when to keep
quiet, just how to arouse curiosity, and when to mention the price!
That is the most critical point! If you have a good book, well illustrated, a good way to begin is to place the book in your customer's
hands and just smile while he looks and then answer questions.

As a rule, it has been found that salesmen do best when they
concentrate upon one or two books, which they can advocate with
skill and fervor. To try to cover more may cause the prospective
customer to hesitate and endanger the sale of any book at all.

In the writing and printing of new books, these are very fine
questions to ask: "Would this book be easy for a salesman to sell
to a villager? Does it contain illustrations that would catch the eye?
Are the sentences gripping from the first?"

Wherever campaigns are now in progress, it is highly important
for every legitimate type of pressure to be used to get at least a few
books into every home containing new literates. Otherwise many
will forget all they have learned. Getting books into homes is a sine
qua non for a literate world.

BOOK PUBLISHING HOUSES

The second type of salesmanship, that of Book Societies and
Publishing Houses, has developed far more than house to house visitation. Experiments in selling books and other literature through a
number of channels are constantly being made. Not all are successful, but there is great need for exploring more channels and for developing those channels for literature already proven successful.

A detailed and objective account of book distribution in Northern Rhodesia here follows.

HOW TO MAKE IT EASY FOR PEOPLE
TO GET HELPFUL BOOKS

By J. R. Shaw

The production of books for Northern Rhodesia is in the hands of the Government Publications Bureau, various publishers, many missions, and the British and Foreign Bible Society.

Books are only useful when they are in the hands of readers. The work of distribution, so that books and readers come together, is the duty of the United Society for Christian Literature. The methods used to help distribution are many and varied.

On the Copper Belt books are stocked and sold at the Kitwe Book Shop and from that center they are sold in the various mine and town compounds at Nkana, Luanshya, Mufulira, Chingola and Ndola by means of book kiosks (booths) and colporteurs (salesmen). From Kitwe books are also sent to missions, bomas, and stores in N. E. and N. W. Rhodesia, i.e. to the Northern Province.

From Lusaka we have tried to serve the rest of the country. The following methods have been tried:

1. From the Lusaka Bookshop itself.
2. Through established missions.
3. Through government centres.
4. Through welfare societies.
5. Through traders, European, African and Indian
6. Through travelling cinema vans.
7. Through advertising and mail orders.
8. Through railway welfare officers.
9. Through the supply of book display cupboards.
10. Through the employment of African selling agents.
11. Through the supply of book boxes to Native Authority Headquarters.
12. By means of a tricycle with display lid on the Lusaka Railway Station.
13. By means of Book Exhibitions at Senior Day Schools, Training Colleges for teachers, nurses and police, and at Secondary Schools.
14. By means of Book Stalls at African Agricultural shows, Native Authority gatherings, Farmers' Meetings.
15. By attending Teachers' Refresher Courses in various parts of the country with an exhibition of books specially suited to their needs.

16. During the long vacation we have supplied students
    at the Government Secondary School for Africans
    with boxes of books suited to their home, people
    and vernacular.
17. We have supplied stocks of books to Government
    Development Centres where courses of various
    kinds are held for men and women and from which
    campaigns of many kinds are organised throughout
    the districts. The distribution of books becomes
    part of the development campaign.
18. By means of the Teachers Journal
19. Through any other reasonable channel.

It should be noted that not all the books read in the country pass
through our hands. Many of the larger missions print their own
books. For example, the <u>Nyanja Hymnal</u>, published by the press of
the Dutch Reformed Mission at Mkhoma in Nyasaland, had a circulation of more than 400,000 in the past ten years.

The following comments on the various methods we have tried
may be of interest:

1. The Lusaka Bookshop. This has become a busy place at which
   most Africans know that they can see and buy books in any vernacular of Northern Rhodesia and also in English. In a year we
   sold 1060 pounds' worth of vernacular books to retail buyers in
   the shop. This shop has also served many Africans who wanted
   English books, and has served also the local European community.

2. Many missions produce their own vernacular literature. It is
   from the missions that we purchase such books and then try to
   serve the scattered peoples of the various languages. To the
   missions we offer the books of the Publications Bureau and of
   other publishers and also school books. The British and Foreign
   Bible Society supplies missions direct with Scriptures. We have
   been sending books to more than one hundred mission stations in
   Northern Rhodesia. From these stations books have been available to the people in many outstations.

   The missions have played their part splendidly in the distribution of books to the people of the areas they are trying to
   serve. One mission employed very successfully twelve travelling
   booksellers in various parts of the country. These men sell the
   books of the mission but they also sell the books of the Publications Bureau.

   One very good point of the work of the missions is that they
   pay for the books they take from us. They do not hold the books
   for a year or two and then return them to us unsold.

Literacy booth at a "mela" (fair), as this one in East Pakistan,
is an excellent way to promote literacy in any country.

3. We have tried to arrange for government centres (Bomas) to be
   centres of book distribution. Success has varied. One Boma has
   an African library. There 43 pounds of books have been sold in
   four years.

   Another Boma has a bookshop which was built by a grant
   from the Publications Bureau. We undertook to stock this new
   centre which is at the Bus Station and near the Government offices
   of the district. A cripple is in charge. The discount we allow
   pays for his wages. In four months we have sold books for 50
   pounds at the centre, which is 260 miles from the railway line.

   Many Bomas have bought books for their Welfare Halls and
   in this way the books of the Publications Bureau were seen and
   known.

4. Some Town Welfare Societies stock books for sale so that the
   members can see and purchase their own copies.

5. From the beginning the writer has felt that the best way to get
   books into the hands of the people was to use established commercial channels. When they have money the people go to the stores.
   If they see the books they want at the stores they will buy.

   We have tried to arrange for stores of good standing to
   carry stocks of books in the local vernacular and in English.

In a few places our hopes have been fulfilled. In 1955 one store sold books in the amount of 249 pounds, another 72 pounds, another, 48 pounds, and another 46 pounds.

In the past, several of the largest trading firms accepted books for selling. The details of distribution and stock-taking seemed a burden to the local staff and repeat orders did not come along. One firm returned to us books for 75 Pounds after having held them for a year. There was evidence to suggest that the books had never left the central warehouse.

Our success with traders has varied. A profit of one sixth is not very attractive alongside the usual profits made in an African store.

6. Another method used to try to get books to all parts of the country was through cinema vans. We sent to each of four vans a tin box of books carefully selected for the particular area. Two of the four provinces have been a success. The other two have failed through human failure. One operator was a few pounds short in his money and was in prison for stealing government property. Another was dismissed and his box and books were missing. Local supervision has evidently been beyond the power of some local officials and so the attempt failed.

7. Another line of distribution was through Railway Welfare Officers. These men travel their sections regularly and we hoped, through them, to serve all African railway employees. The demand for books in the first box surprised the European officials. All the books were sold in four months. We sent another supply and eighteen months later the box was returned to us. It had apparently never been opened.

8. Advertising and Mail Orders. We keep an up-to-date advertisement going in some periodicals. This brings us a large number of orders for books by post. During 1955 such mail orders took books to the value of 350 pounds. This represents many hundreds of parcels and several thousands of books. Many of these books go to Northern Rhodesian Africans who are working outside the territory. Orders come from Wankie, Bulawayo, Johannesburg, The Free State, Goldfield, Cape Town, Namaqualand and Natal.

9. During the past few months a new method of displaying our books has been used. Book cupboards have been supplied by the Publications Bureau to some Bomas and missions. We wrote to each suggesting that now is the time to stock them well so that they can fulfill their purpose. Some of them are now being used successfully.

10. At one big centre on the line we tried the employment of a full-
    time African bookseller. The education department helped us
    with storage and housing. Wages and cost of supervision came
    to 8 Pounds per month and he sold books totaling 12 to 20 pounds.
    He also quickly got behind with his money at the monthly balance
    until his deficit was about 20 pounds. Fortunately, the man's
    father was able to put the account straight.

    Since that experiment we have served that town through an
    Indian store. No supervision is necessary on our part and the
    books are bought and paid for by the trader.

11. Book boxes to Native Authorities. This is a line of development
    which has been greatly helped by the Publications Bureau which
    supplies the boxes.

    We aim to send to Native Authority Headquarters a box of
    books in the local vernacular and in English. This box is in the
    hands of the Authority Clerk. Thus the people are able to see
    and to purchase the books which have been published for their
    benefit. This started well but the clerks have failed to keep it
    going.

12. Two years ago we bought a tricycle and on it mounted a large
    metal box. This is at the railway station everyday displaying
    books in all the vernaculars and in English. Fortunately the two
    African trains of the day are here in daylight. Large crowds of
    people are on the station for several hours either going back to
    their homes from work at Lusaka or going away to other parts
    of the country to search for work. Every day it is a different
    crowd. In a recent month over 700 books were sold from this
    station box. Amongst these books were Scriptures in fourteen
    different languages or vernaculars.

    This is one of our most successful efforts. Supervision is
    easy so there are no shortages. Through it we know that we are
    serving every part of the Federation.

13. We arrange exhibitions of books at Senior Day Schools, Training
    Colleges for Teachers, Nurses and Police at the Secondary
    Schools.

    Not all scholars can buy the books they want, but notes of
    title are made so that one day the desired book can be bought.

14. We arrange for Book Stalls at African Agricultural Shows, Na-
    tive Authority gatherings, Farmers' meetings. These are well
    worthwhile in every way.

15. We find the dates of Teachers' Refresher Courses during school

holidays and visit as many as possible with suitable books. These
are great opportunities as teachers from vast areas are gathered
together. They are the people who guide the thinking of the masses. The teachers are keen buyers if the right books are put before them. At one Scotch Mission centre we sold books worth
15 pounds in one hour and took orders for 10 pounds' worth to
be sent along by post. We think these are very important occasions.

16. During the long vacations we have supplied students of Govern-
    ment Secondary School with boxes of books suited to their home,
    people, and vernacular. In 1955 there were 24 such vacation
    booksellers. They sold books worth 150 pounds in their home
    communities. This is a valuable social service apart from any-
    thing else.

17. We have supplied stocks of books to Government Development
    Centres where courses of various kinds are held for men and
    women and from which campaigns of many kinds are organised
    throughout the districts. The distribution of books becomes a
    part of the development campaign.

18. Recently the Department of African Education has produced a
    Teachers' Journal. It is issued twice a year.
            We have arranged to insert an advertisement order slip into
    each copy telling of the best professional books we can supply
    for teachers and of Scriptures suited to their needs as teachers
    and of the best recent and suitable Christian books. As an ad-
    junct to this we have suggested a simple kind of Book Club for
    teachers. Through their school managers they are to send us a
    sum of money as a deposit. We will then send to them books on
    request until the deposit is spent. This should save the trouble
    of frequent postal orders and registered letters. Some of the
    teachers are two days journey from the nearest Post Office.
            As there are about six thousand teachers who will receive
    the Journal every six months we are hoping that this new line
    of service will develop into a very big thing.
            A personal link with an individual in any part of the country
    can easily become a channel for service to a whole community.

In such a variety of ways do we try to serve the needs of the people. We are ready to experiment in any reasonable manner in order
that helpful books shall be within reach of the people who are becoming literate so quickly. Our major problem is not how to teach people
to read but how to make it easy for them to possess helpful books.

TIN TRUNK LIBRARIES

By Betty Mooney

An interesting variation, and often a stepping stone to a permanent village library, is the "tin trunk" library. Following are excerpts from a pamphlet on tin trunk libraries, published by Literacy
House in Allahabad.

Eight tin trunk libraries have joined the ranks of "Servants of
Indian Literacy." These libraries are going out to all Hindi-speaking areas to offer their services in making the country literate and
in providing keys to better living.

Each library has a tin uniform to protect it against the dust and
hard knocks of village travel and against the rain and insects during
its stay in the village. The bright red of its top adds a gay splash of
color and the seal which it displays declares "Gram Pustakalaya" to
be an official servant of literacy.

Gram Pustakalaya comes bringing the new literates books on
Agriculture, Health, Religion, Child Care, History, Geography,
Handicrafts, Recreation and all the other subjects of interest and
help to him--books to inform, books to inspire, books to enlarge
his experience and show him how to improve his village, books on
different stages so that his reading ability will grow.

Books for the tin trunk libraries have been carefully selected
and graded. Hindi books written especially for new literates have
been collected from publishers all over the country and assembled
at Literacy House for analysis. During the past year, the staff of
Literacy House have examined some 800 books, trying out many of
them on new literates in the villages. From these, 500 were selected
and compiled in ten libraries of 50 books each.

Five libraries are for new literates with from one to six months
of reading experience. Each of the five libraries contains books in
three stages. Stage I books are easy enough for those who have been
reading from four to six weeks, Stage II for the second and third
month of reading and Stage III for up to six months of reading. The
other five libraries are for more advanced new literates and include
books on Stages IV-V, thus taking the new literate through his first
year of reading. (Stages III-IV of the Literacy House publications
would correspond roughly to Stage III materials described in this
Manual.)

Books have been analyzed in regard to appearance, ease of reading, interest, utility and price. Tests of readability were given to
each book. These tests determined the average length of sentences,
length of words, and number of conjuncts. Vocabulary was checked
with the villagers to find out which types were put in first stages.
Only 50 books met all the requirements for the first stage.

Interest is also an important requirement for a book for a new
literate. It may be easy, it may be attractive but if it is not interestingly written it will not be read. Narrative form, direct quotations,
questions and directions to the reader, names of people, personal
pronouns all help to make a book interesting. Tests were devised on
these points.

Many books were read to the new literates to note their reaction.
Those which were found to be dull were discarded. Some have been
included which are not as interesting as they should be but are the
best that can be found on the particular subject. They will have to do
until more interesting books are written.

"What use can it be to the reader?" is the question to ask of any
book which is considered for the library. "Will it give practical information which he can put to use?   Will it inspire him to action?
Will it enlarge his experiences and dispel his superstitions?"

Information given in the books was checked as far as possible to
determine these points:

Is it accurate? Is it up-to-date? Is it useful? Is it new
to the reader? Does it carry one main idea?

Betty Mooney

"Librarian" (left) shows materials from portable Tin Trunk Library.

Books on a variety of subjects of interest to the new literate have been included. In experimental projects it has been found that the three main subjects of interest are agriculture, religion, and biography.

The average price of a book is eight annas (about ten cents). Some expensive books have been included in the more advanced libraries, but as a whole the aim has been to keep the price low. If a book is lost by a villager, it can be replaced by him. Also, the readers can be encouraged to buy similar books for themselves.

Literacy House circulates the libraries in several nearby villages in which literacy work is being carried on. One library is left in a village for two months and then sent on to another village and a different set takes its place. Usually an elementary and an advanced library are circulated at the same time so that there is a constant supply of fresh reading material for new literates of all stages.

In this way the ten tin trunk libraries can serve a circle of five villages for a year or more. Literacy House acts as a center for this nearby area where libraries can be exchanged. *

The literacy worker is responsible for the library while it is in his village but usually he has a committee of villagers to help him. In some villages the books are kept in a reading room and are read by the new literates in the evening literacy classes while the teacher works with the beginners. Other village workers like to have the adults take the books to their homes to read between classes.

In some villages the people come to a central place to get the books; in others the worker takes the box on his cycle from house to house. But in either case those who use the library are expected to pay some small fee either in cash or kind. This gives the members more respect for the library and also provides a small fund to keep the books in repair and to pay for the oil for the reading room light.

The tin trunk library is only the beginning of the village library. It is designed mainly for the new literate, although others may also find the books interesting. In addition to the circulating tin trunk library, each village is encouraged to have a permanent basic library which will serve the whole community--children, semiliterates and the more educated group. But the tin trunk library is a way of making a start--getting people interested and showing them what a library is. If it is a success, they will soon want a permanent library and will take an interest in obtaining more books.

---

* A complete discussion of all aspects of distribution of literature is found in Ruth Ure's (now Ruth Ure Warren) book The Highway of Print. It is based on her years in India, engaged in literature production and distribution. Many of the problems and solutions are similar in other areas of the world. This is a book so valuable, though now unfortunately becoming rare, that it should be in the personal library of everyone engaged in literacy-literature activities. See Appendix A.

GETTING GOOD READING OUT TO THE PEOPLE
IN THE NORTH SUDAN

By Edwin C. Carlson

Opportunities for literature distribution are tremendous in young, newly independent countries. More and more people are becoming literate each year because the powerful five of nationalism demands that education must solve all of their problems and enable them to close the gap of centuries of backwardness. We must now reach the masses with practically the only way open--the printed word.

As old customs are being thrown aside, people in these countries are demanding to read, learn, and find out how to adjust to this "modern world" of progress. Millions of new literates are demanding good reading material that can be helpful and understood. Our Christian duty is to fill that vacuum by getting our books and magazines to these starving minds and souls.

Such an area of change is Khartoum, the capital of the Sudan in East Africa, and the neighboring cities of Omdurman and Khartoum North. These "Three Towns" have a population of 250,000.

I was serving as a short-term teacher in two mission schools in Omdurman. During one of my vacations, I visited the printing press in Malakal in the South Sudan. They have a fine magazine in English called Light. * The main problem of the magazine at that time was circulation. Copies were sent regularly to various mission stations and schools throughout the Sudan, where missionaries and teachers would give the magazines away to anyone who said they wanted one. That's as far as the circulation had climbed. Under that system the hopes of increasing publication and reaching more people with good reading were in vain. They needed someone to "push" the sales with a new and more business-like fashion. As long as people get something for nothing, they won't feel that they are getting something worthwhile. It must cost them something--enough to make them find out what they paid for, but low enough so they can afford it.

I remembered the many books in Arabic and English that were stocked in our Literature Center in Khartoum. Our reading room was small and only a few people actually bought the many books that were available. I was convinced that if the general public only knew that these books could be purchased, sales would boom and the circulation would rise. Returning from my vacation, I was determined to use all my spare time in getting these publications "out" to the man on the street.

* See Appendix A, Periodicals for New Literates. Incidentally, "Light" is one of the most popular names for periodicals for new literates in various parts of the world.

Newsstands Take Our Literature

At the beginning of 1958, I started a new method of distributing Christian books and magazines to public newsstands and bookstalls located on almost every bus stop and street corner throughout the "Three Towns." Most of these newsstands consist of large crude tables with local newspapers and magazines laid on top with stones or pieces of metal as paper-weights. Some "luxurious" stands have overhead coverings and colored lights. During the night, all the literature is locked in compartments underneath the tables.

I contacted all the operators of these newsstands. They were very eager to sell our books and magazines when we offered them a 25 per cent commission and promised to take back all the unsold copies at the end of the month. Some refused to sell the literature because it was Christian and they feared public disapproval. But after a few months, they saw their competitors making nice profits and begged us to let them have all the literature we could give them.

I had set as my sales goal 300 magazines a month. The mission in this area was then receiving only 50. We passed that goal and never had enough literature. We always felt bad when a place sold out of magazines or a certain book before the end of the month. This meant that perhaps someone or many people wanted to buy that certain copy--yet they couldn't because we hadn't left enough at the newsstand! After each sellout, we tried to leave more copies than the previous month to allow for an expected increase.

After one year I had a route of 25 newsstands and bookstalls selling over 2500 books and magazines each month. The buyers consisted largely of Moslems and nominal Christians from the Nilotic tribes of the South Sudan. Both the Arabic and English publications ranged from very easy reading for the new literates and less educated to a high literary standard for the intellectuals. Government officials, merchants, students, and laborers were all buying Christian literature from public vendors on street corners.

At last the general public had the chance to see and buy reading material that had been gathering dust on the shelves of our small reading rooms and isolated mission bookstores. A Moslem could not allow himself to be seen entering a mission library--but nothing prevented him from purchasing a book or magazine from a newsstand where he also bought the daily newspaper.

The circulation of the magazines and books increased so fast that our printing press and Literature Center had trouble keeping up with the fast pace. But they eagerly accepted the new challenge. Special funds and discounts from our mission bookstores helped the finances.

A dedicated Sudanese Christian became interested and has been trained to carry on the work of distribution. Every now and then a

new bookstall would pop up in another part of town. We both would
go and begin a business relationship with the agent.

Keeping Book Sellers' Friendship Is Important

One of the most important factors in the success of this distribution drive was the good relationship that we built up with the selling agents. If he doesn't like you or if you have lost his trust in you,
he won't sell your material. We had to make friends with these
agents to keep them happy. A little gift from the magazine, like an
inexpensive ball-point pencil or extra copies of calendars, helped to
win their friendship. We always had to do some bargaining over
prices and commission rates--but we never quarreled or made them
angry.

With a few more intelligent agents, we tried a different approach
to the selling of books that appealed to the natural Arab talent of
bargaining with customers. We told the agents that we had to have
so much for a book; if he could get more than the usual selling price,
that would be all his profit. As long as we didn't interfere with
Christian salesmen or colporteurs, there were no bad effects. I
don't believe the vendors were able to get much more than the standard prices but they really appreciated our concern for their business enterprise and the local sales techniques!

Many gimmicks can be used to spurt sales. Here's one example.
We had some attractive magazine holders built by a local carpenter
and placed them on the tables to distinguish our literature from the
stacks of others, including communist propaganda. The result was
greater than we expected. One newsstand was sold out completely
in three days, and we were asked for twice as much literature. Sales
boomed about 300 per cent.

Money Matters Are Equally Important

Another important key to good business relationships is the art
of handling accounts. We had to continually revise our system of
bookkeeping due to increasing kinds and titles of books and due to
the discovery of new bookstalls. Later we mimeographed special
forms that had blanks to list the particular book or magazine, the
name of the newsstand agent, and the month.

We also gave a small notebook to agents who had a rather large
business. Then they had a separate book for our accounts with them.

In settling our accounts each month, we made sure that the ven-
dor understood the selling price, the commission, and the number
of books sold out of what we had left with him the previous month.
We would take each kind of publication separately and figure out what
he owed us. For example, if I had left 50 Light magazines at a

Edwin Carlson

A simple rack boosted the sales of <u>Light</u> on newsstands in the Sudan.

certain newsstand last month and he now could find only 10 copies, that meant he must have sold 40. At one piaster each, the total income was 40 piasters. For this particular magazine, his commission was 50 per cent or 20 piasters. This same amount was recorded in his bill. I would then collect the money and leave him 50 new issues, hoping for an increase of 20 per cent. If he had sold all of his 50 copies, I would try to have him take 60 or 65 new issues, depending upon the rate of his sales over the recent months.

It is always better to add up the itemized account <u>with</u> the agent and have his complete agreement on all totals. After we arrived at the amount of money he owed me, I would settle for as much as he could pay me at that time and set a specific time in the next few days when I would come again for the rest of the money. Large bookstalls would usually pay in full right away but the smaller agents operated on a small cash basis and were forced to live from their daily profits. This type of patience and trust helped tremendously to create a workable business relationship--Arab style. In a year and a half, only one regular newsstand agent failed to pay his bill. I consider this easy-going method much better than a strict western business approach.

About half of the sellers were illiterate and couldn't even do simple arithmetic. Settling accounts in this situation demanded even more patience since I didn't know much Arabic myself. Again they had to trust me probably more than I had to trust them.

Several times, agents claimed that books had been stolen from them and they would lose all their profits. After some bargaining, they understood that I also would lose money, so we agreed to share the loss between us.

All the bookstalls didn't agree to sell Christian literature, being either strongly religious themselves or pressured by fanatical Moslem groups. However a few places did accept our literature-- but put it underneath the counter right after we left. Surprise visits to these newsstands revealed their policy. This happened at one of our best locations in Khartoum, right beside a bus stop directly across the street from the largest market. We took back all the literature despite polite excuses and didn't contact him again until several months later. Perhaps a new man would by then take over the location and have a different policy. We were alert to take advantage of such openings.

Books in both the limited and high vocabulary sold well. In Arabic the best sellers were Quo Vadis, The Christian's God, Gospel of Luke (colloquial Arabic), and Stories From the Bible. In English the most popular were Pilgrim's Progress, What Christians Believe, Stories of a Doctor, Story of Jesus, Story of Joseph, and Illustrated Books of the New Testament. The Moody Colportage Library Series and World Books Series (Arabic and English) were very useful.

A Writers' Club Organized

As interest in our Sudanese Christian magazines grew in the North Sudan, there arose a strong need for articles to be written concerning activities, events, and people of that area. I started a Writers' Club in our secondary school and the Christian students responded with great enthusiasm to the call for writers. In our meetings articles were presented by the members for criticism and themes were discussed for future issues. We had to learn to write in short sentences, using simple words; those who knew Arabic could write their articles in both languages. Picture stories were also submitted to the group and later to the editors of the magazines.

The members of this club not only wrote but also started sales and subscription campaigns, reaching other schools, churches, suburban areas, the native market, and even into the government offices in Khartoum. One young man named John Choul sold over 300 magazines each month. We rewarded such feats of salesmanship with ivory pins with a cross carved in and the word "LIGHT" written in both Arabic and English on the top and bottom. As these Christian men would sell literature, they also witnessed to the buyers, answering questions about their faith and giving their testimony boldly and simply.

Chapter 16

How to Discover What Interests
New Literates

What vitally interests the villager? This is the first question any writer ought to ask if he expects his writings to be read. Again we may turn to the schools for help. Students are enthusiastic when asked to help in this inquiry and they reveal good judgment. The method that has been used for schools and conferences of students is to say:

"There will be silence for five minutes while you all write the subjects that you believe would most interest illiterate villagers." At the end of five minutes say: "Now, of all the themes you have written, mark the one you consider most interesting." Then let each person name his first choice while somebody writes it on the blackboard. At the end, all the lists may be collected.

Each student should be pledged to write on one of the topics written on the blackboard. The student should be told that the article which he submits will be taken into consideration in deciding upon his school grade. If carelessly done, it should be returned again and again until it meets a high standard. If written ten times, the student is learning high ideals of writing.

After articles have been published in a journal, there should be a thousand or more reprints of the articles of permanent value, and these should be placed in appropriate boxes under such captions as Health, Agriculture, Songs, Folklore, Useful Recipes, Child Welfare, Economics, etc. When there are enough pages, say fifty or sixty, bind them in a small booklet. If the articles are interesting, the new literates will enjoy rereading them and will cherish them under their new cover.

If several hundred village schools were asked to suggest themes for the periodical, they would contribute a very useful list. We have met with enthusiastic response whenever we have tried it. High schools, colleges and churches also respond with zest and produce valuable ideas.

Here are a few sample subjects for magazine articles submitted by students and at a literacy conference:

147

A model wedding
When to marry
How to increase income
Smallpox
Calves' diseases
Baby's eyes
Rats
Water smoke-pipe (Hooka)
Gambling
Oppression
Purdah
Songs
Wrestling
Birth control
Village Industries
Snake bites and what to
    do when bitten
Reducing taxes
Water supply
Better roads
Cattle diseases
Improved homes
An ideal village
A good soldier
Irrigation canals
Native tobacco
Itch
Plague
Spinning
Opium
Plows
Congress
Drowning
The Bible
Hindu Classics
The Koran
Current news
Gossip
Pilgrimages
Cinemas

Caste
Gandhiji
Quarrels between mother and
    daughter
How to stop quarrels
Better prices
Court trials
Laws
Funeral feasts
Prayer
Jewelry
Home remedies
Cooperative banks
How to get out of debt
Manure cakes
Selling girls
Harvest
Seeds
Life after death
Stories of many kinds
Tricks of beggars
Mother-in-law
What they say at the tank
    (water hole)
Communal relations
Weights and measures
Land measurements
Cholera
Morality
Ethics
Worship
Money lenders
Markets
Prices
Rain
Stories of saints
Sports
Ghosts
Proverbs

In addition to students, professional people who have been working with the villagers should be asked to name the topics that would
be of interest. Pastors, teachers, social workers, sanitation workers, census takers, government officials and others can be ques-
tioned. Their opinions should show more maturity and insight than

the young students, as they have visited and perhaps lived in the villages and know the villagers' problems more intimately.

GO TO THE PEOPLE!

Finally, don't fail to go to the people themselves. Find out what they think they need to know and want to read about. The person who really wants to know the people must live among them for some time, talk with them, make friends with them, and so begin to understand their problems. While living in the village, be observant of the following:

1. What do they talk about most?
2. What are their problems?
3. What information would help them meet these problems?
4. What songs do they sing? What stories and poems do they recite?
5. What kind of humor do they have?
6. What kind of people do they admire and respect the most?
7. What are some interesting stories and anecdotes about people in the village?
8. What have the people in this village learned that they can pass on to someone else?
9. What are some interesting things about the location of this village? Is there something of historical interest? Is there some special handicraft? What about the birds, plants, animals of the village--can they be put into stories?
10. What are the superstitions and customs of the village?

If information on the villagers' needs are from at least three sources mentioned--students, workers with the villagers, and villagers themselves--some interesting discrepancies will be found.

Mr. Samuel Habib, of Literacy House, Minia, Egypt, polled 600 villagers and about 25 professional workers with the villagers as part of a survey for his master's thesis at Syracuse University School of Journalism. One of the questions asked was just what we are here concerned with: What subjects do you want to read about?

Each of the villagers who answered Mr. Habib's questionnaire (which was sent to the village pastor or teacher, who then asked the questions of the villagers) had a choice of his favorite topics from a list of about 100. Among the topics was sanitation, which failed to receive a significant vote from the villagers. The same list was submitted to the professional workers with the villagers. Their votes put sanitation at the very top of the list.

Two points of view are represented here: that of the professional
workers who look at the village and see what it might be like if the
gutters were clean, if privies were built, if mosquito-breeding ponds
were drained; and that of the villagers themselves, who, not having
known anything different, are not aware of what benefits changes in
certain areas would bring to them.

Topics for writing should be sought from every possible source.
We should, of course, give the villagers what we think they need to
know. But be careful! Literature is not like a pill we try to stuff
down sensitive people's throats, for they won't swallow it. The adult
new literates are not like children in school, who are assigned a
chapter for the next day, and have to read it by threat of failing a
quiz on it. The adults are on their own. They pick and choose....
and they won't choose a pill instead of a bonbon.

The tragedy is that already there are, in many areas of the
world, stock piles of literature that just won't sell. They're pills
that people don't want. Perhaps they are not on interesting subjects,
perhaps they are not written simply or with high interest, or are
not illustrated attractively or well printed. A missionary on furlough
from a Near East country told us recently of just such a case: a
warehouse full of dozens of pamphlets, each in a printing of several
thousand--but less than a hundred of any of them have been sold!
And he had just been appointed the new director of the literature
program!

FIRST PRINT WHAT THE PEOPLE WANT

The success of magazine and book publishers in the United
States and Europe depends very largely on the ability of the editors
to feel the pulse of the nation and know what people want to read
about. Have there been articles in the newspapers about flying sau-
cers lately, and is everyone talking about them? Then you will find
a number of articles in many magazines, and even books about this
intriguing subject. Is an election coming soon? Then there will be
articles about the candidates, the parties, the issues. Are there
new discoveries in medicine which will soon benefit everyone? Then
you will find numerous articles explaining them in detail.

Well-written articles on subjects of high interest tend to bring
forth a long series of articles and books on the subject. The resur-
gence of interest in religious matters in the United States is attested
to by the unending succession of magazine articles, syndicated newspaper columns, books, radio and television programs....or could
it be that the frequent concern with religion in print and on the air
has been the cause of, rather than the result of, the public renewal
of interest in religion?

The interplay of cause and effect is very hard to trace. The moral of this, for those of us concerned with the new literates, is that, by writing about what they are interested in, we are not necessarily kow-towing to their whims. The lesson we should have learned by now is that, all through the Each One Teach One process, we begin where the illiterates--or new literates--are. Begin where they are, with their interests. Then lead them gradually into areas of thinking which are new to them, but which we and other professional people know will benefit them.

We need articles written on thousands of themes. Some people suppose that a dozen books will bridge the gap between literacy and standard literature, but this is a serious mistake. Put yourself in the place of the new literate. When you go to a library, you may care to read only one book from an entire shelf of a hundred. Another man would probably choose a different book. Illiterates are even more difficult to please, because they have not yet learned to read for pleasure. The subjects must be such as will naturally intrigue them, and in which they can see an immediate application to their own and their family's lives.

How enormous this task is of supplying these literates with reading matter, very few people have even begun to suspect. Unless it is to be more than an ineffectual, pious wish, every competent individual and agency must cooperate.

Can attractively presented literature, written about what greatly concerns potential readers, be made to "sell"? Currently successful ventures in Africa hurl a ringing "yes" to that question.

Trevor and Grace Shaw, a journalist man-and-wife team from New Zealand, gave up their profession in their homeland after the war to go to Africa. Their source of inspiration: reading about literacy campaigns and the hunger for literature on a scale never before known. They resolved to devote their journalistic skills to bringing reading matter to "the unreached man on the street." A principle which they hold to strongly is that the writing should be by Africans for their fellow Africans.

In May 1951, the Shaws* began work on the first issue of African Challenge, published in cooperation with the Sudan Interior Mission in Nigeria and, at the outset, with backing from friends in New Zealand. In the five years since the first issue of 5,000, African Challenge (printed in English) has had a spectacular growth--to the present circulation of 140,000, the largest circulation of any newspaper or magazine in all of Africa! A Yoruba language edition is now being published.

The Shaws have pioneered again, with a magazine in French, Envol (In Flight), published at Leopoldville, Belgian Congo, for

---

* Their own thrilling story is told modestly in a little book, Through Ebony Eyes, by Trevor and Grace Shaw, Lutterworth Press, London.

French-speaking Africans in Belgian and French areas. Magazines
based on the <u>Envol</u> pattern were started in 1958 in the Kikongo and
Lingala languages of the Congo; other language editions are being
planned. It is expected that material specifically for the new literate
will be included in these periodicals as the demand for these articles
grows. (See Appendix A for listing of these and other periodicals.)

A young student in a training college said: "I aspire to write for
the masses. I shall not imitate present day writers, but shall break
away from their style and develop a style as clear as a mountain
spring." If that young man persists he may rest assured that what
he writes will be read by millions and that his influence will be vast
beyond his wildest dreams. The future of the world is with men and
women who know how to play across the heartstrings of the armies
of new literates who will come, hungry for great ideas clothed in the
simple tender words they have always spoken.

Chapter 17

How and Where to Get the Facts

HOW TO INTERVIEW

If you want your writing to help people, the facts must be accurate. One good way to get facts for the subject you want to write about is to interview an expert on the subject. It is good to know something about the subject before you interview him. You can read a book on the subject. You may list some questions you want to begin with. Other questions will come to you as you talk with the expert. The expert will enjoy talking about his subject. He will tell you things you may not find in a book. He will make the facts alive with his enthusiasm and with interesting little stories. But he will probably use many big words and technical terms. If you don't understand what he is saying, you can always say, "Give me an illustration." Guide his discussion by asking questions which apply to the particular village situation in which you are interested.

Your job is to "pick the expert's brains." Find out all he knows on this particular subject. But don't bring in too many subjects. Ask your questions so that he will give you the information which best suits your story. You will get more information than you need. Your next job will be to sift this information. This will be done after the interview. Take notes on the facts he gives. Write a sentence or two which will help you to remember the illustrations he gives. You should be able to get all the information you need within 30 or 45 minutes. He is a busy man, so don't keep him longer. Thank him for his time and tell him what a big help this will be to the villagers.

The next job is to sift the facts. Pick out the facts which are most important. Make an outline of these facts in logical order. Decide the one important lesson you are going to teach in this story. Make a note of illustrations you can use. Be sure to make this outline while the facts are still fresh in your mind.

The next job is to write the information simply and interestingly. Here you will throw out all the expert's big words and put in simple ones. The expert helps get the facts right, but you are the expert who must write them for the new literates.

153

Remember:

1. Be familiar with the subject.
2. Ask leading questions.
3. Find out all you can.
4. Take notes.
5. Keep the interview short and snappy.
6. Sift the facts.
7. Make an outline soon after the interview.
8. Think of illustrations and human interest
   to put across these facts.

And when you have finished your simplified version of what the expert told you, _always_ check back with him, or with someone else well qualified in that field, to make sure your simplified writing has not distorted or misrepresented any of the facts. Most information _can_ be told accurately in simple language, but check with the experts before printing!

It is better not to print sermons or lectures for new literates. People will listen to sermons sometimes, but they don't like to read them. Our experience is that a story or a song or a drama is always best.

Even when we want to teach the facts about health and agriculture and home life, we make up stories about a man who learned to read. He read the secrets which books contain, became healthy, wealthy and wise, happy and famous.

While writing Anand The Wise Man, we asked the health, agriculture, and home economics experts in each country what they were trying to tell the people. Then we made a story out of what they told us. We wrote it in the language of the people. This is one good way to prepare simple literature. The experts give us many ideas that we can depend on to be true, yet are fresh and new to the people. Our art is, then, to put these ideas into exciting stories that are packed full of interest and contain useful information.

On pages 155 and 156 is a story* which came from experts and was rewritten to be made simple. The new words in it are those which, because we have kept careful count since the primer, we know that the new literate has not yet come across. Note that each of the new words is repeated several times. In fact, the main ideas are repeated several times too, once by reading from the book, again by what Anand says, and again perhaps by what his wife Sevati says.

---

* All the examples of articles for new literates included in this text are
in larger type. In a book or periodical for new literates, articles
should be printed in large type, perhaps 12 point at least. Detailed
recommendation concerning the graphic presentation of material for new
literates is beyond the scope of this text.

Anand Reads About Flies

There were many flies in Anand's house.
Flies sat on Anand's food.
Flies' feet were on his food.
Many, many flies sat on his food.

Anand read his book about flies.
The book said,
Flies put their feet in filth.
Their feet are covered with filth.
Flies eat filth.
Fly babies live in the filth.

There are many germs in the filth.
The germs are on the flies' feet.
The germs are in their mouths.
They fly to your food.
They eat your food.

The germs are in their mouths.
The germs get on your food.
The germs are on their feet.
The germs get on your food.

You put the food in your mouth.
The germs make you sick.
They give you dysentery.

Anand said, "I am sick.
I have dysentery.
The flies gave me dysentery.
They have germs on their feet.
They have germs in their mouths.
The germs made me sick.
The germs gave me dysentery."

The neighbor said,
"The baby is sick.
My baby has diarrhea.
Did flies give my baby diarrhea?"

Anand said,
"The flies made your baby sick.
The flies gave your baby diarrhea.
Diarrhea came from filth.
The flies brought it on their feet.
The flies brought it in their mouths.
You must kill the flies!"

Revati said, "We must kill the flies!"

Anand read his book. It said,
You can kill the flies with gamexane.
Put gamexane in the house.
Put gamexane on the wall.
Put gamexane on the filth.

The neighbor put gamexane in the house.
He put gamexane on the filth.
He killed the flies.

New Words

(Words Not Found in the Hindi Primer)

flies   feet   filth   mouth   sick   baby

dysentery   diarrhea kill live cover gamexane

The new literate loves to read the repetition, when it is varied
a bit, or when different characters say it. It gives something of the
flavor of the epics and ballads which they love, in which there is
repetition--a sort of verse and chorus effect. So, what to western
eyes and ears may seem boring repetition, is to the new literate
easy and delightful reading. And it is good teaching, too, for every
fact is repeated again and again. Psychologists say that after we
have heard or read a fact five times we begin to believe it!

SIMPLIFYING TECHNICAL MATERIAL

A great number of technical brochures and booklets are printed
by various governmental departments in many countries, and by a
number of organizations, such as insurance companies, health

agencies, transportation companies, etc. With little more trouble
than writing a letter or a post card, one can often get a number of
pamphlets at no charge or for a small amount. Many of them deal
with subjects which can be related to the needs of the people for
whom you are writing.

In the United States you can get on the mailing list to receive
announcements of all pamphlet titles published by the U.S. Government Printing Office. Simply write to the Superintendent of Documents, Government Printing Office, Washington 25, D.C., and request to be put on their mailing list. The variety of titles which they
print will surprise you. Dozens of other government and private a-
gencies publish pamphlets on a wide variety of subjects*. These contain accurate information, written in language we can understand.
But it is still much too hard for the new literate.

Let us look at a short passage in the style of some of the technical materials published, and see how we would go about rewriting it
for the new literate.

> One cannot exaggerate the probability of incurring
> illness from having drunk from a river, lake or well of
> questionable purity. If it is found necessary to drink wa-
> ter from these sources, the impurities may be removed
> and the germs killed by prolonged boiling of the water,
> and by storing it in a safe covered container used for no
> other purpose. The water should boil vigorously for at
> least five minutes before being stored. A separate dipper
> should be reserved for dipping from the container, and
> should not be used for drinking.

As you grow in ability to write and rewrite materials, you will
develop your own techniques. At the beginning, however, definite
steps of procedure may be of great help. Look at the passage above
again and consider the following steps:

1. Read the original material all the way through for
   general understanding.
2. Read a small section at a time, once or twice, till
   you are sure you understand the main points.
3. Just what is the author trying to say? List the main
   ideas. List the subordinate ideas as parts of each
   main idea.
4. In the original article, examine the words used.
   Underline or circle those words which are not in
   the word list you are using.

* See Appendix B for names and addresses of agencies preparing pamphlets
  on a great variety of subjects.

Here is the version of that short article, as written in a group session by a class at Chautauqua in Writing For New Literates.

Drinking Water -- For You and Your Family

Do you drink the water in the river? Do you drink the water from the lake or from the well? If you do, you take a chance of getting sick. There are many diseases in that water.

Boil Water
This Way . . .

Let it bubble five minutes or more.

But that same water can be easily made into good water. The water must be boiled. To boil means to heat the water very much. It is not enough just to see steam rise from the water. The water must bubble.

It is not enough just to see bubbles on the bottom of the pan. The bubbles must rise to the top of the water. You will see bubbles and steam rising.

Let the water bubble on the fire for five minutes.

NOT
This Way

This water is not boiling enough.

Pour the bubbling hot water into a jar. This jar is used only for boiled water. Never put any other water into this jar. Put a top on this jar to keep out dirt and insects.

Use a separate cup to take water out of this jar. Don't drink from this cup. Pour the water into your own cup. Then drink from your own cup. Never use your cup to take water from the jar.

New Word: bubble

This article was printed in a model periodical for new literates, Read and Grow. The only new word in this story, not found in the Streamlined English Word List, is "bubble," which is used a number of times. More about word lists later.

RESEARCH CALLS FOR THE COOPERATION OF US ALL

You should keep in touch with organizations which are promoting literacy, and with training schools. Missionaries especially will want to work closely with the Committee on World Literacy and Christian Literature, 475 Riverside Drive, New York 27, New York. Workers in government campaigns and campaigns sponsored by other agencies will find that World Education, 45 East 65th St., New York, will be of assistance.

The School of Journalism at Syracuse University, and the various literacy organizations are engaged in perpetual research, not only in sources of materials, but all aspects of literacy and literature. We are eager for you to know what is being developed in the way of good reading matter, so you will be able to get it and have it translated into your own languages.

It is very good also to be in touch with your government. Nearly every department of education, health and agriculture is seeking useful reading matter. This will need to be rewritten for the new literates. The Ministries of Education are supposed to be developing special literature for the new literates. You and they can be of aid to one another.

In fact, in the whole program of literacy, you should keep in touch with your Ministry of Education and any other organization that teaches illiterates and publishes simple material. Sometimes the information is dry and tedious; but if so, you can take that dry material and rewrite it simply and print it with attractive illustrations, and you will gain the gratitude of both the government officials and the people. But be sure to get their approval before printing.

Sources of reading matter for the new literates are all about you. By interviews and by reading books and pamphlets you can uncover much of importance for your new literates.

Let us emphasize that it is highly important for you to cooperate with all who are teaching illiterates--everybody who will cooperate with you.

Need For Literacy Libraries

At the present time there is no one library in the United States, or elsewhere, which houses literacy and literature materials from all around the world. That there is a real need for such a storehouse is being felt by many organizations. Among these is the Missionary Research Library, 3041 Broadway, New York 27, New York, which has plans to enlarge its collection of literacy materials.

The United Nations Bookstore, United Nations, New York, will help locate any materials published by UNESCO. A number of universities are organizing UNESCO libraries; the UN Bookstore will send you a list of these on request.

Chapter 18

Experience with Two Knotty Problems: Alphabets and Languages

THE QUESTION OF ALPHABETS

The question of improving alphabets is interesting to most teachers and absorbing to some. Nearly all the ancient alphabets are in need of reform, some of them in very great need. But those who desire to make a country literate--the readers of this book--should be warned not to dissipate their efforts in trying to employ a reformed alphabet in their texts unless it has the endorsement of the government and also general public approval.

Experience has taught us the sad lesson that reforming alphabets is one of the most difficult and rarest changes in the educational field. People change their vocabularies constantly. Every year some words come in and some go out. But spelling goes on forever!

There are a few exceptions. Spanish was changed by the Spanish Academy in 1880, and millions of Spanish-speaking people have found that language among the easiest in the world to learn to read. About the same time, the dialects of the Philippines adopted a perfect spelling, eliminating even the few imperfections of the Spanish alphabet.

During the time of Kemal Pasha Ataturk in Turkey in the 1920's, the Arabic alphabet was discarded and a perfect Roman alphabet was adopted--one of the most perfect in the world. Lenin in Russia threw out the irregularities of their alphabet. Such a change is possible under a rigid dictatorship. It has not happened in a democracy in this country. For in this matter of spelling, the people decide, and they stick by the spelling which they learned in school, no matter how hard it is.

While we were in Egypt preparing the textbook which has been widely used ever since, Dr. William Hambrook, advisor to the Ethiopian government, came to Cairo and asked us to come up to Ethiopia and help them. We went. We found that the Ethiopian alphabet had 250 letters, not representing pure sounds, but syllables. For example, there was one letter for "ba" and a totally different letter for "bi." This is called a syllabary. If we had a letter for each syllable in English, we would have about 250 letters.

When we went to interview the Emperor, we told him that it would be far easier to adopt five vowels. He told us to do it. So we made one of the finest sets of lessons in the world. Ten thousand copies were printed. But after we left, the Coptic priests said that the entire Coptic alphabet was sacred and they would not allow the new book to be used. So our reform attempt failed.

In the Hindi (Devanagari) alphabet in India, they have a rather good alphabet, but then they complicate it by adding many "conjunct" letters, which are combinations of two consonants in a form that do not look like either one. Why do they do this? Because behind every consonant is the short "u" sound as in "but" unless some other vowel is written. So our English word "strict" would be pronounced with Hindi letters "suturikut." They get around this by taking a small piece of "s," a small piece of "t," and a small piece of "r," and putting one over the other like this:

s
t
r . The same with "k" and "t" at the end of the word: k͟t.

We will now attempt to write "strict" as we would have to write it if we followed the Hindi style:

s   k
r it .

(The "k" is used instead of a "c," which has two sounds in English: "s" and "k.") A group of scholars spent twenty years improving the Hindi alphabet, adopted it officially--and nobody uses it!

English unquestionably needs respelling more than any other language. This is especially true since it has spread all the way around the world and has become the lingua franca of mankind. The fact that the United Nations is in New York spreads English even farther. Logically EVERY reason favors respelling. But in practice English spelling is not making any important changes. Changes that do take place are haphazard, usually immaterial and sometimes dead wrong. For example, "lite" is no improvement over "light" phonetically, unless every common word with "ight" is also changed --"sight, right, might, fight, night, tight"--because "ight" is always pronounced alike.

Literally hundreds of people are working to produce a regularization of English spelling. ANY of their suggestions would be better than the present spelling--if agreement could be reached and the newspapers and book publishers would begin to print books in that way.

The only argument that has any validity against respelling English is that we would not be able to read the books now in print. They would soon look like the old English books to us--Beowulf and Chaucer.

IT ISN'T HARD TO MAKE ENGLISH SPELLING EASY

Over the past fifteen years a study of English has shown that
English is not as chaotic as we formerly thought. There is a lot of
phonetic regularity in English--once one learns the rules.

In Streamlined English, * our Primer for adults, we don't try
to reform English spelling, but we do teach adults to read English
through an understanding of its phonetics.

Streamlined English has gone through several editions and is
gaining in popularity each year. In the Hawaiian Islands, for example, the Department of Education uses Streamlined English for teaching English to the adults of many races in those Islands. It also finds
specific use for the book in each of the grades of the Islands' schools:
word building in one grade, phonetic drill in another, etc. Teaching
illiterates by television, begun in Memphis, Tennessee, and now in
use in several cities, is also based on this book.

In order to know which spellings are "regular," we counted the
ways of pronouncing and spelling vowels in 7, 5000 different English
words, containing 14, 400 syllables. The analysis of this word study
is found in the Teacher's Manual of Streamlined English.

In the summer of 1959, at Chautauqua, New York, we conducted
a short course in simplified English spelling. We prepared a text,
English Spelling Made Easy for the World. * This book proposes perfectly regular spelling for English, with as few changes as possible
from present spelling, and with no additional letters or marks not
already found on everybody's typewriter. The entire Book of Mark
has been respelled, and it is so easy that anyone can read it right
off. Several persons have told us that they never really appreciated
this Gospel before reading it in our revised spelling. The enthusiasm
of the class at Chautauqua and everyone we meet convinces us that
the time is here when people all over the English-speaking world
will demand that we reform present spelling madness.

Regular Ways of Spelling English Vowel Sounds

In the following list, most of the spellings of vowel sounds will
look familiar. Only one new mark, a slanted line (/) is used after
a vowel to show that it is a long vowel. So the long sounds of "a, e,
i, o," and "u" are spelled thus: "a/, e/, i/, o/," and "u/." We
respell the word "two" this way: "tw/," to differentiate it from "too."

The only other spelling that may look strange is that for the
sound in "book" and "woman." We adopted "uu" for this sound, which
is used by both the American and the English societies for simplified
spelling.

All the other respellings are old friends:

* See Appendix A.

Short Vowel Sounds				Long Vowel Sounds			
a	arr		at carry	a/ ae ai ay		a/ble graet	
e	err		end merry			maid day	
i	y irr		pity mirror	e/ ee ea ey		be/ bee eat key	
o	orr ar		hot sorry car	i/ ie y/ igh		chi/ld tie my	
u			us			high	
ur	er ir		burn her bird	o/ oe oa		o/ver toe oak	
				u/ ew		mu/zic few	

Digraphs and Diphthongs

oo w/		boot tw/ (two)	
uu		buuk wuuman shuud (should)	
or o/r oar		for fo/r (four) oar o/r (ore)	
aw au ong		law cauz (cause) long	
oi oy		oil boy	

Let's try writing a poem most of you know in the new spelling. Here is "God's World," by Edna St. Vincent Millay, as you are used to seeing it.

> O world, I cannot hold thee close enough!
>
> Thy winds, thy wide gray skies!
>
> Thy mists, that roll and rise!
>
> Thy woods, this autumn day, that ache and sag
>
> And all but cry with color! That gaunt crag
>
> To crush! To lift the lean of that black bluff!
>
> World, world! I cannot hold thee close enough!

Now let's write Millay's poem this way:

> O/ wurld, I cannot ho/ld thee clo/s enuf!
>
> Thy/ windz, thy/ wi/d gray sky/z!
>
> Thy/ mists that ro/l and ri/z!
>
> Thy/ wuudz, this autum day, that a/k and sag
>
> And awl but cry/ with culor! That gaunt crag
>
> Too crush! Too lift thu lean uv that black bluf!
>
> Wurld! Wurld! I cannot ho/ld thee clo/s enuf!

Does it look hard? It may look odd to you, but read it aloud to yourself. You will find that sight and sound go hand in hand. This is a great delight to the foreigner who is learning to read English!

ROMAN IS A PRACTICAL SCRIPT

The Roman script is practical. Note this distinction: it is <u>not</u>
the Roman alphabet that is at fault in spelling English. Because of
centuries-old influence of many languages on English, it is the way
we <u>use</u> the Roman alphabet--our spelling--that gives us trouble.

A good system of spelling in almost any language of the world
can be developed with the use of the 26 letters in the Roman alphabet, with perhaps a few added symbols from the International Phonetic Alphabet. Many influential leaders in India, for example, have
reached the conclusion that the Roman script is India's best solution.

The Advantages of Roman

1. With the addition of a few marks and letters used in
   the International Phonetic Alphabet, it can serve any
   Indian language, and practically any language in the
   world.

2. It can be spelled phonetically, without exceptions and
   without conjuncts.

3. It can be learned in much less time than any Indian
   alphabet, in one-fifth the time needed to learn Urdu
   or Telugu and less than half the time required to learn
   Devanagari or Tamil.

4. Having one alphabet would tend to unify all India. Since
   the Roman alphabet is used by far more nations than
   any other, it would serve to keep India in touch with the
   rest of the world.

5. It requires far fewer letters in printing presses and
   much less space than do the Indian dialects.

6. Presses could save great expense in type. They could
   print anything in Indian and in English or other Western,
   African, or Malay languages with no additional type.
   Most Indian presses now print English books, magazines
   and newspapers, and therefore are now equipped for
   Romanization.

The Objections to Romanization

1. Sentiment: India wants her own invention; this is also
   true in many other countries.

2. Literature: There is not much literature printed with
   Roman script in most of the Indian languages. This is
   also true in other non-Roman language areas.

This second objection is not so important for the literacy campaigns as it appears to be. There is next to nothing easy enough for villagers in most of the Indian alphabets. The lack of appropriate literature, which the three hundred millions of new literates will need in order to reach the present standard literature, is almost as acute in Indian alphabets as in the Roman alphabets.

One practical way for the Roman script to win its way against sentiment would be endowment to subsidize literature to be printed with Roman letters, ranging from charts and primers to transliteration of the classics. At first the educated reader would probably consider this literature slow-reading, unfamiliar, and unsightly, but his difficulties would quickly disappear--indeed, with a few hours or days of reading.

The battle of alphabets and languages is not won by arguments. In a democracy, it is the script that people confront day by day as they go about their work and play that wins, no matter how scholars may expound. In every language in which there is a literature (though only a very small percentage of the people may be able to read it) tradition and sentiment will hold fast to the present spelling system and alphabet. Only in languages which have been reduced to writing in this century, and in which there is only a small body of literature, is there much chance of revision according to the latest scientific thinking. These are the literacy facts of life; we shall have to live with them and work with them the best we can.

WHAT LANGUAGE SHALL WE USE?

Studios clinic e metabolic essava executate pro promover le clarification del effectos de Rauwolfia serpentina in patientes in varie phases de morbo vascular hypertensive. Le serie del patientes observate consisteva de 10 ambulante casos in le phase non-complicate del morbo, 10 hospital-istate casos in le phase accelerate, e 4 casos in varie stadios studiate in le section metabolic del hospital sub un regime constante de fluido e de dieta.

Discouraged? Here's the translation:

Clinical and metabolic studies were undertaken to throw further light on the effects of Rauwolfia serpentina, administered to patients in various phases of hypertensive vascular disease. Observations were made on 10 ambulatory patients in the uncomplicated phase, on 10 hospital patients in the accelerated phase, and on 4 patients in varying stages of their disease studied on a metabolic ward under constant fluid and dietary regimens.

Interlingua Is Its Name

You've just been reading (or trying to read) a language which
scientists from all over the world use in their international meetings. It is called Interlingua, a new language used, for example, in
the Second World Congress of Cardiology in Washington, D.C. Perhaps it isn't quite right to call it a new language because you can
read most of it easily. So, it evidently is similar to something with
which readers of English are familiar. It has a great deal in common
with other languages based on Latin. As many scientific terms are
from Latin origins, you can see the value of Interlingua to scientists
and medical practitioners.

For a language like Interlingua to be easily learned and easily
used, it must be simple. The complicated conjugations like those
you struggled with when you studied Latin or French or Spanish are
streamlined. The different endings for masculine and feminine, object and subject, singular and plural are eliminated. In many ways
the language has been reduced to the bare essentials: subject, verb
and object. And note, too, that they use the numeral "4" instead of
writing it out. That way one person reads to himself "quatro," a-
nother "quatre," another "vier," another "four," etc.

The object of such a language is to make as straight a channel
as possible for a person in one part of the world to tell a person of
another part of the world--in speech or in writing--what is on his
mind. There are no sand bars to get grounded on while we are trying to talk--like the endless rules of conjugation in existing languages.
There are no rocks to founder on, no sharp turns in this channel of
communication to trap the unsuspecting newcomer.

The old arguments of "mental discipline" and "learning how to
think," which are used to prod the schoolboy into learning "amo,
amas, amat" seem ridiculous as a means of learning how to communicate. Of course, those memory exercises are just for that: mental
discipline. But when we want to communicate as directly as possible
with someone else who may speak a different language, then we need
to meet easily on some common ground without having to jump dozens
of amo-amas-amat hurdles.

Esperanto is another language which clever people devised,
based also on Latin. It was popular 20 or 30 years ago, and still
has its speakers in many parts of the world.

What are these languages and how do they serve us? They are
examples of what is called a lingua franca, which means literally a
Frankish tongue. The lingua franca is a hybrid language, based on
Latin. But now the term is commonly used to mean any hybrid language. There are two outstanding examples of linguas franca in
Africa: Hausa, spoken by millions on the west coast, and Swahili,
spoken in half a dozen countries of east Africa.

Pigeon--But Not A Bird

Here is another one, which doesn't have a Latin base by any means, but has enough in common with English so that you should be able to make it out. The sentences are numbered so you can refer to the translation easily.

1. I gudpela samting turu sapos yumi ken sikul kuik long rid na rait.

2. Long onem liklik taim baimbai igat sampela titsa i kam bilong long-wei peles, Amerika.

3. Dr. Laubach i kam Lae bilong painim out ol pasin bilong mekim ol dispela samting.

4. Dr. Laubach kam wok liklik taim long Lae Lutheran Mission.

5. I go lukim oli ken makim ol sikul wok bilong ol enamel long ol neitiv bilong dispela peles.

And here is the translation into everyday English.

1. It's a very good thing to suppose we (you-me) can in school (sikul) quickly learn to read and write.

2. In (long) a little (liklik) time soon (baimbai) a teacher fellow will come from a far-away place, America.

3. Dr. Laubach comes to Lae to find out all fashions to do this fellow   (literacy).

4. Dr. Laubach will work a little time in Lae Lutheran Mission.

5. He ("He" is "I", pronounced "ee") will see how to make the schools work among (ol enamel) all the natives of this place.

Isn't it fun to read? And what fun it is to hear a news broadcast on the radio, or to read the newspaper. This was a news item in a weekly mimeographed newspaper published by the Australian Administration of New Guinea. The language is called "Pigeon, " or in their spelling, "Pigin." It is made of some words from various dialects of the coastal peoples of New Guinea, plus a lot of English and some German, for New Guinea was German territory before World War I.

The word "fellow" (pela) is used to denote a single item from a class of that kind, so "one teacher" is a "sampela titsa. " "It's very true" is "I (he) gudpela sumting turu."

There is no possessive case, so you can't say "the boy's hat;" you say "hat bilong boi." On the wooden privies scattered around the town of Lae you see "Bilong Boi" or "Bilong Mari" (Mary being the name for all women). The word "bilong" also is used for "comes from," or "among," or "to do," or to indicate some other kind of relationship.

The missionaries and New Guinea pastors preach in Pigin, and the newcomer can understand quite a lot of even the first sermon, though it is often hard to keep a straight face. "God" is "Numba Wun pela bilong top side."

We have seen in Interlingua an example of a lingua franca that has a world-wide use, and in Pigin a lingua franca with use among tribes on one island, New Guinea. Other areas of the world have lingua francas. There is Creole in Haiti, made of French and Haitian Indian dialects. It is about the simplest language from a construction point of view of any in the world, hence ultra easy to teach to read or to speak. In East Africa, there is Swahili, a widely used language, and in West Africa there is Hausa. In Sierra Leone, Liberia and other areas where English is influential, there are varieties of Pigeon English, in no way similar to the Pigin in New Guinea, but still easy for an English-speaking person to get on to.

Why doesn't Interlingua or Esperanto sweep the world? Why don't these other lingua francas completely dominate their areas? One reason is to be found in the pride which we all have--and rightly so--in our own local dialect. My wife is from North Carolina, and nothing so thrills her as to meet and talk with another Carolinian far from home; nothing does she fear more than that she may lose the music of Carolinian English after living for some time in "Yankeeland."

The Bostonians love their speech and believe it to be far superior to that of other Americans. Yet some scholars tell us that the "best" American English is spoken in Westchester County, New York. What is good speech? Is "ideer" and "cah" (for car) of Boston essentially any prettier than "deez" and "youz" of Brooklyn? Or, if Brooklyn had been the cradle of American arts, music and letters, would its speech not now be the "best" in America?

Let people keep their pride in their own dialects. That is fine. And let them smile at the incongruous or humorous things about the lingua franca in their area, for any language made from several others is bound to seem odd to many at first. But let us who wish to work with language for communicating review our notions about one language being "better" than another, to see if after all they have not been founded on rather flimsy or even false concepts about culture. Let us keep asking ourselves always, "What will best serve our new literates?"

A second reason that Esperanto, or Interlingua, or any other

"His scurrilous tongue incited me to engage him in a
bout of fisticuffs—and dat's de story in me own woids."

THE SATURDAY EVENING POST

lingua franca, will probably never sweep the earth is that language
is always bound closely to national power and economics. As long
as the Anglo-American influence is felt in the remotest corner of the
earth, English will stay the nearest thing to a world language. It
may not be something to be desired, but it is a fact. The smaller
lingua francas, as Hausa, have become so wide-spread because of
the economic influence of their originators, the Hausa Tribe, who are
the traveling merchants in a large part of West Africa. The origin
of the term "trade language" as a synonym for lingua franca can
easily be seen; for the traders were the only persons who moved
from one tribe to another, and who developed and spread their "language of trade."

The trade languages are being used more and more by publishers.
For it is obvious that it is much more practical to print a book in an
edition of , say 10,000 in one language, than in five or six different
language editions of 1,000 to 2,000 each. And if the five or six tribes

speak a common language, as is often true, the case for publishing
in the lingua franca is even stronger.

In teaching adult illiterates, though, it is much easier to teach
the Primer in their mother tongue; for then they are learning only
one new element--reading. If the spelling of the Primer is the same
as that of the trade language, then the new literate, after finishing
Stage I and Stage II, will be able to read the trade language about as
easily as his own mother tongue. The tendency in mission publishing
concerns, as in the Belgian Congo and neighboring French and Portuguese areas, is to write and publish only a few titles in the small
tribal dialects, more in the larger tribal dialects, and still more in
the lingua franca.

This is practical; but there are a number of emotional, cultural
and anthropological aspects which cannot be neglected. Both foreigners and nationals are divided in opinion as to how much to use the
trade language for publishing. Here are the sentiments of an educated
African, Joseph Samba, a teacher at the Seminary of the Mission
Evangelique Suedoise at Ngwedi, French Equatorial Africa:

> If these European scientists, who love the peoples of
> our continent, take an interest in the study of our languages,
> why does not the African wake up from his sleep ? It is time
> for us to understand the importance of our mother tongue
> and to try to preserve it. We, the Congolese of the Lower
> Congo, have a beautiful language, the Kikongo, with its
> different dialects. It contains moral treasures; it is rich
> in verbs, in expressions, etc. It is a real language, wor-
> thy of a people, a gift from the Heavenly Father. It is the
> inexhaustible heritage from our ancestors. It is time for
> us to understand the importance of our mother tongue and
> to try to preserve it.
> Unfortunately this is not what all Congolese do. Many
> of them are losing their language. I know of young women
> of the Bakongo and the Balari who do not know the language
> of their parents. If addressed in Kikongo, they smile and
> answer in Lingala (a widely spread trade language). Along
> the railway from Brazzaville to the Ocean, in Leopoldville,
> and especially at Matadi, I know Congo families where
> Kikongo is not spoken any more. Lingala has taken its
> place. Or, what is even worse, they prefer the artificial
> language called Kituba (a rudimentary trade language
> based on Kikongo). When the old parents speak in Kikongo,
> they are answered in Lingala or Kituba. These poor Congo-
> lese who think they are civilized are ashamed to speak the
> language of the Basenzi (the non-civilized people of the bush).
> Poor people who have lost contact with their country!

Funny civilization it is!

Would a Frenchman accept that his children speak English or Esperanto instead of his mother tongue? And would a Swede living in Paris let his children lose the use of Swedish in preference to French? In "Mputu" every people has its own language and preserves it jealously. Those are the best citizens who keep and cultivate their mother tongue.

In conclusion, I appeal to your good judgment. It is very important that a child worthy of its ancestors should speak the language they have given him in heritage, and that he jealously love it. It is therefore logical that this language be spoken in the family. Shame to the family which loses the use of its mother tongue.

Advantages of Lingua Franca and Tribal Dialect

As writers and publishers for new literates in many parts of the world, we will have to make decisions in this matter. This summary of argument for the lingua franca and for the tribal dialect will be of aid. And when decisions have to be made, don't forget to ask yourself again: "What will benefit the new literates most?"

	Reasons for Using LINGUA FRANCA		Reasons for Using TRIBAL DIALECT
1.	Aids in getting a better job in government and private business.	1.	People are happier in their own dialect.
2.	Government or social pressure against use of dialect.	2.	Women use dialect more than men.
3.	More literature available.	3.	People learn better if the words are familiar from childhood.
4.	Easier access to foreign culture.	4.	Mental block might develop if lingua franca is taught first.
5.	More economical production of literature.	5.	Develops tribal pride.
6.	Unites the people with a single language.	6.	Use dialect as pre-literacy course to lingua franca.
7.	Better educational opportunities.	7.	Better for religious purposes.
8.	Easier for missionary, teacher, publisher.	8.	Makes Christian message less foreign.
9.	Helps to develop world citizens.	9.	Helps appreciation of traditions of one's own people.
10.	Aids in understanding rest of world.	10.	Language association with one's past experiences.

Our chief concern is to teach others to read the printed word, and to write for them. No written language is perfect. Some of them, as English, are far from it; others, as Spanish, Turkish and Korean, are much better. But we will have to teach the illiterates how to read the existing written language. It is fun, of course, to play at improving the alphabet. But let's not allow ourselves to get so involved in theoretical arguments that we bring upon ourselves popular disapproval or even official censure.

Maybe you've wondered how this chapter fits in this book. Well, remember our job is to communicate with the new literates, and to help them communicate with one another and with the rest of the world. Until the day mankind develops mental telepathy to the point where present means of communication are outdated--like the radio, the pen and the printing press--we'll have to get along with what science has developed so far. And we mean the science of the mechanical and electrical aspects of communication, and the science of language and writing.

If a language in any area of the world serves the people, use it. Language is what sets us apart from the beasts. But when language, for some fancied or artificial reason, becomes our master, it is time to tell ourselves again what language and writing are for--to serve us and our fellowman.

We are helping men and women become master of this servant of great value when we teach them to read and write, and train writers for them. Let's see this goal clearly. Let nothing deter us from it.

Chapter 19

How to Make and Use Word Lists

In this chapter and the two that follow, we will take up three "musts" in writing for new literates:

1. We must be sure that each article we write is on the proper grade level. To know that, we need a word list. This chapter shows how to make and use word lists.

2. Each article we write must be simple and clear. Chapter 20 tells how to write clearly.

3. Our writing must be on the proper grade level, must be clear--and it must also be interesting! Chapter 21 tells how to make writing interesting.

WHY WE NEED WORD LISTS

The literacy problem is a double-headed giant--<u>making</u> people literate and <u>keeping</u> them so, and nobody yet knows which will prove more formidable. Before a campaign begins, we are tempted to believe that the second problem will somehow solve itself when we come to it. Experience is proving, however, that this is not the case. <u>Keeping</u> a country literate seems likely to be the more difficult problem of the two.

The first obstacle we encounter is the fact that nearly all the adult books and journals in Asia and Africa are too difficult for new literates. A teacher said ruefully: "I have made some people literate; but they cannot read!" This is not as absurd as it sounds. After an illiterate has learned to read syllables and can pronounce every word he meets in conversation, he may honestly be called "literate." But he will not be able to read standard literature until he has learned the meaning of many new unspoken words, for many ancient Asiatic languages employ a large classical vocabulary in writing which is never spoken by illiterates. The student must also learn many new

prefixes and suffixes which are employed in writing but which illiterates never use in speaking.

Illiterate villagers in six leading language areas of India were
asked to tell what words they understood in: 1. The Book of Acts,
2. A standard newspaper, 3. A typical classical book. These were
their answers, when hearing the materials read aloud:

In Hindi (Devanagari script)

> Acts--one word in 16 unknown
> Newspaper--one word in 9 unknown
> Classic--one in 11 unknown

In Urdu (Persian script)

> Punjabi Acts--one word in 28 was unknown
> Urdu Acts--one word in 24 was unknown
> Sixth standard story book--one word in 34 was unknown
> Milap, a newspaper with wide circulation--one word in
> 14 unknown

This indicates that Urdu is much more satisfactory in Biblical
translation, but not in newspaper.

India does not differ from other countries in the world which
have a small aristocracy of readers. We find the same cleavage between spoken and written Arabic in Egypt. As a country becomes
literate the written and spoken languages will tend to become closer;
they will level up and level down, just as they have done in the West.
In Europe, Latin was the written language before the people became
literate. The gradual process by which people began to read the spoken languages of Europe is a fascinating study. But today we cannot
wait for such a slow evolutionary process. The chasm between "literacy" and "standard literature" must be bridged at once.

There are cases where the objective of the writer will be to introduce new literates to the literary word so that they will be able
to read "standard literature."

An example has come from Miss Sally Anstey, Hyderabad State,
India. As she was working with her Indian colleagues on a book of
Bible stories, she says:

> "I suddenly saw what we could do to help the learner
> from the first stage and follow-up readers which use vil-
> lage words, over to the Bible words. Even the simplest
> Bible passage includes many unfamiliar words and forms--
> for example:

> "There are at least two words in Telegu for "jungle":
> the village common word, adivi; and the Bible word, not
> even known by some villagers and never used, aranyamu
> or aranyapradeshamu.

"So we have used first the familiar word the new literate
has read before:

Jesus went to the jungle (adivi, known, previously read word).
Jesus went to the jungle (aranyamu, new word) .
Jesus prayed in the jungle (aranyamu).
Jesus prayed for me in the jungle (aranyamu).
Jesus prayed for you in the jungle (aranyamu).

"Thus we introduce each new Bible word only one
at a time, and use the new word four times in quick
succession. "

When we speak of using only words which villagers understand
we must at once ask: "What words do they understand?" The answer
is not as easy as it may at first appear to be. A writer may know
the colloquial language of his own immediate neighborhood, but he
probably does not know how many of those colloquial words are used
in other regions. Spoken language sometimes changes within a ra-
dius of twenty miles. In every language area there is need for the
preparation of a "basic" list of the most frequently used words, such
as we now have in English and the other principal languages of the
West.

Rather we have need of two word lists, one at each end of our
problem. At one end is the illiterate--we must find the words he
uses in everyday speech. At the other end is standard literature--
what are the most common written words which the illiterate must
learn before he can read newspapers, magazines and ordinary books?

HOW TO PREPARE WRITTEN WORD LISTS

To prepare the two lists needed we must follow two wholly different methods. The first, the basic written words, can be obtained
by counting words in books, magazines, and newspapers which are
being published for the educated people of the language.

This is a rather straightforward, but arduous task. It is a task
which can be made easier if a number of assistants work with you
on it. One person may be assigned to read a certain magazine for
a period of a month or six months; another, a newspaper, every
issue or at regular intervals for a period of about a month; still others can read books which are currently popular.

As each person reads his assignment, he will keep a tally of
the number of times each different word occurs. One way to do this
is to copy the words from a dictionary in a row down the left hand
column of wide pages. Then as each word appears in the writing, a
mark or tally is put beside it. The fifth mark would be a diagonal

line through the first four. This makes counting the totals much
simpler.

Another way of keeping count is to have a pile of blank cards,
perhaps 3 by 5 inches, and as each word in a piece of writing appears
for the first time, it can be written in the upper left hand corner of
a card. The tally can be kept on the card for that word as indicated
above.

Someone should be designated to combine the various countings
of the assistants into a grand total. This could be done as the assistants read, or it might be done at the end of each two weeks or month.

Soon after the counting has begun, it will become evident that
many words need not be counted every time--words such as "the,"
"and," "to," "in," and similar articles, prepositions, and connec-
tives. In fact, it would become evident very quickly which are the
100 most frequently used words in that language. Those who do the
counting will soon become so familiar with the words that they will
not have to keep referring to this list.

Should you count every word as a different one? Probably not.
You may decide to count a word with varying suffixes as only one
word, but where it has varying prefixes, to list each prefix as a
different word. If the body of the word changes, like "is" and "was,"
"man" and "men," each form should be listed separately.

The accuracy of this written word list will depend upon how
many books, magazines, periodicals are read. If funds, personnel,
and time are limited, you may wish to do a count of only, say, three
or four issues of a half a dozen popular magazines and newspapers,
and perhaps two or three chapters from each of about 25 books.
Even a limited count should give you a pretty accurate picture of the
first 1,000 most common words in the standard literature and help
you to judge which are the least frequently used words.

One of the most exhaustive word counts is the Thorndike-Lorge
count of 30,000 English words. They and their graduate assistants
at Columbia University spent a number of years counting literally
millions of words and keeping accurate tallies. In their Teacher's
Work Book of 30,000 English Words, you can tell exactly the rating
of any word. The first 500 and the second 500 have been used by us
to help develop the Streamlined English word list of about 1,700
most common words in English. This is the list used in practice
writing in English for new literates found in the following chapters.
This list is in Appendix C of this text.

In a number of the other larger languages of the world there
are word lists taken from the literature. Notice this about the per-
manence of a word list: every language constantly takes on new
words and drops old ones. So a frequency count done ten or fifteen
years ago will have to be adjusted in the light of the new words that
have come into the language. A study of, for example, the word

"atom" will illustrate this. In the dictionaries and encyclopedias of twenty years ago, the word got only a few lines; now there are several paragraphs in the dictionary and more than a page in most encyclopedias, and the word is used daily in newspapers and maga-zines.

HOW TO DEVELOP A SPOKEN WORD LIST

The second type of word list--that derived from the conversa-tion of illiterates--is illustrated by the many working vocabularies prepared by foreigners for their own use in learning to carry on conversation. None of these, however, meet all the requirements, though they are of great value as a basis for a more scientific list. Their defect is that they do not cover a wide enough language area. Word lists from all the dialects of a language area need to be com-pared and checked with dictionaries and with illiterates themselves.

The procedure for those desiring to make a spoken word list is as follows:

1. Hold a small conference of linguists who are in close touch with village literates. Decide upon the number of sub-dialects spoken by illiterates in the area covered. Then select the best available linguist in each subdialect area to be studied.

2. Let a committee collect all dialect word lists and literature word lists, and prepare a composite list, making sure that it indicates the region in which each word is spoken. Supply the chosen sub-dialect research workers with this composite list.

3. Each research worker will go through a dictionary of his language, marking those words, and only those words, which he has heard his illiterate neighbors use.

4. Each research worker will call together 10 illiterates, paying them a small hourly wage: 3 men, 3 women, 2 boys above fifteen, 2 girls above fifteen. He will try out on these ten persons, each word in the word list and those he selected from the dictionary. He must say: "We desire the most common thousand spoken words. So raise your hands at each word. If you believe everybody knows the word, raise your hand when I say 'well known.' If you think not everybody knows the word raise your hand when I say 'not.' You are judges. Be sure to vote for not what you know, but what everybody knows."

Then each word is read, thrown into a short sentence or phrase, and the vote is taken. He will record how many vote

well known. If only one votes well known, he will write "1" after
the word. If 6 vote well known, write "6." If all favor it write
"10." If nobody wants it, write "0." So continue to the end of the
mimeographed word list and the dictionary. The record can be
written with pencil, in the dictionary, beside each word voted on.

5. The research worker may now either prepare the list of words
   chosen by his ten illiterate helpers; or if he is too busy, send
   his marked dictionary and mimeographed word list to a Central
   Recording Office for them to tabulate his results.

6 The Central Recording Office (one secretary is enough) will make
  a form for tabulating words, in the following manner. Secure a
  large sheet of paper wide enough to contain a 2-inch column for
  each sub-dialect reporting, plus a column for the words as they
  appear in the dictionary. The dictionary words in dictionary
  form are written in the left hand (first column).

SAMPLE FORM FOR TABULATING SPOKEN WORDS
Malay Language and Philippine Dialects

As in the Dictionary	Dialect A		Dialect B		Dialect C		English Definition
babaji	7	babai	2	. . . . .	4	babae	woman
babuj	2	baboy	5	baboy	3	baboy	pig
bajad	4	bayad	8	bayad	2	bayad	brother-in-law
baju	10	bayo	3	bayo	7	bayu	pound
bakul	9	bakol	6	bakol	6	. . . . .	basket
balay	3	. . . . .	8	balay	8	balay	house
balu	5	balo	9	balo	10	balu	widower
balik	1	balik	3	balik	9	balik	return
balut	6	balot	4	balot	2	balut	wrapping
banir	10	banig	7	banig	5	banig	mat
banut	2	banut	6	bunut	6	bunot	coconut husk
barah	3	baga	9	baga	8	baga	lungs
batu	9	bato	5	bato	5	batu	stone
batah	6	basa	10	basa	3	basa	wet

The preceding form is used for Malay. Each subdialect has its own column with the same word spelled as it is pronounced in that district. Before each word is placed the number of illiterates who voted for it in that district.

7. When all words have been thus listed, the next process is to classify them. List 1 will consist of those words which both appear in the dictionary and have the vote of all illiterates. List 2, words in the dictionary that are known though not accepted unanimously (number of votes should be noted), in all districts. List 3, words in the dictionary that are known in all but one district (district where unknown should be noted). List 4, in all but two districts. And so on.

   The first two thousand words derived in this manner--if that many words are common to most districts--will constitute our basic spoken list, arranged in four columns: 1 - 500; 500 - 1,000; 1,000 - 1,500; 1,500 - 2,000. These are the lists which should be used in preparing the total literature program: 1-500 for the Primer and Stage II; combined 1-500 and 500-1,000 for Stage III; and for Stage IV, gradual introduction of the remaining words on all the lists.

   A word list showing frequencies in several subdialects will shed much light on the problem of the use of the lingua franca, which we discussed in the last chapter. Indeed, the production of literature in vocabulary common to several subdialects will in itself be building a sort of written lingua franca.

8. The list should now be compared with lists made by book word counts in order to make a third list, consisting of the most common words found in books but not on the spoken list. This third list is compiled easily by eliminating, from the written word list, words which appear in the spoken list. What remains will be the words we must gradually introduce into our first and second readers and our newspaper for new literates--not more than one such word in twenty, repeating each new word as soon as convenient five or more times.

So we should have three lists:

   1. The words used in "standard literature."

   2. A list of words used in everyday speech, and also used in literature.

   3. A list of words found in literature, but not in everyday speech.

This is the ideal, though we realize that in some cases literature

will have to be produced in the absence of all three lists. Even
with only one word list, that of words in literature, if they are
rated according to frequency of usage, we have a valuable tool
to aid the writer for new literates.

HOW TO USE WORD LISTS

The old textbooks for primary school are deadeningly difficult.
Modern educators believe that in writing readers for children only
one word in thirty, or, at most, one word in twenty ought to be a <u>new</u>
word. At least nineteen words in twenty ought to be words that have
already been used. Old-fashioned primers have been inspected in
which on an average every second word was a new one! New words
piled upon one another in this fashion make the page difficult and in-
comprehensible.

This is as true for adults as it is for children. The mind, being
occupied with the recognition of new words, has no time to grasp the
meaning of the passage. If, however, new words are introduced spar-
ingly, the mind can comprehend their meaning. The reader develops
the important attitude of expecting an interesting message from the
printed page. The well-known law of learning then comes into operation, namely, that the mind tends to repeat that which gives satisfaction. Reading thus becomes a habit and a pleasure.

Complaints are frequently heard that new literates often revert
to illiteracy, also that there is very little demand for literature on
the part of many literates. May this not be due to the fact that many
literates never have had access to booklets or periodicals which they
can read without hesitation and understand without difficulty? One
who has never experienced any pleasure or profit from reading cannot be expected to demand much literature.

To stop this relapse into illiteracy, a literature must be created,
written on the third and fourth grade levels, but <u>adult in content</u>.
When writing for adults, follow the same three principles that writers of primers for children use:

1. Keep the number of new words down to one in twenty
   but keep introducing fresh, interesting material.

2. Use each word introduced in the text at least five
   times, soon after it first appears--more times if
   possible--since five is the minimum number of rep-
   etitions required for the memory of a new word.

3. Use the most common words first, as far as possible,
   and the less common words later. This must not be
   followed so strictly, however, as to interfere with
   interest in the story.

In most primary schools of the world, only 250 to 500 words are taught the first two years. During the first four to six years, the child learns to read the 2,000 or 2,500 words in the average everyday adult vocabulary.

The job in writing for new literates is to build up the adult's reading vocabulary, in a matter of weeks or months. This takes the child years to do. Keep in mind this basic difference: the child is learning to speak new words as well as to read them; the adult learns only to read new words. But until the adult has seen a word in print --several times and in several combinations with other words--it is a new word.

This is so hard for us who are good readers to understand that it bears repeating. When you, the students of this text, have had considerable experience observing new literates trying to read what you have written for them--then, and not until then--will you fully believe this statement. Until that time comes, take our word for it! If you can achieve the goal of writing with utmost care in presenting new words, you will be almost assured of success in writing for new literates.

"Why this concern for 'new literates'?" you may ask. "Aren't there enough 'regular literates' for whom to write, in the free-flowing manner to which I'm accustomed?"

Well, let's look at India, for example. How many of the "regular literates" there do you think can read "regular literature?" Government educational reports have shown that only 2 per cent of all the literates of India have reached the high school level (that would be two-tenths of one per cent of all the people in India, or about a half million people).

It would seem, therefore, if these figures are correct, that nearly all the literature to be found in the libraries of India is read by not more than 500,000 who have reached high school. Only about 5 million, or 20 per cent of the literates, have reached middle schools. There are not many magazines and still fewer books easy enough for them. For the 20 million who have studied, but have not gone beyond fourth grade, there is next to nothing easy enough except school books, and many of these are so dull that students loathe them.

Let's look, now, at the United States, with its millions of "highly literate" people. Here are some of the periodicals they read, with their corresponding school grade levels:

Grade 13 and up	None
Grade 12	Atlantic Monthly
Grade 11	Harper's
Grade 10	Time
Grade 9	Reader's Digest

Grade 8   <u>Ladies' Home Journal</u>
Grade 7   "Confession" type magazines
Grade 6   Comics

Perhaps you ladies didn't realize at what grade level you were reading! How many of us read the two magazines mentioned at grades 11 and 12? Should we not admit that for recreation--and for information--we read on a pretty low grade level?

The lower the grade level, the greater are the circulations of periodicals in that group. It is a powerful comment on the literary stature of this country that the often not-so-funny comics (in "books" and newspaper supplements) far outnumber every other group of journalistic publications.

Yet, <u>content</u> need not deteriorate, as it has in this country, just because the material is written within a small vocabulary. The huge commercial success of the sixth-grade materials should give us great hope--for we need to prepare a vast amount of literature two or three grades lower. And it will be "degraded literature" only in the sense that reading ease is increased for our friends, the new literates. The literature which we create--and which we'll be helping others to create--will be uplifting, practical and highly interesting.

Does it sound impossible to create a literature on the fourth-grade level? It is not only possible, but it is the <u>only solution</u> to the problem of keeping the new literates literate.

To fix in your mind clearly the various "stages of literacy" and for easy and repeated reference, study the chart found on page 184. Then read carefully the sample of writing in each stage.

An Article In Stage I

Let us first imagine the hardest possible condition under which to write with a word list. Suppose that the student has no recognition vocabulary at all. Then every word is a new word the first time it is used. In writing a second reader in English, called <u>Making Everybody's World Safe</u>,* this supposition was followed. The first chapter, then, has a number of "new words." By the end of the 49 chapters, some 1,500 words have been used.

On page 183 is the beginning of Chapter 1 in the reader. Each new word is underlined. Is each new word used at least five times? It should be. (As only part of the chapter is written here, the repetition of some words may occur soon after where we stopped quoting.)

---

* See reference in Appendix A.

The Nations Have United

The nations have united. They united to win the war.
They won the war. Now they have united to win the peace.
They are now called "The United Nations."

The United Nations have not won the peace. Not yet.
They have won the war. The peace is not yet won. They are
now trying to win the peace. They have called many meetings
to try to win the peace. And they are trying to end all wars.
They have not ended all wars. Not yet.

If the nations can end all wars they can win the peace.
And if they cannot end all wars, they cannot win the peace.
They cannot have peace if they have wars. So they have
called many meetings to try to end wars.

New Words

the	nations	have	united	they	to
win	won	now	peace	are	called
not	yet	is	trying	many	meetings
and	end	all	if	can	so

As was pointed out earlier, words like "end" and "ended," dif-
fering only in suffix, are counted as one word.
Of course, in this piece of writing the principle "use not more
than 5 new words in 100" has been violated. But remember, it was
assumed the reader did not know any words. If this had been written
on the Thorndike-Lorge first 500 word vocabulary, there would have
been only 6 new words: nations, united, win, won, peace, meetings.
If it had been written on the 1,000 word vocabulary, there would
have been only 3 new words: united, win, and won.
So it can be seen that the job of fitting our writing to a word list
is much more exacting in Stage II than in Stage III.
Most of the practice writing for new literates in classes is done
in English. To approximate the various stages of writing we have
more or less arbitrarily set these standards:
Stage II   The first 500 words in the Thorndike-Lorge List
Stage III   The first 1,000 words in the Thorndike-Lorge List
Stage IV   The total list of 1,700 Streamlined English Words

Use of Word Lists in Different Stages

Materials	Cumulative Word Count	Use of Word Lists	Length of Time Spent by Student
Stage I			
The Charts and Primer.	100 to 300 words, depending on the language. (Exception is Streamlined English; 850.)	Primer building is not the job for writers for new literates. However, it is done with extreme care, using only the most common words.	Student may take from two weeks to six months on Primer, depending on language and individual pace.
Stage II			
Anand, The Wise Man Series, and Story of Jesus Series.	Builds up to 1,000 , or even 1,500 in some languages.	Careful control of words is still called for. Each chapter in the series is in its proper sequence, adding 8 or 10 new words to the cumulative count.	Students may take four to six months to read either series. Stage I and Stage II are usually taught by tutorial or class method.
Stage III			
Pamphlets on many subjects; magazine or newspaper, or special section of them for Stage III.	Can assume a knowledge of 1,000 to 1,500 words.	Materials are not in a sequence, as in Stage II. But care should be taken not to use more than 5 words in 100 not found in word list.	New reader is now on his own. He may spend three or four months in Stage III. In fact, new readers should find Stage III materials of interest all the time.
Stage IV			
This is "general literature" for new literates; books, pamphlets, magazines and newspapers in constant stream.	Can assume knowledge of 2,000 to 2,500 written words --or the vocabulary of the everyday speech of the people.	Still trying to keep new words down to 5 in 100; technical material can be rewritten, "standard literature" can be simplified and its interest heightened.	The highest reading level most adult new literates will achieve. This is the "Reader's Digest" level for them.

The "Streamlined English Word Lists," composed of the first 500 most common, and the second 500 most common on the Thorndike-Lorge List, and about 700 other "Useful Words," is printed in Appendix C.

An Article In Stage II

Perfect Religion

By G. Lee Stewart

"If any man thinks he has religion but speaks anything wrong, his religion is wrong. Perfect religion with nothing wrong before God is this: go to help people who need you, and to keep away from the wrong in the world."

James 1: 26, 27.

What is religion? Is it to write on paper what you believe? Is it what you feel? Is it what you say and do before God? Is it what you do to others?

Perfect religion has all of these. Religion is to hold back and not "speak anything wrong." It is to love by going "to help people who need you." To be perfect in religion is also "to keep away from the wrong in the world."

In this new day how will you use your religion?

New Words
(Not on First 500 Word List)

perfect   religion

Is it not amazing what can be said with only 500 words? Only two words were outside the first 500 word list. "Perfect" is used four times, including the title, which is all right in a short piece like this. "Religion" is used nine times.

This article deals with abstract values. But concrete examples are given, as they are all through the Bible, to help us relate the abstract to our own experience. More about "abstract" and "concrete" will be found in the next chapter.

An Article In Stage III

Let us now look at an article done on the 1,000 word list. This is from <u>Community Development</u>, an experimental magazine produced by one of the classes at the Syracuse University School of Journalism. Samuel Mentee, on scholarship from the Government of Liberia, was the "editor" of the magazine, and is now helping to produce literature for the new literates of Liberia.

What The Agriculture Office Does

Most of the people of Liberia are farmers. The work of farmers is called agriculture. Agriculture is the most important work of our country.

Our Government knows how important agriculture is to Liberia. The Department of Agriculture of our Government is studying the problems of the farmers.

Our Government knows that the farmers have little money, and that they are already busy. The Government is showing the farmers new and better ways of farming.

The Government wants all the farmers of Liberia to learn better ways of farming. So our Government has already done two things:

1. It has brought to Liberia different kinds of
    plants from many countries. These plants
    give more fruit and more grain than Liber-
    ian plants. If these new plants are used here,
    they will bring more fruit and more grain
    to Liberia.

2. The Government has put an office in several
    parts of the country. This is the Agriculture
    Office.

In each Agriculture Office is a man who will
help the farmers with their problems. This
man is there to help you, if you are a farmer.
So do not be afraid to go to see him. He is
the friend of the farmers. He wants to be
your friend.

So, you see our Government has two plans:

1.   It wants to help all the people in Liberia.

2.   It wants to help you to become a better farmer.

New Words
(Not on First 1,000 Word List)

agriculture   grain

The word "Liberia," while not on the list, would certainly not
be a new word to the new literates in Liberia. Generally, you should
count proper names as new words, but you do not have to be so careful to repeat them five or more times, as this might make an article
awkward. If new names are the central characters of your story, or
the location of the story, you will have no trouble repeating them
several times.

An Article In Stage IV

In this stage, in which all of the "general literature" for new
literates is written, there is a large list to give you a great deal of
freedom in writing. All the articles in practice writing quoted in
this book are based on the Streamlined English Word List, which
totals about 1,700 words. In your writing abroad, after you have
developed your word lists, you may have about 2,000 common words
with which to work.

On page 188 is an article from Read And Grow, another experimental magazine prepared by a School of Journalism summer class.
Read this story. Compare the vocabulary with that of the preceding
stories. Note that, while there is only one new word, the larger
word list was used as a basis for this story.

Your word lists will grow considerably with usage. If in Liberia,
for example, a periodical is published which includes articles month
after month on farming and on government and on international affairs,

Save Your Soil

Do you have a farm?
If you do, you have
to work hard to save
your soil.

The heavy rains
carry away the soil.
People have to work
hard to keep the soil.

Before the heavy
rains come, you can
help save your soil.

Plant some kind
of grass. The grass
will hold the soil.

When the rains are
over, plow the grass
under the soil.

This is GOOD. The plow went around
the hill. When it rains, the water goes
into the ground. The soil is saved.

The grass under the soil will make the soil strong and
good. This good soil will hold more water than weak soil.
Weak soil, without grass under it, is very poor soil.

Is your land on a hill? If it is, plow along the hill, NOT
up and down the hill. This will help to hold the water. Some
water will go into the ground. It will not run off so fast.

This is BAD. The plow went up and
down the hill. When it rains, water
runs off quickly, taking soil with it.

Another way to hold
the soil on the side of
hills is to dig ditches
for the water to run
down. The ditches will
take the water into a
river or into a lake.

Save all the soil it
is possible to save.
Don't let heavy rains
carry your soil away.

New Word
(Not on 1,700 Word List)

ditches

words like "agriculture" and "education" and "United Nations" and several dozen others may be added to the lists.

As you work with the words on your list, you will become so familiar with them that you won't have to check with every sentence you write. Write fast, as the inspiration and pressure of your work dictate. Then go back over your work, looking for the big long words which have sneaked in through your subconscious. With practice, you will more and more automatically choose the right word--the simple word--the first time you write your article.

Let's end this rather long chapter on word lists with a word of warning: the mere use of a word list in your writing will not in itself make your writing good. Simple writing is something more than just avoiding hard or unusual words. The word lists confine the canvas of your writing to definite limits. The art of simple writing is to develop freedom within those limits. You will experience a great new joy as you develop your art of simple writing. The new literates will bless you for the clear and interesting articles, stories--even poems--you will write.

Cogitate (pardon the slip!)--think on these things.

Chapter 20

How to Make Your Writing Simple

Read the following selection on a mountain top. Or, if there is no mountain top handy, pretend you are on a mountain top, and let your mind's eye see what the story tells:

There is a lovely road that runs from Ixopo into the hills. These hills are grass-covered and rolling, and they are lovely beyond any singing of it. The road climbs seven miles into them, to Carisbrooke; and from there, if there is no mist, you look down on one of the fairest valleys of Africa. About you there is grass and bracken and you may hear the forlorn crying of the titihoya, one of the birds of the veld. Below you is the valley of the Umzimkulu, on its journey from the Drakensberg to the sea; and beyond and behind them, the mountains of Ingeli and East Griqualand.

The grass is rich and matted; you cannot see the soil. It holds the rain and the mist, and they seep into the ground, feeding the streams in every kloof. It is well-tended and not too many cattle feed upon it, for the ground is holy, being even as it came from the Creator. Keep it, guard it, care for it, for it keeps men, guards men, cares for men. Destroy it and man is destroyed.

Where you stand the grass is rich and matted, you cannot see the soil. But the rich green hills break down. They fall to the valley below, and falling, change their nature. For they grow red and bare; they cannot hold the rain and mist, and the streams are dry in the kloofs. Too many cattle feed upon the grass, and too many fires have burned it. Stand shod upon it, for it is coarse and sharp, and the stones cut under the feet. It is not kept, or guarded, or cared for; it no longer keeps men, guards

190

men, cares for men. The titihoya does not cry here any
more.

The great red hills stand desolate, and the earth has
torn away like flesh. The lightning flashes over them, the
clouds pour down upon them, the dead streams come to
life, full of the red blood of the earth. Down in the valleys
women scratch the soil that is left, and the maize hardly
reaches the height of a man. They are valleys of old men
and old women, of mothers and children. The men are
away, the young men and the girls are away. The soil
cannot keep them any more.

Do you know what it is? It is the opening page of <u>Cry, The Beloved Country</u>, by Alan Paton. To comment on its beauty would be
as absurd as to try to explain the fragrance of a rose. It is simple;
it is beautiful beyond any further "singing of it."
Alan Paton has caught the beauty and simplicity of Africa, and
further on in the book he catches the beauty of the idiom of the African speech. The best lesson we could prepare on simple writing is
to tell you to read Paton's whole book, or, if you have, read it again.
It is the only argument, and the final argument, needed to use with
those who still complain that simple writing is beneath them; that
only with the full play of their stock of multi-syllable letters can
they express themselves in beautiful and complete language. Simplicity is beauty!

By way of contrast, read this:

"Eight and seven-tenths decades ago, the pioneer
workers in this continental area implemented a new group
based on an ideology of free boundaries and initial conditions of equality. We are now actively engaged in an over-
all evaluation of conflicting factors . . . We are met in an
area of maximum activity among the conflicting factors .
. . to assign permanent positions to the units which have
been annihilated in the process of attaining a steady state.
This procedure represents standard practice at the admin-
istrative level.

"From a more comprehensive viewpoint, we cannot
assign--we cannot integrate--we cannot implement this
area. . . The courageous units, in being annihilated .
. . have integrated it to the point where the application
of simple arithmetical operations to include our efforts
would produce only negligible effects. . .

"It is preferable for this group to be integrated with
the incompleted implementation . . . that we here resolve
at a high ethical level that the deceased shall not have been
annihilated without furthering the project--that this group
. . . shall implement a new source of unhampered activity
--and that political supervision composed of the integrated
units, for the integrated units, and by the integrated units
shall not perish from this planet."

How far did you read before you guessed what it is? It's Lincoln's "Gettysburg Address" intentionally "lumbered up" by Prof.
Richard D. Fay of Massachusetts Institute of Technology. He did
it to ridicule some of the elephantine language used by sociologists.
Compare, for example, "political supervision composed of the integrated units, for the integrated units, and by the integrated units,"
to Lincoln's simple, majestic, "government of the people, for the
people, and by the people."
Now, just for fun, let's look at the same portion of the "Gettysburg Address" as President Eisenhower might have delivered it
"off the cuff." An anonymous White House newsman wrote it, in much
the same style as Ike's celebrated talks during his weekly press conferences.

"I haven't checked these figures, but 87 years ago,
I think it was, a number of individuals organized a government set up here in this country...based on a sort
of national independence arrangement and the program
that every individual is just as good as every other individual.

"Well, now, of course, we are dealing with this big
difference of opinion--civil disturbance you might say--
though I don't like to take sides and name any individuals.
The point is naturally to check up, by actual experience
in the field, see whether any governmental setup with a
basis like the one I was mentioning had any validity,
whether that dedication you might say by those early
individuals has any lasting values.

"But if you look at the overall picture of this, we
can't pay any tribute--we can't sanctify this area--we
can't hallow, according to whatever individual creeds
or faiths or sort of religious outlooks are involved. It
was those individuals themselves, including the enlist-
ed men, who have given this religious character to the
area.

"We have to make up our minds right here and now,
as I see it, that they didn't put out all that blood, per-
spiration and--well--that they didn't just make a dry run
here that all of us, under God that is, the god of our choice,
shall beef up this idea about freedom and liberty and those
kinds of arrangement and that governments of all individuals,
by all individuals and for the individuals shall not pass out
of the world picture."

THREE NAMES FOR A DREADFUL DISEASE

There is a disease that has crept into the writing, not only of
sociologists and other technical men, but also of popular writers,
journalists, government and business writers. This disease is ready
to creep into the literature now being created in many countries,
especially if the masters of the long word and the windy phrase are
allowed to set the style of writing in those countries.

This disease goes by several descriptive terms: "lumbered lingo," "gobbledygook," and "tapeworm English." Or, each of them
might be considered a different form of the same disease.

You "lumber up your lingo" when you fill your writing with fifty-
cent words, which stick in your mind, but which you may or may not
be using in the correct way. Somehow it seems to lend a flavor of
scholarship to the writer who measures the quality of his writing by
the density of the big words in it. It is dense, without a doubt!

I remember while we were in Korea a high-school boy came to
me one day, carrying a Dictionary of Big Words, filled with words
of the increase-your-word-power variety. "Please, sir," he asked,
"what are this word?" And he pointed to a word; perhaps it was
"ambivalence." This ambitious boy was starting in the front of the
book and learning as many big words as he could, though he could
not yet speak a simple English sentence correctly. I admire his am-
bition, but am afraid that another lingo lumberer is in the making!

"Gobbledygook" refers to the round-Robin Hood's-barn way of
saying even the simplest thought. Just how much of the gobbledygook in the fine print on insurance policies, contracts, mortgages,
etc. is deliberate one can only guess. One can hardly blame lawyers,
accountants and other professional people for protecting their own
profession by writing in a style that only another lawyer or account-
ant, with several years of special training, can read. But when we
are trying to say something clearly and directly--not to confuse, but
to communicate--then out goes the gobbledygook!

"Tapeworm English"--that's the meandering style of writing in
endless sentences that seldom make a clear point. Have you stood
on the edge of a desert and followed a small stream with your eye?

It wanders around until finally it disappears. That's the way with
tapeworm English, or tapeworm any-other-language. The sentence
may start with an idea, perhaps just a little one. But instead of
sharpening up that idea, and letting it sparkle by itself, the tapeworm
sentence goes on and on until the original idea is lost in a desert of
words.

There is one good remedy for the tapeworms in your writing:
chop them up into short, clear, complete bits. Better yet, don't let
the tapeworms get into your writing in the first place. Before you
start a sentence, know where it is going to stop. And when it is
done--stop!

Fortunately, more and more people are learning about this
dread disease, which you can call by your favorite name. There
are "doctors" of readability, whose prescriptions we shall get in a
few pages. Journalists and writers of popular books are less sus-
ceptible to lumbered lingo than are others.   For the fact that one is
a "popular" writer shows that, perhaps unconsciously, he knows
how to write clear and concise language that holds the reader to the
end.

The scientists and professional men are now being told of the
disease in their writing. In an annual meeting of the British Association for the Advancement of Science in Liverpool, England, the
scientists were told they were "illiterate, inarticulate and irresponsible."

Ritchie Calder, Chairman of the Association of British Science
Writers, justified his harsh judgment of scientists this way:

1. "They are illiterate, because the test of literacy is
   the capacity to communicate ideas, and in these days
   of specialization, scientists are the hostages of their
   own professional slang.

"B. C."

New York Herald Tribune

2. "They are inarticulate because they cannot, or do not bother to express themselves intelligently."

Scientists may claim as an alibi that they are too busy to learn other vocabulary than "their own professional slang." But you and we who are concerned for the new literates have no such alibi.

We have something to say. We have a reading public in mind whom we have studied and know well. We are building the public's reading ability with carefully controlled word lists. The scene is set, therefore, for good communication. The rest is up to us as writers. Let us examine a few of the ways we can improve the "telling power" of our writing.

KEEP SENTENCES SHORT

One does not have to reach far to find a tapeworm sentence that could be chopped into smaller bits. Looking in my wallet, I find my driver's license and turn it over to read the small print (have you read yours lately?):

Duty to Report Accidents

The operator of any motor vehicle, involved in an accident resulting in death or personal injuries in any degree, or damage to the property of any one person in excess of one hundred dollars, shall, within twenty-four hours, forward a report to the Department of Revenue, Harrisburg. Failure to report accidents may result in suspension of operator's license."

The first sentence in that bit of instruction has 49 words. I can read it, and after the second or third time, can figure it all out. But can the thousands of men and women who didn't get beyond the fifth or sixth grade? And, even if every licensed person can figure it out, with some difficulty, why not write it so it can be figured out at the first reading? Let's try:

You Must Report Accidents

If you operate any motor vehicle, and are in an accident, you must report it, if:

By Johnny Hart

I COULD HAVE SWORE IT WAS A MIXED DRINK.

hart

1. The accident results in death.
2. The accident results in any personal injury.
3. The accident results in damage of $100 or more
   to the property of any one person.

   You must send a report of the accident within 24
hours to the Department of Revenue, Harrisburg.

   If you fail to do this, your operator's license may
be suspended.

Instead of 49 words in one sentence, there are now five sentences, with a total of 61 words. Just by cutting the sentence length,
and adding the "1, 2, 3," it has been cleared up considerably. No
attempt to change the words was made, as they may be used in a
certain legal sense.

How long should sentences be for the new literates? We suggest
an average length of 8 to 10 words. This does not mean that every
sentence should be only 10 words long. That would be very monoton-
ous to read. We all like variety. Nothing puts one to sleep quicker
than the regular clickety-clack of a train on the rails, or the sonor-
ous voice of a preacher who never alters his sentence length or his
intonation--or trying to read an article with little variety in sentence
length or structure. Variety keeps us awake. The book or magazine
that you take to bed and read long after the town has gone to sleep
will have variety in sentence length. But the average length of the
sentences will be short.

Look at the paragraph I just wrote. Two sentences have only
four words. One has 44. But the average is only 14, and I'm not
writing for new literates here. And I didn't get the idea of counting
the words till almost the end of the paragraph. So it wasn't a "rigged"
paragraph just to prove a point.

How do American magazines rate in average sentence length?
Here are the ratings, sampled over several years, of different classes of magazines:

		Average Sentence Length
"Pulps," like "confession" magazines and men's outdoor magazines		12-15
Reader's Digest		14-17
News magazines, like Time		16-17
"Class" magazines, like Atlantic Monthly, Harper's		20

And it will be noticed that the publications with the shortest sentence length have the largest readership. The total of all the "Class"
magazines is not even one million; the total of all the "pulps" amounts
to many millions. Reader's Digest has a circulation in the United

States alone of ten million. Of course, there are many factors which account for circulation, such as the low taste and "confessional" nature of the pulps.

But the role that sentence length plays may be more clearly seen in this analysis of sentence length compared to reading grades in school. The McCall-Crabbs Standard Test Lessons in Reading have been given millions of American school children. The test shows what sentence length children in each grade can read with understanding (not to be confused with what level they enjoy reading):

School Grade	Average Sentence Length
12	20
10	18
8	15
6	14

From the experience of successful magazines, and the knowledge of the reading skills of American graduates of the public school system, we can gain a great lesson. The most popular magazine in this country--and in the world--The Reader's Digest, is written on the eighth or ninth grade level.

We wish to write for those who have had no schooling as children, and only a few months of reading instruction as adults. An average sentence length of not more than 10 words should be our rule. Let us never violate that rule!

USE THE SHORT AND EASY WORD

We have already talked at length about word lists. They will keep us from going too far astray in our use of words. But even within the word lists there is plenty of choice between the long word and the short. In English, the shorter word is usually the more common. That will generally be found true in most other languages, perhaps, I suppose, because people naturally want to say the most in the shortest amount of time and with the least amount of breath. So "end" is more common than "terminate," "go" is more common than "proceed"--and the list of comparisons goes on indefinitely. For your amusement you might make up a list of synonyms, and see if, nine times out of ten, the more commonly used one isn't the shorter one.

There is a ring of sincerity in short words. Everyone looks with suspicion on a person whose speech is always liberally sprinkled with platitudinous polysyllabifications. How do you get to know someone well? Not by maintaining your artificial politeness and careful use of big words, as you do when being interviewed for a new job. But you learn to use the short, polite words of everyday speech.

Sometimes we wonder about the sharp line of distinction between students and professors in colleges. Many professors honestly try to get to know their students, but their trouble may lie partly in their stuffy vocabulary. A student may come in some morning and say, "Gee what a rain!" If the professor answers something like, "Indeed, it is undoubtedly the most disagreeable precipitation of the season," you know he hasn't succeeded in getting "next" to his students. Or, as the psychologist puts it in his scientific lingo: "The barriers to empathy become temporarily insurmountable."

Drama lies in the short words. The next time you go to the theatre, try to keep a tally of words used over four syllables long. The fingers of one hand will suffice for the tally. For drama reflects life, and life is composed of short, common words. Winston Churchill, leader and orator, had the knack of coining phrases to stir men's hearts. Can you think of any more powerful words to rally a country in its darkest hour than these three: "Blood, Sweat and Tears!"

Become a friend of the short word--the common word. For it is your friend.

WORDS ARE PRECIOUS--DON'T "PAD" YOUR WRITING

The greatest art in writing we have learned in our school days is "padding." But let's not blame it all on the schools, but also on our whole attitude toward writing. "Gee," we think, "I ought to write a letter home. But what will I say. Nothing's happened here in a month." And so we start with an empty page and fill it with empty words. As long as we keep that kind of writing strictly in the family, it's quite all right; for even a page of "empty" words helps maintain and improve the family "empathy," to use the psychologist's term. But let's keep it in the family!

Or, perhaps, in our younger days, we had to write a 500-word theme on Columbus--and it's due tomorrow! We really didn't know anything about Columbus except that the year 1492 stuck in our heads. So we sat down and began something like this (Writer claims no responsibility for historical accuracy.):

On or about the month of December in the year 1491,
the man whom history calls Christopher Columbus had just
about come to the conclusion that there must, after all, be
something away out beyond the western horizon, farther
than any sailor had ever sailed. So he proceeded to go up
to the capital city of Madrid to arrange for an audience with
his old friend, Queen Isabella. The Queen, who had, on one
occasion or another, aided and abetted the earlier voyages
of Columbus, listened with rapt attention.

Does it sound like a high-school theme? Has anything been said in it? It wouldn't take long to write 500 words of that kind of padding. And the chances are, if the padding were polished up a bit on a second writing, it might get a fairly good grade for "fluidity of language," "sentence balance," or "choice of words."

But you and I know it's just a padded piece of nothing. There are at least a dozen padded phrases: "on or about," "the month of," "in the year," "whom history calls," "had just about come to the conclusion," "away out beyond,". . . you find the rest. In fact, you'll "just about come to the conclusion that" it's all padding!

For the fun of it, make up a list of padded phrases you may have used, or heard others use. Or, in the books by the various doctors of readability (see Appendix A) there are long lists of padded phrases and padded words.

Pick up any textbook you had in college. How much in it is concrete stuff you can get your hands on and which you can remember? How much is just padding? This book is intended to be a definitive text, or a "how-to-do" book. So it behooves us (an uncommon word, but an apt one here) to wield the blue pencil harshly on all the padding before we seek a publisher. The blue pencil is the greatest enemy of padding --and the writer's great friend, second only to the common word.

Enough padding on padding.

USE THE ONE-TWO-THREE TO HIT THE MARK

Boxing fans are familiar with the cry, "Give 'im the ole One-Two-Three!" It's a sequence of punches that often hits the mark. Writers have punches to give, too. And too often we hide our punches somewhere in a long sentence or a solid paragraph. Boxing fans like the One-Two-Three because it's out in the open where all can see it. Let's bring our punches--things we have to say--out in the open, too.

In writing to instruct, the One-Two-Three--and the Four-Five-Six-And-So-On are especially valuable. Let's see how the One-Two-Three steps in how to produce good eggs are hidden in this paragraph, taken from a popular farm magazine:

Farm practices were studied by several experimental
stations to determine just which practices are necessary
to produce clean eggs. Some of their findings indicate that
frequent gathering, at least three times daily, is the most
important factor, as most soiling comes from the hens'
feet. Dry litter helps keep the hens' feet clean. Adequate
ventilation and adding new litter to the old built-up litter,

and stirring, keep the litter loose and dry. Nesting material needs to be clean and dry. Granular types of nesting material, such as shavings, sawdust, ground corn-
cobs, are better than coarser types such as hay and straw.
Plenty of nesting space--one nest for every four or five
birds--is necessary. Layers should be confined to keep
eggs clean.

The class in writing for new literates went to work on the article
from which that passage is taken. In addition to simplifying it, some
of the details were omitted that were not considered essential for
farmers, for example, in Africa. The introduction to the article
showed why the farmers need clean eggs: because they will bring
higher price in the market. Then the One-Two-Three technique was
applied.

How You Can Get Clean Eggs

1. Make the nest of clean material.

2. Make the nest of shavings, sawdust or ground-up
    corncobs.

3. Collect the eggs at least three times every day!

4. Keep the material dry.

5. Keep the material fresh. Add new material, and
    stir it up.

6. If the nest is always clean, the hen's feet will
    stay clean.

7. Give the hens plenty of space. One nest for 4
    or 5 hens is good.

8. Keep laying hens by themselves.

You will notice how, all through this book, whenever we had
several related things to say, we used the One-Two-Three punch.
Diagrams and graphs are other ways of freeing the important facts
from the prison of the paragraph. Free your facts. Put them in a
form every reader can see quickly, and they will stay with him
much longer.

USE ACTIVE VOICE AND ACTIVE VERBS!

The attention of the reader should be drawn to the fact that the use of the active voice is to be highly recommended over the use of the passive tense. It surely is! Now--putting it actively--we highly recommend: Always use the active voice.

One of the secrets of the "success courses" to which so many people subscribe is that they teach you to act and speak in a positive manner. You learn to feel positive, and to act and speak the way you feel. The person with inner strength of his convictions usually has the outward positive manner.

Our whole program of writing for the new literates is a positive one. They are on the way to a better life through reading good, positive literature. If we don't believe that right down deep inside, then we are in the wrong business. If we do believe that the whole future of the new literates is positive, then let us speak and let us write positive! (The strict grammarian may insist on saying "positively" --but somehow positive seems much stronger here.)

In English, writing in a positive and active way is not hard. It consists in simple subject-verb-object sentences. They are strong and they are clear. You always know who or what it is we are talking about, what is happening, and to whom it is happening. And don't hang a lot of participial phrases or clauses on the strong stem of your sentence. For that weakens the whole structure. If each of these secondary thoughts that come to your mind is worth the saying, give it an active sentence. These active sentences, neatly strung together, will help line up our positive thoughts clearly, like pickets in a fence.

Some writers jumble their thoughts together in long, disorderly sentences. Their readers have trouble distinguishing one thought from another, just as you would have trouble distinguishing one picket from another, if they were in a huge jumbled pile. The good writer arranges his thoughts in orderly fashion, like the fence maker arranges his pickets. Then each thought, like each picket, stands out clearly as an individual, yet contributes continuity to its neighboring thoughts which come before and after it.

Let's look at this pile of words:

My collection of National Geographic Magazines, which had been started when I was born, and which I had carefully added to every year since I was old enough not to have to have my parents do it for me, was greatly enriched by my grandfather, who, having subscribed to the Geographic himself since he was ten, left me in his will complete sets from 1889 to the year I was born.

It sounds a bit like modern Dickens. But, then, he was a master of English and never would have written such a hodgepodge. Did the writer have clearly in mind what he wanted to say before he put the first word on paper? You be the judge of that. Everything is so jumbled it is hard to find the idea that the author was most excited about when he wrote it.

Probably it was the gift from his grandfather that prompted him to write this. Let's start this way, then:

My grandfather willed me complete sets of the <u>National Geographic</u> Magazine from 1889 to the year I was born. My grandfather was only ten when he started collecting the Geographic. My parents started my collection when I was born, and I have carefully added to the collection every year since I was old enough to do it myself.

From the jumble of ideas in the first version, we have lined up the ideas clearly in four sentences. The word "and" serves to start the last sentence. For not only periods, but commas and semi-colons may divide thoughts into separate sentences. We did not use a strict chronological order for the ideas. We put the most interesting one first--the one we think excited the author most. Then a "flash back" to bring in a little background, followed by the last two sentences that give meaning to the whole paragraph.

The revised version of that paragraph illustrates several of the principles of which we have just been talking:

1. The voice is active all the way through.
2. Sentences are shorter--14 words average per sentence in the revision; 71 in the original.
3. Dangling clauses have been eliminated.
4. Active words used.
5. Padding thrown out ("willed me" instead of "left me in his will").
6. The whole passage is shorter--57 words in the revised against 71 in the original.

Some languages, by their construction and by the culture of the people, may give trouble in writing in the active voice. In Maranaw, the language of the Moros of the Philippines, where Each One Teach One began, the people often speak in the passive voice.

Instead of saying, "Please pass the bread," you should say in polite society something like, "Please, by you the bread to be passed to me." It just isn't proper to say "Pass the bread," even with a polite "please" somewhere in the sentence.

And visitors in Japan and other countries of the Orient have often seen signs such as this:

> Please, to beg your humble pardon so that the
> grass may be nourished by Mother Earth not
> to trod hereon.

Quite a contrast to our signs: "Keep Off The Grass" (with or without "Please").

In Kabul, Afghanistan, the sign was seen--pardon me--we saw a sign in a shop window:

> ## Crockery Be Hired Here.

Much more to the point, but still passive!

Read the ads in American newspapers and magazines. The ad writers are the masters of writing in the active voice. We have much to learn from them.

With the active voice, use active words. In the Daily Orange, a newspaper published by journalism students at Syracuse University, there is a rule: "Never use any form of the verb TO BE in headlines." For "is" is such a weak, unexpressive word--and so much overused. One can relate in dull terms the whole life history of a man with "is": "He was born, he was confirmed, he was married. Now he is dead and is buried." You don't portray man just a little lower than the angels with a dull, dead verb like "is!"

You can get many strong, active verbs from your word lists, for active verbs are often common words. For an interesting exercise, go through the Streamlined English Word List and check the active verbs, especially those which can be used as synonyms for "is."

WRITE IN CONCRETE TERMS

As you try hard to write in the active voice and use verbs of action, you must also speak in concrete, specific terms. For the clarity and strength of your positive approach in writing will lose its vigor if you use abstract terms. The last sentence has at least three abstractions, so let me say it stronger this way: You want to write clearly and be positive, don't you? Then use the active voice and active verbs--and your thoughts will be propelled directly to the thousands who will read your writing with interest and understanding.

You have seen recruiting posters for the armed services. Do they say something like: "The presence of yourself would be of benefit to your country, due to the exigency of the times and the sacrifice

which patriotism demands of everyone. " They do not! At least one
of the most used posters showed a bearded Uncle Sam pointing
straight at you, saying, "I want you. " No beating about the bush.
No weakening of message in abstractions.

What are abstract words? Some you can class by their endings:
"--ness" (happiness, healthfulness), "--ence" (presence, quintes-
sence, inconvenience), "--ment" (payment, advancement). By putting those endings, and others, on good, strong words, you change
them into floating abstractions. And there are hundreds of abstract
words--words which sum up the essence of a quality, or enlarge a
specific into a whole universe full of that particular class of thing.

"You, " "I, " "he, " "she, " "we. "   They are all specifics.
Sum them up and you have "man" or "mankind", an abstraction.
The Pigin of New Guinea doesn't go in for abstractions. Even a
word such as "we" (hardly an abstraction in our sense of the word)
is broken down into its more specific parts, "you-me" (or, if you're
a strict grammarian, "you-I").

"But isn't the ability to think in abstract terms a monument to
the development of man's thinking prowess?" you might argue. Certainly it is. And when we recommend that you avoid abstractions,
we are not trying to discredit the growth of you-me-they (mankind).
You can't avoid abstractions entirely, nor should you. But when you
use abstractions in a lazy and hazy way, instead of pinning down
what you want to say in concrete terms that relate directly to the
reader, you have no alibi.

Let's look at this example. Here are the introductory remarks
to an article on prenatal care.   It was published in a handsomely
printed magazine in Africa, and contains ten excellent suggestions
for care of the expectant mother. But do you not agree that it loses
its punch with this opening?

PREPARING FOR YOUR BABY

Very few African women consider the inconvenience,
discomfort, and pain of child-bearing too great a price to
pay for having a baby. However, even in spite of the advancement in provision of maternity centres and proper
care during pregnancy and delivery, it is still an ordeal.
But the joy of having a child is well worth all the trouble
it costs.

The child's health before birth is closely connected
with the mother's health. The questions of the right kind
of food, what to do, and what not to do are very important.
The following suggestions may be helpful as a guide during
the time you prepare for your child.

Child-bearing is a perfectly normal function and

therefore the rules of ordinary health should be followed.

How many abstract words do you count? There are at least 20, counting even small words like "joy" as an abstract. There is a lot of padding. More active verbs could be used. The sentences are too long--so several principles we have been talking about were violated.

The class in Writing For New Literates discussed the article, before rewriting it: If "very few African women consider the inconvenience, discomfort and pain of child-bearing" then why talk about it in at least three sentences?

Is the maternity center a real place? Members of the class from Africa said there are many maternity centers. They are run by the government in the Belgian Congo and neighboring countries. If we want to encourage women to go there, then let's not hide the Maternity Center. Capitalize it and capitalize on it. (Maternity Center was treated as a new word, so was repeated several times.) Here is the simplified version as it appeared the experimental magazine Read And Grow:

Before Your Baby Comes

Are you going to have a baby? The Maternity Center will help you. The Maternity Center will help you before your baby comes. The Maternity Center will help you when your baby comes. The Maternity Center will help you after your baby comes.

But you have important things to do before your baby comes. Your good health helps your baby.

You should know what things to do. You should know what things not to do. If you want good health, do these things:

1. GET FRESH AIR · Get fresh air in the day. Get fresh air in the night. Stay out of crowds.

2. DO EASY WORK. Do your usual work. But don't lift heavy things.

3. REST EVERY DAY. Lie down one hour in the middle of the day.

DO NOT lift heavy things. You may do everyday work.

4. KEEP CLEAN. Clean your body with warm water every day.

Eat many kinds of
fruits. Eat all food
aggreable to you.

5. KEEP HAPPY. Be pleasant
with your family. If you are happy,
this will help your baby to be happy.

6. EAT GOOD FOOD. Eat different
kinds of food. Eat as much as you want.
Don't try to eat more than you want.
Fruit is always good for you. Some women think that fruit is bad for you when
you are pregnant. But this is not true.
Eat any kind of food that agrees with
you.

7. DRINK MUCH WATER. Drink much water to have
good health. Some women think much water is bad for you
when you are pregnant. This is not true. You need the water
to clean out your body. You need enough water for you and the
baby.   Drink a cup of clean water every two hours. Be sure
you drink clean water. Boil your water to make it clean.

8. USE A BABY SUPPORT. When your baby gets very
heavy you need support. Get a wide baby cloth. Lie down on
it. Draw the cloth close around your body. Pin the cloth
close. Wear it all day.

9. DO NOT WEAR TIGHT THINGS.
Your clothes should not be tight. Do not
wear anything tight around your legs and
arms. Your blood must be free to move.

10. KEEP YOUR MOUTH CLEAN.
Clean your teeth well every day. Always
clean your mouth with salt water after
you eat.

DO NOT wear tight
things. Wear a big
baby cloth support.

- - - -

A good mother does these important
things. A good mother goes to the Maternity Center. Be a good mother.

New Words
(Not on 1,700 Word List)

pregnant   Maternity Center

BLAZE A TRAIL THROUGH YOUR WRITING

We have been discussing, so far, ways you can make individual sentences and paragraphs come alive and tell their message. You also need a way of leading your reader with your strong, positive hand through your writing. You can't afford to lose him somewhere in paragraph Number 1, or even in Number 10.

You all have at least one friend, I'm sure, whose conversation gets you jittery after a while. He (or she) never seems to finish one sentence without getting off into another thought. And while you may still be thinking about one thing, the conversation has flitted about like a butterfly from blossom to blossom, until you are hopelessly lost. Friends like this you may love dearly, but their conversation may leave you exhausted.

And have you not read something recently, only to find that you get lost half way down a page, and have to backtrack to pick up the thread of the thought. It might have been your mind that wandered, but the chances are it was the author's mind that darted about, perhaps very keenly, but without leaving a clear trail behind him for you to follow.

A way to avoid losing your reader is to mark the trail clearly. In the woods, at every important turn, the guide chops a white blaze on a tree. You can blaze a trail through your writing by using some word or phrase near the beginning of each paragraph which says: "The trail goes this way." And this blaze should point both ways-- back to the thought you have just finished, and forward to your new thought.

What are some of the trail-blazing words? All the connectives-- "and," "but," "so," "in order to," "therefore," "however," "yet"-- are fine trail blazers. And if you have a guilty feeling, instilled in you somewhere in grade school, about starting a sentence with "and" or "but," there's no time like right now to start ridding yourself of that feeling.

The pronouns are good trail blazers. Each paragraph, and each sentence, too, should tell us again just what or who it is we are talking about. So use "he," "she," "they," "it"--and "you-me"--if your language calls for it.

Don't forget the nouns, either. If you are writing about your Uncle John, you can refer to him in several different ways: "Uncle John," "my uncle," "Uncle." It's better not to use the pronoun "he" over and over, but mix in pronouns and nouns. Then the reader knows at all times just who or what you are talking about.

There are a number of expressions you can use as trail blazers. "Well!" adds to the excitement of a statement just made, as well as pointing to a new line in your thinking. Or a milder "Well, then" does the same job for you.

You can address your reader: "Think of that!" or "Have you
wondered. . ." or "However. . . ," or "Let's see, now" are just
a few of the connecting phrases you can use. They flag the reader's
attention, in case it may have wandered, and point the way your writing goes next. One warning is in order. Don't overdo these attention-
getting phrases. Make sure they serve a purpose and are not just
padding.

In the following article the trail-blazing word or words near the
beginning of each paragraph are underlined. They do not all fit the
categories just mentioned, but they point the way from the thought in
the previous paragraph to the thought in the one just beginning.

AFRICA

Africa is a very large continent. It is a very important
continent too.

There are many different kinds of people in <u>Africa.</u>
There are many different kinds of people in America. There
are many different kinds of people in many countries of the
world.

It is not important that there are <u>different kinds</u> of
people. It is important that people can learn from each other.
Those who have learned new things can teach others.

People in Africa are <u>learning</u> that other countries need
things from Africa. And Africa needs things from many
other countries.

What does <u>Africa</u> have that other countries need? Africa
has palm oil. It has mahogany and cocoa. It has many fruits.
It has gold and diamonds.

Africa <u>needs many things</u> from other countries too.
Africa needs cloth. It needs bicycles and lanterns. It needs
many things made by machines in the countries of Europe
and America and Asia.

The <u>people in Africa</u> want to buy all these <u>things</u> from
the people in other countries. The people in Africa want to
sell things to people in many other countries.

People in Africa and in the rest of the world need to learn more about each other. They need to know more about what other people need. Then they will be able to buy each other's things better. They will know what people in other countries need.

When the people of Africa know what other people want, they can make the things. They can grow many of the things in their fields. They can learn to make many other things on new machines.

Yes! We all need to learn more about people in other countries. In this paper you may read about people in many countries of the world.

New Words
(Not on 1,700 Word List)

palm oil   mahogany   gold   cocoa   diamonds

bicycles   lanterns

These are but a few suggestions to help you develop a clear and direct writing style. Books are written every year on effective writing. You will want to read some of them, and do the many practical writing exercises they present. Some of the more practical books we have examined are listed in Appendix A. You should own and study hard at least one of them.

HOW EASY IS IT?--READABILITY YARDSTICKS

Suppose you have practiced writing simply and directly, using the suggestions in this chapter and others you have found elsewhere or developed yourself. You read over the article you have written. "That looks easy," you think to yourself contentedly, for you and I both get a contented and satisfied look when we see our creative work on a neatly typed sheet or on a printed page.

But just how easy is it? An experienced photographer can judge distances pretty closely and will come within a foot in guessing a distance of 14 feet or 19 feet. But he still relies on a yardstick, or an optical device to "find the range" for precision work. After considerable writing experience, you may be able to state accurately that a certain piece is written on a third grade level, or that it would be easy for a new literate in Stage III to read. Yet, for the new writer, the faithful use of a readability yardstick will help him get the feel of writing at any given Stage.

A number of readability formulas, or yardsticks, have been developed, for use in writing for various grade levels in American schools, and for use in writing for adults. A glance at several of them will show what elements they all agree are important in measuring readability.

The Gray-Leary formula (1939) predicts reading difficulty (ease and difficulty being on opposite ends of a continuous scale) on five points:

1. Proportion of different "hard words."
2. Proportion of prepositional phrases.
3. Average sentence length.
4. Proportion of pronouns.
5. Relative number of different words used.

The Irving Lorge formula (1939) uses the same first three elements as in the Gray-Leary, but gives them different relative weights in arriving at the answer on the ease-difficulty scale.

The Rudolf Flesch formula (1946) is based on:

1. Proportion of prefixes and suffixes.
2. Average sentence length.
3. Relative number of references to people.

The Dale-Chall formula (1948) is based on:

1. Average sentence length.
2. Percentage of unfamiliar words (those not on the Dale-Chall list of 3,000 words known by 80% of fourth-grade school children).

A second Rudolf Flesch formula (1949) is based on:

1. Average number of syllables in 100 words.
2. Average length of sentences.
3. Relative number of references to persons.
4. Proportion of personal sentences.

The Robert Gunning formula (about 1950) is based on:

1. The proportion of hard words.
2. Average sentence length.

A third Rudolf Flesch formula is based on two elements of readability he calls "realism" and "communicative energy." It is derived by a count of:

1. Proper names or titles of places, persons, etc.
2. Nouns denoting human beings.
3. Pronouns and pronominal adverbs.
4. Numbers and words expressed in figures.
5. Colors.
6. Words specified or individualized by preceeding words.

The elements on which all these experts will agree are important in measuring reading ease are:

Average sentence length.
Average word length (in some formulas used synony-
          mously with word difficulty).

A second consideration, which is separated in some formulas, and combined in others, is: what elements make for reading interest? The formula-makers will agree on the importance of these two:

Number of words indicating specific people or things.
Number of proper nouns and pronouns.
And (not agreed on by all), number of personal sentences.

TWO FORMULAS OF VALUE TO WRITERS FOR NEW LITERATES

The Flesch Formula

The formula which we have used the most, in classroom practice and in writing for new literates, is the second formula by Rudolf Flesch (1949). Easy application of this formula is made possible by a visual scale not published in this text. Here are step-by-step instructions to use the Flesch formula.

To obtain a good picture of the reading ease of an article, select several "sampling places," at least one near the beginning, one in the middle, and one near the end of the article. Longer pamphlets and magazines should have a number of "samplings" taken, at least one sample for every 1,000 words.

The over-all score for an article or a pamphlet will be the average score of all the samples you measure. To get the average, add up all the individual sample scores, then divide by the number of samples.

How to count each sample:

1. Count 100 words (this is the "sample" to be measured).
2. Count the total number of syllables in those 100 words.
3. Figure the average sentence length in those 100 words. Do this by counting the number of sentences in the sample (if the 100th word falls before the middle of a sentence, do not count that sentence; if the 100th word falls after the middle of the sentence, that sentence is counted in the sample).

This is the equation for finding average sentence length:

$$\frac{100}{\text{Number of sentences}} = \begin{array}{l}\text{Average number of words} \\ \text{per sentence.}\end{array}$$

4. Consult Table I in Appendix F. This table has most of the possible answers worked out for you.

Your answer will be a number between 1 and 100. A score near 100 rates "Very Easy;" and the lower the score, the greater the difficulty, until it reaches "Very Difficult" near the bottom.

Students of this text who are not native-born speakers of English may have some difficulty in telling just what a syllable is. This rule-of-thumb will help you: Each time you change from one spoken vowel to another, count that as a new syllable. Usually, though not always, there is a consonant in between. "Operate" has three spoken vowels, thus three syllables: "op-er-āt" (the final "e" is not spoken so is not counted). Similarly, "opiate" has three spoken vowels, thus three syllables: "op-i-āt" even though there is no consonant between two of the vowels.

For fast counting of syllables in a sample, count only the "extra" syllables in the long words, then add the number of "extra" syllables to 100, which is the minimum number of syllables you can find in 100 words.

Counting A Sample

For practice, let us see just how the Reading Ease score of the following sample is found. This symbol, /, is placed just after the 100th word. Each extra syllable has a small number above it; the total number of syllables is 100 plus the last number. Each mathematical step is worked out for you.

Before Your Baby Comes
(Printed in full on pages 205-206)

Are you going to have a baby? The Maternity Center will help you before your baby comes. The Maternity Center will help you when your baby comes. The Maternity Center will help you after your baby comes.

But you have important things to do before your baby comes. Your good health helps your baby.

You should know what things to do. You should know what things not to do.

If you want good health, do these things:

1. GET FRESH AIR. Get fresh air in the day. Get fresh air in the night. There/ is not much fresh air in a big crowd.

Total number of syllables in the 100 word sample: 128

Number of sentences in the 100 word sample: 13

$$\frac{100}{13} = 8 \quad \text{(approximately)}$$

Average number of words per sentence: 8

Reading Ease Score: 90

How did we find the Reading Ease Score? Turn to Appendix F, Table 1, in the back of this text. Along the top of the page are various syllable counts; find 128. Down the left side of the page are average sentence lengths. You will find 8 at the very top. Just under the 128, and level with the 8, is the number 90. This is the Reading Ease Score. If you have a copy of Dr. Flesch's book, How to Test Readability, (see Appendix A) you will be able to use his visual Reading Ease Scale. The Tables and the Scale both give the same answer.

How easy should your writing be? Let's suggest two rules-of-thumb:

1. Articles for new literates should have an average rating of 90.   Individual articles may range between 85 and 100. This range can be attained only by writing with very short sentences, and with as short words as possible. The reader with only a few months' experience should be able to read in this range.

2. Reading matter for better readers should have an average rating of 82.   Individual articles may range in difficulty between 75 and 90. This should ensure easy reading by most of the readers, while at the same time not offending, by its ultrasimplicity, the better educated readers.

It may be expected, also, that many of the better readers will enjoy reading the very easy materials for the new literates. And, if there is not a great gap between the readability range of all materials in a newspaper or periodical, the new literate will be encouraged to try reading other articles besides those especially designed for him.

These rules-of-thumb may be expressed in this diagram:

RECOMMENDED READABILITY RANGES

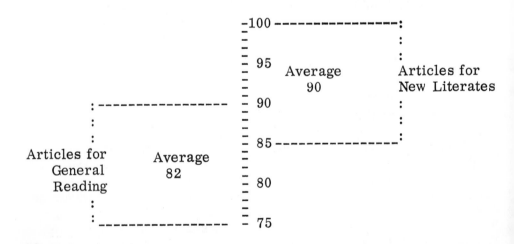

BEWARE
OF THE
FOG

Copyright PUNCH, London

The Gunning Formula

The Robert Gunning formula is very easy to count and compute and deserves more use in writing for new literates. Mr. Gunning speaks in terms of a Fog Index, a most descriptive term!

The fogginess in writing comes from the number of hard words. Hard words were found, at first, as they were by the other formula makers, by counting prefixes and suffixes and other word particles. But most laymen, in using the formulas, had trouble identifying the various "fixes," and found the counting very tedious.

So Mr. Gunning decided that it wasn't so much the nature of the extra syllables we hang on our English words, but merely the existence of them, that makes the words hard.

How to use the Gunning formula:

1. Select a sample of 100 words.
2. Find the average sentence length.
3. Count the number of words of three syllables or
   over. (Do not count proper nouns, easy compound
   words like "book-keeper," or verb forms in which
   the third syllable is merely the ending, as, for example, "directed.")
4. Add average sentence length to the number of "hard
   words."
5. Multiply the sum by .4 (four tenths). This gives the
   Fog Index.

The equation for step 4 and 5 is:

Number of "hard words"
     Plus
<u>Average number of words per sentence</u>

Sum of the above multiplied by .4 ⁔ The Fog Index

Let's, for practice, find the Fog Index of the sample on page
213. We have already found the average number of words per sentence to be 8.

Now let's count the "hard words" (words of three syllables or
more). We find "Maternity" and "important," thus making two hard
words. "Maternity" occurs four times, but, from several class discussions, and after careful consideration, we decided to count this
hard word only once. Its very repetition makes it easier each succeeding time it occurs.

Here's how the Fog Index formula works:

Number of "hard words:"   2
    Plus
Average number of words per sentence: <u>8</u>
                                   10
Multiplied by the constant   <u>.4</u>
        The Fog Index: 4.0

The Gunning formula is excellent for writing materials in English for adults. The Fog Index, as you can see in the following chart,
is identical with grades in school. Studies have been made which
demonstrate that adults tend to read materials on the same grade
level as the last school grade they attended. While the article,"Before
Your Baby Comes,"looks almost "too easy" to students of this text,
remember there are perhaps 15,000,000 (that's FIFTEEN MILLION)

adults in the United States who cannot read that article.

Here are the Fog Indexes for reading matter for various school grades of the United States:

College, freshmen to graduates	13-17
High School, freshmen to seniors	9-12
Eighth Grade	8
Seventh Grade	7
Sixth Grade	6
Fifth Grade	5
Fourth Grade	4
Third Grade	3
Second Grade	2

Mr. Gunning has had a great effect on simplifying writing of news by press associations and by numerous newspapers. For a more complete understanding of his formula, and for a very practical how-to-do-it book, see his Technique of Clear Writing (Appendix A).

HOW PRACTICAL ARE THE FORMULAS?

The chief difficulty with all the formulas is that they are calibrated for the American public, from school children to literate adults. They are not sensitive enough in the higher extremes. They will immediately indicate that a piece of writing is "easy"--but how easy? Our concern is not in being assured that an article is "easy" for a high school graduate to read. We must know that it is also "easy" for the new literate, with only a few months' reading experience. That means it must be ultraeasy for the good reader.

So these formulas are comparatively rough measures, just as a house thermometer is a rather rough instrument for measuring one's body temperature. The house thermometer will let you know when the day is hot or cold, but will it tell if your body is a degree, or a fraction of a degree, above or below normal?

In the same manner, these formulas very quickly show whether your writing is "hot" (easy), or "cold" (difficult). When you use these formulas, don't be satisfied unless you practically run right off the scale and "blow the top off" the thermometer. This means that everything you write should rate "Very Easy" by the Flesch Formula (80 or above) and should have a Fog Index of less than 6 (preferably 4 or under) by the Gunning Formula.

The readability formulas are especially valuable to the beginning writer for new literates. When you have had considerable practice in writing, you will begin to get a "feel" for writing simply, and will know, with considerable accuracy, whether you are writing on Stage II, III or IV. Even then, a suitable formula should be used occasionally to help offset the tendency, so gradual as to be unnoticed by the writer, to become more and more complicated.

It is hoped that many students of this text will later teach others to write for new literates, in English and in other languages. In such a training situation, the use of a formula is highly advisable, to help create the discipline in your students to write with simplicity and interest.

ADAPTING ENGLISH READABILITY FORMULAS
TO OTHER LANGUAGES

What elements that make for reading ease and interest in English can be measured in a similar manner in other languages? Graduates of the Syracuse University School of Journalism and professors have found that these elements may be measured with almost the same weight as they are in English: sentence length, use of concrete words, personal references, and number of unfamiliar words.

With regards to the latter, the unfamiliar or "hard words," it has been found that one cannot merely call the <u>long</u> words <u>hard</u> words as we do in English. For in many languages, in a choice between synonyms, the more familiar may be the longer one, and the "harder" word may be the shorter one. So, one has to be wary of assuming that he can put the three-syllable words, or even longer words, directly into the Gunning Formula as "hard words." Nor can one always be assured of accuracy by putting the total number of syllables in a 100-word passage into the Flesch Formula as it is designed for English.

Prof. J. Maurice Hohlfeld, of Hartford Seminary Foundation, spent a year in Iran, working on literacy and literature problems, including the adaptation of the Flesch Formulas to Persian. Dr. Hohlfeld reported that the Reading Ease Formula, except for the word length factor, can be used directly in Persian.

At the Syracuse University School of Journalism, two students worked on the problem of adapting the Flesch Formula to Egyptian Arabic. Samuel Habib, an Egyptian, and Graham Leonard, an American with two years' speaking experience in Arabic, worked on the project for a graduate journalism class in readability. They found, as did Dr. Hohlfeld, that word length was the only element that required any great change. Mr. Leonard has since worked on a literacy project in Jordan, and is studying the problems of readability in Arabic in greater detail.

At Literacy House, Allahabad, India, Miss Elizabeth Mooney

reported success in using the Flesch Formula in Hindi, without any major change. The correlation of word length to word difficulty in Hindi is evidently similar to that in English. Dr. Flesch visited Literacy House in the spring of 1955 to teach readable writing, and would have aided in finer adjustment of his formula to Hindi had he not become ill while there. Initial trials indicate that this adjustment may be made with little trouble.

One semester we conducted a special course at Syracuse University School of Journalism for a UNESCO team from Ghana. During this course we made an attempt to adapt the Flesch Reading Ease Formula into two languages of Ghana, Fante and Ewe. We compared average word lengths in those languages with English, using translations of identical materials. Ewe and Fante are both much more polysyllabic than English. So we made an adjustment in the Reading Ease Scale to allow for this difference. With the Adjusted Reading Ease Scale in each language, a reliable Reading Ease Score may be found. A report of this experiment is available from us, though it is presented with a statement of its limitations, for many aspects of readability have not as yet been touched.

We feel that a great need exists to adapt English readability formulas into other languages, or, better yet, to develop new ones in those languages. There is a great unexplored area here, waiting for persons looking for problems for Ph. D. dissertations.

Two Readability Formulas in Spanish

Two formulas developed by Dr. Seth Spaulding are especially interesting to all concerned with writing for new literates. The Spaulding Formulas consider elements like sentence length and the use of a Spanish word list. By his formulas you can measure reading ease in terms of various stages in a graded series of literature.

The first Spaulding Formula is concerned with sentence length and with the frequency of usage of each word in the sample tested. The frequencies are found in the Milton Buchanan A Graded Spanish Word Book, which is to Spanish what the Thorndike-Lorge word count is to English. This formula, as Dr. Spaulding admits, takes a great deal of patience and hard work, as every word has to be looked up, and a numerical equivalent given to it. Then it is put into the formula.

The second Spaulding Formula is much easier to work. In this formula you proceed as follows:

1. Compute average sentence length as you have for every other formula.
2. Find the words that are not on the Buchanan first 1,500 most used words in Spanish.

3. Divide the total number of words in the passage
   (easiest if 100) <u>into</u> number of words not on word
   list. This gives you a decimal.
4. Consult the diagram provided with the formula for
   the answer, thus avoiding computation.

The answer will be on a scale with "Hard" at 200, and "Easy"
at 10. All material for mature adult new literates should rate not
higher than 40 on this Spaulding Scale.

Dr. Spaulding studied at Ohio State University under Prof. Edgar
Dale. He spent several years with Pan American Union where he
guided the development of a number of excellent adult graded pamphlets on economic, health and social matters. He was recently with
the Burma Translation Society, a work supported in part by the Ford
Foundation. At publication time of this text, he is Executive Director
of the United States Commission on Literacy, a division of the Department of Health, Education and Welfare. Requests for the Spaulding
formulas may be sent to the authors of this book.

One last word to conclude this chapter: Making your writing
easy is not done by formula. There is something within you which
only practice over a period of time will bring out as writing skill.
Use the formula with discretion; don't allow it to be your master,
but your servant. When used with wisdom, the readability formula
will serve as your invaluable ally in the long task ahead--developing
a literature suitable for the millions who have yet to come into the
light of literacy.

Chapter 21
How to Make Your Writing Interesting

When one tries to tell others how to make their writing interesting, he immediately lays his own writing open for inspection. Is this book interesting? We would naturally like to see it on the best seller lists, like A Man Called Peter or The Power of Positive Thinking. But the chances are it won't be, because the subject matter isn't of interest to hundreds of thousands of people. There is a new magazine, Sports Illustrated, which has already gained about a million readers. It is well written and beautifully published, but I just am not interested enough in sports to do more than casually leaf through the magazine once a month in the barber shop.

The subject matter, then, is perhaps the most important element in creating interest. The more scholarly of you readers would have plowed through this book even if it were written in a highly technical style--if you were interested enough in the subject. But we are trying to write in an informal and conversational manner, and still not sacrifice the accuracy of the information of this book.

We write this way because we enjoy writing this way, and because we believe in what we preach. We believe that any subject should be written so as to invite you to read it--not dare you to. We are frankly trying to encourage you and hundreds of other men and women to teach and write for the new literates and semi-literates in every country. Even if this subject interested you intensely, a dull book might kill your interest. An "interesting" book (if we have achieved this goal) will encourage you to go further in the study and practice of the art of simple writing.

We have spoken at some length of ways of finding what subjects interest our readers. We have spoken about how to write a subject on the proper level for their stage of reading, and how to express ourselves clearly. The next question is: How can you make a naturally interesting subject even more interesting to read?

For, in writing for new literates, you want to do about the same things we are trying to do with you in this book: (1)You want to encourage the more "scholarly" readers to forge rapidly ahead. (2) You want to catch and hold the interest of a lot of other readers who

would yawn in the first paragraph of a dull article and go back to
sleep.

To interest people in what you write, you have got to put "Human Interest" in it. Human Interest can be put in small places in
your writing--in your phrases, sentences and paragraphs. And Human Interest can fill a longer article or book. You'll find in the next
few pages a few of the techniques for increasing Human Interest in
your writing.

What is Human Interest? It is the something in writing that appeals to you and to me when we read. We don't want to go too deeply
into the psychological motivations of reading, and of everything else
we do. But there is little point in denying that we do serve self when
we read--whether we are looking up the recipe for that chocolate
cake, studying the instruction book that came with our new camera,
reading an assignment for school, glancing over the morning paper,
or eagerly curling up with the new novel that just came from the
book club.

Reading serves us in many ways. Reading can serve the new
literate in many ways, too--perhaps in more different ways than it
serves us. The problem is to help the new literate see, as soon as
possible, just how each article will serve him. Or, if the value of
the article is not apparent at the very start, then the writer must
present his message in such a way that the reader will be intrigued
into reading it.

This, then, in perhaps over-simplified terms, is Human Interest. Human Interest might be called the "Personality" in writing.
It's the personality of the writer showing in his writing. And you
cannot say exactly what personality is any more than you can say
what a person is. Those are concepts that escape being pinned down
with words. For personality, and the person behind it, are products of spiritual convictions, attitudes towards life and experiences
in life. Become familiar with the writings of a person, and you know
the person. This has been true with the few eminent writers whom
I have met after having "read" them.

You have seen courses advertised to help you change your per-
sonality--act and feel successful, make friends, influence others.
We here prescribe a few techniques for making friends and influenc-
ing people--that is, being successful in your written expression.
The techniques are offered with a warning. No matter how well
learned or flashily displayed, the techniques will never quite ring
true if the personality behind them is not true.

We are not trying, in this text, to influence your personality,
as a prospective writer for the new literates. Your personality--
your soul--is your own domain.

We are, however, suggesting some ideas which will help you,
as a human personality, to write for other human personalities.

A FORMULA FOR HUMAN INTEREST

Of the formula brewers in the preceeding chapter, the only one who specifically prescribes a way to measure Human Interest is Dr. Flesch. The amount of Human Interest in your writing depends on how often specific persons are referred to. These persons may be characters actively engaged in a story, persons mentioned incidentally in an article, or even the reader himself.

To measure how often persons come into your writing, you count two types of personal references: personal words and personal sentences. "Personal words," according to Flesch's Human Interest Scale, are:

1. Names of people.

2. Pronouns which refer to specific people.

3. Nouns which refer to persons of a specific gender. "Nurse," "wife," "husband," and similar words would count as personal words. But "teacher," "citizen," or "European" would not count since the gender is not apparent.

These three are rather minute measurements. They are individual words which you can learn to sprinkle through your writing. A larger measurement is the "personal sentence." The personal sentences are:

1. Quotations. The quote marks indicate actual words spoken by a character in a story, or by a person referred to in an article.

2. Direct address to the reader. Sentences like: "Think of that!" or "Let us look at this more closely." This is the type of sentence that comes into a good lecturer's speech, and it can be worked into your writing too.

3. Questions asked of the reader. "Have you ever wondered. . . ?" or "What would you say if . . . ?" We feel that the writer is talking directly to us when he asks us to think about a problem. The question brings the reader's attention back to the article, and gives him the feeling that the writer is depending on him personally.

Using the Formula

Let's see how the Human Interest formula works, by measuring the article, "Before Your Baby Comes," found back on page 213.

Let's look first for the personal words. There are no names of
people, but there are pronouns, "you" and "your," which surely
point to a specific person, the reader. Within the same 100-word
sample we counted out before, I see "you" 9 times, and "your" 5
times, for a total of 14. As the sample is 100 words long, the 14
is already in per cent, so this sample has 14 per cent Personal
Words.

There is only one personal sentence, the opening question, "Are
you going to have a baby?" There are 13 sentences in the sample.
Here is the equation to find the per cent of Personal Sentences in
the sample:

Number of Personal Sentences in the Sample: 1
              Divided By
Total Number of Sentences in the Sample: 13
      .07
13) 1.00   Per Cent of Personal Sentences   7

Now turn to Appendix F, and find the Human Interest Table.
Along the top row are numbers for various Per Cents of Personal
Words. Find 14.

Down the column at the left are numbers for Per Cents of Personal Sentences. Find 7. There is no 7, so use 8. Follow along the
line to the right until your eye is right under the 14 column. You
will see the number 53.

Human Interest Score: 53

Note that this score is for one sample only of "Before Your
Baby Comes." For a good picture of the Human Interest of an article, or a longer book, many samples are necessary, as in the case
of measuring the Reading Ease.

The score of 53, as you can see on scale on the next page, is
right in the middle of what Dr. Flesch calls the "Very Interesting"
range.

Here's a rule-of-thumb for writing for new literates: The Human Interest score should never be below 40, no matter what the
subject matter may be.

In your writing, if the first or second drafts fall short of the 40
score, rework them, putting in more personal references, and more
personal sentences. Don't be afraid of making your writing "too personal."

It's important, when we write for new literates--or for anyone
--to make it easy for them to read. It's perhaps even more important to make it interesting. With his first yawn, you've lost your
reader. Keep your writing always in the Very Interesting and Dramatic ranges, and you shoo away your readers' yawns.

RECOMMENDED HUMAN INTEREST RANGES

```
- - - - - - - - 100 - - - - - - - -
         :                              :
         :          90 -                :
         :                              :
Dramatic             80 -               :
         :                              Writing for
         :          70 -               New Literates
         :                              :
- - - - - - - - 60 -                    :
                                        :
Very             :                      :
Interesting :    50 -                   :
         - - - - - - 40 - - - - - - - -:
              :
Interesting :    30 -
              :
              : - - - 20 -
Mildly Interesting :
              - - - : 10 -
         Dull :
              : 0 -
```

MAKE YOUR WRITING DRAMATIC

Always aim to make your writing "Very Interesting," even "Dramatic." You will not find it difficult to achieve this. The liberal use of personal words in your writing will do the trick for you. Often in testing your writing you will not find any personal sentences in the sample tested, for in writing some types of articles it is hard to bring them in. But if you use lots of personal words you can still keep the Human Interest up in the "Dramatic" range.

A "drama," by its very definition, is in the "Dramatic" range. When you read a drama, every sentence, aside from a few to set the scene, is a personal sentence. Every sentence is in quotes, that is, the actual words of a person. You would find 100 per cent personal sentences in reading a drama.

Other types of writing may be dramatic in somewhat less degree. As the writer of a story, you spend more time on "setting the scene," and less on speaking through your characters. But the characters must speak--that is, there must be drama in your writing--if it is to be highly interesting. Generally, the more characters speak, the higher the "dramatic" interest.

The next time you read a novel, analyze your own reading. Don't
you often skim lightly over the long paragraphs of description, reading just enough to get a general idea of the situation? Then, when you
find a series of quotations your interest quickens, and your reading
slows almost to conversation speed to allow you to appreciate the
feelings of the characters who are speaking.

We could cite a number of values of the use of conversation in
your writing. These four may be of most value to you:

1. Conversation is in the idiom of everyday speech. The
    reader will feel more "at home" with the conversation
    than he will with even the well-written straight narrative.

2. Conversation brings an intimacy into your writing.
    The reader almost immediately feels that he knows
    the "real person" in the character the writer has
    created. The reader feels as if he were in the actual
    presence of the characters who are carrying on the
    conversation.

3. Conversation rings with authenticity. Because the
    characters appear so real to the reader, he believes
    what they say. The writer can present two sides to
    an issue by creating characters who speak "in char-
    acter." The writer can "write into" his characters
    attitudes and comments he never could say directly.
    The reader will think about what a character says,
    though the same thing said directly by the writer often
    would have little effect, or even an adverse effect.

4. Conversation carries the story along fast, and occurs
    at or near the peaks of action, while the descriptive
    passages build up the background. So when you read,
    skimming between conversations, you are looking for,
    and finding, the peaks in the story's action.

A fifth value of conversation is its appearance on the printed
page. The quotations of each person should be started in a new
paragraph. Thus the page of solid type will be broken up into more
easily read sections, making the page more inviting to read. This
is perhaps more a concern of the editor and the layout person than
the writer, but the writer who uses a lot of conversation will be
aiding the editor, layout man and printer. Variation in visual
appearance of the page is almost as important as variation in the
writing itself.

It should be noted that the use of quotation marks is a convention
in English. Other languages may have different marks to indicate

quoted speech, or none at all. The point is that, if a sentence is clearly shown to be the actual words of a person, it is a personal sentence. For example:

John said, let us go home quickly.

That is a personal sentence, and regardless of the method of punctuation, the reader will quickly learn to recognize it, and similar sentences, as quoted conversation.

HOW TO PUT DRAMA IN YOUR STORIES

You can use techniques just mentioned with great effectiveness in writing almost any kind of article or story. In the next chapter you may examine how personal words and personal sentences have been used. These techniques are equally effective with fiction and nonfiction articles. Up to this time we have been mainly concerned with nonfiction articles, and how to increase reading ease and inject human interest into our writing.

Let us now look at fiction. Drama implies a story, with its characters and conflicts and resolution. We cannot become masters of dramatic story telling without initial genius and a great deal of practice in writing. An introduction to story writing follows, prepared by Margaret Lee Runbeck, well known for her many magazine short stories and books. Miss Runbeck taught her writing techniques at Literacy House in Allahabad, India, and, before her death in 1956, was greatly interested in helping train writers for the new literates.

DRAMATIC STORY TELLING

By Margaret Lee Runbeck

This section is offered in a most humble spirit. But the fact is that no matter how "simply" one may write, no readers will be found unless the writing is also "fascinating," or at least "interesting."

The writing which has endured and has had the greatest influence throughout the long history of literature, is truth told as story-- fables, parables and lively myths. Some of the world's greatest fiction was created to be a vehicle for truth. Almost any truth can be entrusted to survive if it is carried in the "secret pocket" of a story. People who are not yet prepared or willing to accept the truth will remember the story if it is clever enough. The truth will stay safe in the mind of the reader, until he has grown enough so he can understand the story concealed in its "secret pocket."

The principles of story telling and story writing are simple and
so instinctive in the psychology of the human race that people recognize immediately that they are true. Fundamentally, the definition
of a story is "people in a troublesome situation who find their way
out."

There are but two kinds of stories:

1. Those in which someone must decide between two
   courses of action.

2. Those in which someone must accomplish a task or
   win some reward.

A story is gripping or not, according to the size of the danger
which threatens the main factor. Situations must be shown as
important to the characters. If the characters do not care deeply,
the readers will not.

Early in the story the readers must know there is "dramatic
question." The story is ended when the reader has the answer to
the dramatic question.

Every story divides into three parts:

1. Beginning. The presentation of the worrisome problem
   which makes the reader face the dramatic question for
   himself.

2. Body. Battling back and forth between the hero and
   the obstacles which stand between him and success.
   This may be long or short, with alternate defeats and
   triumphs for the hero. But defeats must be stressed
   or there will be a weak drama. Each defeat leaves
   him worse off than before. Triumphs are only breath-
   ing spaces which do not deliver what they promise in
   victory. The body has a climax in the "black moment"
   when ultimate defeat seems certain. Then the hero
   pulls himself together with all his force and turns the
   tide of disaster by some strength in his own nature.
   Victory must come from within the hero.

3. End. The shortest section, showing only the outcome
   of the hero's turning of the black moment into permanently improved situation.

The reader wants to see what is happening. He doesn't want
to be told about it. So the story must be a succession of scenes,
as in the theatre. Each scene has in miniature the same structure
as does the entire story; that is, it has a "scene question," a minor
struggle and a conclusive act which answers the scene question.

Also each scene must be rooted back into the main question of the story. At the end of each scene we must know definitely whether the hero has gained or lost by that scene. There must be a line or two which tells the score.

The main character must be likable. We must want him (and those he loves) to win. He must be somehow like ourselves, so we will understand him. The opposing characters can be drawn in a few lines, and must be impressively dangerous and strong, so we will fear our hero's chances are poor.

A story is most effective when information is given out a little at a time, not dumped unexplained upon the reader. No item should be included unless it contributes to: 1. the likableness of the hero, 2. the danger from the enemy. Each fact included in the story must be like a block, building on one side (yes, he will win) or the other (no, he cannot possibly win).

Every fact on earth can be made interesting, if we will make it come to life. This is done by showing what it does to people . . . how it makes them fear . . . love . . . hope . . . be angry . . . be joyful.

People read fiction with their emotions. They want to feel. They don't want to think while they are feeling. But after the story is finished, the mind comes into action. If the mind is not satisfied that the story is logical and believable, the reader is disappointed. So we must appeal to emotion. At the same time we must be constant so the mind will not protest. Readers want to be entertained but not fooled.

To write good fiction, one must love the world and find it challenging and fascinating. One must enjoy the thousands of fragments of plot and setting all round us. And besides that, one must love those who will read the finished story. There must be a partnership between writer and reader, and this partnership, like most others, is based on love and the desire to please.

Chapter 22
Writing Several Types of Articles

In this chapter we present examples of different types of articles
for the new literate. Some have been written by literacy writers
abroad, others by individuals or committees in classes in the United
States in writing for new literates. They all, even when bearing a
single name as author, were subject to group discussion and were
revised several times.

Some of these articles are intended to persuade, others to
inform, others to inspire, and still others to entertain. Remember
that these are but examples. Will one article cause you to change
your way of thinking or working or believing? Hardly. But think
of each article as a ripple on a broad stream of literature. In a
constant stream there is great power. The power of the printed
word lies in its continuing on and on in an endless stream. The
stream of literature for new literates has hardly begun. But we believe that articles like these will swell a stream of literature into a
powerful force for the good of the new literates.

As you read these articles, and the comments, see how the
techniques in the last two chapters have been used. Can you do
better? Very likely you can, for none of them are supposed to be
perfection. Try rewriting one or two, to see if you can make them
easier and more interesting. Then give a Gunning or Flesch test to
the version here and to your revision. Read the two versions to a
friend for comments and opinions which readability tests alone will
not give you.

Keep in mind that, in presenting all of these stories in pamphlets
or periodicals for new literates, illustrations would be used. Illustra-
tions--line drawings or photographs--add to the attractiveness of the
articles, and also aid greatly in the teaching. In this chapter, however, we are concerned primarily with the writing.

The following is a translation from Hindi. It is Chapter 10 in
Volume II of <u>Anand, The Wise Man</u>. It is, in miniature, a reflection
of the whole Anand book, in which Anand, the hero, battles with many
obstacles. In this chapter the hero himself is not beset with troubles,
but is able to help a friend. This is a story of decision.

STORIES OF PERSUASION

An Old Custom Wastes Money
By A Committee Led By Margaret Lee Runbeck

Comments

One day Anand saw his friend Mohan and knew that he was very sad. "Why are you looking so sad, my friend?" he asked.

Characters introduced.

Mohan said, "My father died last week."

Problem presented.

Anand then also looked sad. They went to Mohan's house to talk. Mohan did not have much money. He had some debts to pay.

"How much will you spend on nukta?" Anand asked him.

"Nukta" is a funeral feast.

Mohan said, "I will have to spend 500 rupees on nukta. That is a big trouble to me, for I don't have 500 rupees."

The problem is lack of money-- of universal concern!

Anand said, "You should not spend so much money on nukta. You would have to get the money from a money lender and that would not be a good thing to do. You are still in debt."

Mohan looked even sadder now. "What shall I do?" he asked.

Body of story used in questioning and debating.

Anand said, "It is time for us to end some of the old customs. I do not think we should spend so much money on nukta."

Mohan asked, "Why do you think that, Anand?"

"We should not waste our money on people who have food. We should give our

food to people who need it. Many people
need food. The people who have food need
nothing from us.''

Mohan's face looked happier. ''Yes,
that is what I think. It is foolish to give
food to people who do not need it. It is a
foolish custom. New times must make
new customs that fill our needs. Now we
should give food only to the people who do
not have it. There are many of those in
India.''

"Black moment"
comes just before
decision is made.
The hero shows a
strength of will in
opposing tradition.

Mohan went out of his house and said
to his neighbors, ''I am not going to spend
500 rupees on nukta. I do not want another
debt. I will buy some food to honor my
father, but I will give it only to the poor.''

Mohan's decision
is the climax of
the story.

At first the neighbors did not like
what Mohan said. But they thought about
it, and talked about what Mohan did. It
did seem a better way to honor the dead.

That is how new customs are born.
People use their minds to think new
thoughts. New thoughts change the old
customs. This is only one of the customs
that are now changing in India.

Story is related to
the reader through
the neighbors. If
this story stimu-
lates discussion it
has achieved its
purpose.

New Words

(Not in Primer or Anand Book to this Point)

nukta   spend   debt   need   honor   custom

There is great inertia in age-old customs, as the one mentioned
in the story above. You have to overcome almost as great inertia
when you urge people to try new methods of doing their work. Your
writing must show at least three things:

1. Show the advantages of the new method in terms of more food,
   better health, or more income.

2. Show just how the new method is done.

3. Tell the reader how he can start using the new method, where he can obtain it, and how he can afford it.

In India, one of the simplest of improvements in farming methods is the use of the moldboard plow, which is a steel plow with a wing that turns over the earth much more effectively than the old "country plow" which has been in use for centuries. Following are two articles for new literates. Both use a fictional approach. Which do you think is more effective? Would a straight essay or lecture be better in this case?

Story No. 1

Why Use A Moldboard Plow?

By Don Flaten
Class Member in Writing For New Literates

Manu and Anand were farmers. They raised wheat on their farms. One day Manu said to Anand, "Your field of wheat looked very nice all summer. Did you get much wheat from it?"

Anand said, "Yes, it gave more wheat than ever before. The man from the agricultural school showed me how to plow it with a moldboard plow. When I did that, it gave more wheat than ever before."

Manu said, "That is very good. It is good to get so much wheat. But tell me, what is a moldboard plow?"

Anand said, "The moldboard plow is a new kind of plow. It does a better job of plowing. Its point cuts deep. Its wide wing turns over fresh earth. It covers up the old, tired earth and grass. This makes a fresh, clean field for the wheat to grow on. It makes the wheat grow better than ever before."

Manu said, "My old plow does not cut deep. It does not turn up new earth and cover the old. Where can I get a moldboard plow?"

Anand said, "The man from the agricultural school will rent you one for only one large measure of wheat."

Manu said, "I must go to the agricultural school and get this moldboard plow. Then I, too, can have wheat grow better than ever before."

Manu went to the agricultural school. He got the moldboard plow and it plowed his fields deeper. It turned up fresh earth and covered up the old, tired earth.

His next gathering of wheat was very good. Manu brought one large measure of wheat to the agricultural school and he had much wheat left over for himself.

New Word
(Not on the 1,700 Word List)

Moldboard plow

Story No. 2

What The Moldboard Plow Said *

By Mildred Jenkins
Class Member in Writing For New Literates

Dangre, the farmer was very sad. He had not been happy all day. The farmer was so sad because his little children were hungry. He had many boys and girls. Dangre wanted his boys and girls to grow strong and well. The boys and girls needed much food.

Dangre grew wheat on his field to make food for them. Dangre must grow more wheat for his boys and girls. How could he grow more wheat? His field was very small. His country plow was old. The soil was old. Dangre could not buy anything to make the soil fertile.

Next week he must plant his wheat. How could he make more wheat grow on his field? Dangre was still sad when he went to sleep that night.

---

* In this story, the conventional English quote marks are omitted. Though this omission may concern the good English reader, it doesn't bother the new reader. Many of the languages in which similar stories will be written have quite different marks-- or no marks at all -- for indicating spoken words.

Now Dangre had a dream while he was asleep. In his dream he saw a bright new moldboard plow. The moldboard plow was like the plow he saw at the school the week before. And in his dream, the farmer heard the moldboard plow begin to speak.

This is what the moldboard plow said: You are very sad, Dangre. You are sad because your children need more food. You want to grow more wheat so your boys and girls can have food. You do not know how to grow more wheat. But I can help you grow more wheat on your field. Then your children can get well and strong. Next week you will plant your wheat. Let me help you.

I am at the school, the moldboard plow said. Come and get me. You can pay rent for me. You pay the rent in wheat you grow. The rent will not be much. I can work fast for you. I will do good work for you. I am a steel plow.

I can plow deep and wide with my steel point. Your country plow cannot do this. Your country plow does not have a steel wing. With my steel wing, I can turn much soil under. I leave your field clean.

Your country plow must plow your field twice. I plow only once. After I plow, the soil is deep. The soil is clean. The seed can grow deep. The little wheat plants will grow strong roots. The strong roots will make strong plants.

Much grain will grow on strong plants. You will have plenty of wheat. You will have plenty of wheat to pay the rent for me. You will have plenty of wheat to feed your boys and girls. You will have plenty of wheat to feed your oxen which pull me. Then you will be happy.

Be sure to ask the school teacher about me soon. Next week you plant your wheat. Let me help you.

Then the good farmer awakened. He remembered his dream. He wanted it to come true. He wanted his children to have more food. He wanted his boys and girls to be strong. He wanted them to be happy and well.

So Dangre went to see the school teacher. The teacher
let him rent the moldboard plow. The next week he planted
his wheat. The moldboard plow went deep and wide. He
plowed very fast. The soil was deep and soft. The little
wheat seeds had a soft bed. Soon they began to grow in their
soft beds. The warm sun helped them grow. The water and
the soft soil helped them grow.

It was not long until Dangre had plenty of full wheat
grains. He paid rent on the plow with some of the wheat.
His boys and girls had plenty of food. His oxen had food and
grew strong so they could pull the moldboard plow fast and
easily. Now Dangre is happy. Dangre is glad he had a
dream about the moldboard plow. Dangre is glad he followed
his dream.

New Words
(Not on the 1,700 Word List)
moldboard   rent

Song is a powerful force to weld a group spirit and bring in an
atmosphere of cooperation. Doesn't every group you belong to,
from your nation down to the tiniest club, have its song? If stories
like the ones above were being used in a village development project,
then would not a collection of songs, like the one following, be valuable?
      You can imagine the villagers gathering in the dusk, singing a
few songs written to their favorite tunes, and then watching slides or
movies or demonstrations of new ways of working on the farm or
around the home.

Here is a song, to be sung to the tune of "Home On The Range."

I've A New Moldboard Plow

By Alec Brooks
Class Member in Writing For New Literates

Verse: Be gone, country plow! I've a new moldboard now!
         And I'll plow just once but so well,
         My farm will be green as it never has been --
         My new moldboard turns green manure swell.

Chorus:
>Plow and you'll soon see
>The new plow is better for you.
>The oxen are still as they get their full fill;
>Your wheat will be food for them too.

ARTICLES ON CLEANLINESS AND HEALTH

As an experiment, committees from a summer class in Writing for New Literates tried three ways of presenting the same health material. The original material was found in a pamphlet on home sanitation, published in English.

Original Version

Keep dishes clean.

>Bacteria can live on dishes which are merely rinsed off in lukewarm, greasy dishwater and wiped on soiled towels.

>Clean dishes are more attractive.

>Use hot, soapy dishwater to remove all bits of greasy food and all deposits from the mouth which stick to the silverware and cups and glasses.

>When there is illness from contagious disease, try to keep the patient's dishes separate.

>Dishes may be dried without towels by rinsing (if possible with hot water) and draining.

Cleanliness in the kitchen.

>The scientific housekeeper prides herself that her kitchen is the cleanest room in the house.

>Fight pests by getting rid of damp, dirty places and by keeping all food out of their reach.

>All garbage should be covered and emptied often.

>Dispose properly of all kitchen waste. Parts of the garbage may be fed to hens or pigs. Others may be burned or buried. The important thing is to get rid of the waste without breeding flies or attracting rats and mice.

First Presentation

The first presentation is Question and Answer. This is a popular way of getting across a lot of information. You see it in many
magazines. There is added value to the Question and Answer article
if a person well known and well qualified in the field writes it. A
well-known baby specialist, for example, or a doctor, or a theolo-
gian, or a lawyer, or an agricultural expert can write a series of
articles of this nature. If they are published regularly in a magazine,
the readers may be encouraged to send in questions to be answered in
the articles.

Why Clean My Dishes?

Question: Why should my dishes be clean?

Answer: You eat from dishes. They are safe and
healthy if clean.

Question: How shall I clean my dishes?

Answer: Use hot soapy water. Grease sticks to dishes.
Soap takes away grease. Take away grease and spots
with soap and water. Hot soapy water takes away grease.
After this put hot water on your dishes. This hot water
takes away the grease and soap.

Question: May I use a cloth to dry my dishes?

Answer: No. Not if you can put hot water on your dishes
after cleaning them. That is best. Any cloth, if used,
should be very clean.

Question: I live with my aunt. My aunt is very ill. How can
I keep from getting her illness?

Answer: Find some dishes to use just for her. Scrub
her dishes with sand mixed with salt. Rinse them in hot
soapy dishwater. Place them in a pan of boiling water.
Boil them for five minutes. Turn them upside down. Do
all this every time she finishes eating.

Wash all your aunt's bedding and clothes with soap suds.
Wash her clothes alone, not with other clothes . Hang

them in the sunshine. Screen her room from flies. Wash
your hands after you wait on her.

New Words
(Not on 1,000 Word List)

cloth   dish   grease   soap

Shoo Fly!

Question: Why should I keep flies and little animals out of
my house?

Answer: Flies and little animals are pests. These pests
cause sickness. Every time these pests touch your food
they may cause you, your husband, or your children to
get sick.

Question: How can I keep pests out of my house?

Answer: It is hard to keep the flies and little animals
out of the house. But you can keep them away from your
food. You can keep all your food in covered containers.
Keep all the food covered tightly in containers. Then
the pests cannot touch it.

Question: What shall I do with the food that is left (waste)?

Answer: Cover the waste in a container, too. But put it
out on the ground often. Your animals will eat some of
it. Cover what is left with earth. See that the waste does
not bring flies and little animals to the house.

Keep every place in the house clean and dry. Pests
don't like clean, dry places.

And they keep away from houses where there is no food
for them.

Say, "Shoo fly! Shoo fly! Shoo fly! Shoo fly!"

New Words

(Not on 1,700 Word List)

pests   containers shoo fly

Second Presentation

The second presentation, by another committee in the class, is a dialogue between a mother and her daughter, in this instance, with Burmese names. If this were to be presented as a single story, more background would be needed. But if the characters in this story were familiar to the reader, then the story could begin as it is written here.

How would the characters become familiar to the readers? If there were a series of articles built around this family, the main characters would soon become familiar. Appearing in a magazine twice a month, or even once a month, the family would soon seem like real people. This is the technique used so effectively in the comic strips and in the "soap operas" on radio and television. Once the reader or listener gets interested in the central characters, he can hardly bear to miss an episode.

We would expect our family of characters to do more than merely continue a weepy melodrama or not-so-funny comedy. Our family of characters may get into weepy or hilarious situations, but its main purpose is to teach. We can teach, through this family, practically anything that is of vital concern to similar families who will read the stories.

Two short skits follow. Each might appear in separate issues of a magazine for new literates, with a clever illustration. Or, each could well be presented on radio (or television, in many countries within a few years) as one- or two-minute skits.

When Mother Helped With The Dishes

A Burmese mother and her daughter, NawSu, are talking.

NawSu:	Tonight I will wash the dishes, Mother.
Mother:	Good! I will go out and sit.
NawSu:	No, Mother, you will watch me.
Mother :	Why should I watch you?
NawSu:	Today teacher told us all about washing dishes.
Mother:	I know all about washing dishes. I have washed many, many dishes. What can you show me?
NawSu:	You will see. Here are the dishes, Mother.

Mother: Here is water in the basin, NawSu.

NawSu: No, no, Mother. That water is not clean. That water is not very hot. We must have very clean water. We must have hot water. We must have soap.

Mother: Why must we have such hot water, NawSu?

NawSu: Teacher told us about germs. Do you not re-member, Mother? Remember when I was very sick? The doctor said the sickness was from germs. Very hot water can kill many germs. Soap can kill many germs.

Mother: Good. Here is very hot water. Here is soap.

NawSu: Now look again, Mother. We must wash away every bit of food from the dishes. We must wash away every bit of food from the cups and spoons.

Mother: That is fine, NawSu. Clean dishes look pretty. Here is a towel. I will dry the dishes.

NawSu: No, no, Mother. The towel is dirty. Here is more hot water. I will pour very hot water on the dishes. We need not dry the dishes.

Mother: That is funny. Do you like wet dishes?

NawSu: No, Mother. Dishes will dry when water is very hot. I must keep the dishes in a clean place.

Mother: Well, I am willing to try anything once!

Watch Out For A Sick Person's Dishes

NawSu: Mother, listen again. I learned something more. If someone is sick we must keep his dishes away from the others. We must not wash the sick person's dishes with the other dishes.

Mother: Why all that trouble? I don't see any difference
               in the dishes.

NawSu: We may get the sick person's germs from his
               dishes. If we do not keep his dishes away, we
               may become sick, too.

Mother: You are a good teacher, NawSu. Now I will be
               the teacher. I will tell you how to wash dishes:

               We must use hot water and soap.
               We must wash the dishes very clean.
               We must pour hot water on the clean dishes.
               We must have clean towels.
               We must not wash the dishes of a sick person
               with the other dishes.
               We must keep the dishes in a clean place.

NawSu: That is very good, Mother. You are a good
               teacher, too. We are both good teachers.

New Word
(Not on 1,700 Word List)

towel

Third Presentation

A third committee in the class wrote, rehearsed, and presented
a playlet to the class. It received enthusiastic applause. Plays are
meant to be staged, but they also have a place as literature. If this
play were to appear in a magazine for new literates or in a pamphlet,
it might encourage groups to put it on. Would it also be read by the
average new reader? Some special instructions would be necessary
for him to read a play. Words like "prologue" and "scene" would
have to be explained or omitted.

The cast should, perhaps, be introduced before the play begins,
with a few words about the kind of person each one is. It might be
expecting too much of the reader to grasp the nature of each character purely from his spoken words. However, in a play such as
the one that follows, where motivations are on the surface and inner
conflicts are not apparent, the reader should have little trouble in
following the story.

A debatable point arises from the use of a half-legendary, half-real hero in this play. Some writers feel that it is good to use a name familiar from the folklore of the culture as the hero of the story. The people have heard stories about the legendary hero, and love to read a new one. The admiration of the hero which the people have will carry over into the new story or drama. They will take seriously what the hero does, in somewhat the same way children take it seriously when they see Popeye eating a can of spinach, and see the strength that comes to him. We should certainly avoid the exaggerations which are so evident in the comic folklore of America, for the new literates believe literally in what they read.

Use Legendary Heroes with Caution

This, then, is the first warning in using legendary heroes: avoid exaggerations. The line between fact and fiction, between truth and exaggeration, is not clear at all. Adults, who have known of the exploits of their legendary heroes from childhood, may already think of the stories more as fantasy than fact. What, then, will they think of new stories woven about their mythological heroes?

A second word of warning: treat legendary and religious personalities with respect. In many cultures the legendary heroes are half religious, half legend. The writer who would take the hero and create new stories about him is perpetuating the fiction, and making light of elements in another religion. If the new reader continues to look on stories of his own heroes as more fiction than fact, will he not also feel the same when he reads stories from the Bible? The writer who wants to present in a believable manner the men and women from his own religious literature should treat with respect the figures from literature or legend of other religions and cultures.

The advantage of using legendary personalities as our heroes is that they increase tremendously the dramatic impact of our presentation. We are using characters already high in the interest of our readers, and they may be expected to read new stories about them with eagerness. There is little need for the introductory build-up, over a period of months, perhaps, to introduce "unknown" characters to the public, such as NawSu and Mother in the preceding story.

So, the disadvantages may about balance the advantages. Writers in each culture will have to judge whether they can do anything of this sort. The following story, from the folklore of America, should raise no religious question. After reading this once, read it again, while substituting in your mind some other legendary hero with which you are familiar. Would the story then be effective against the cultural background which you know?

. . . Now, turn the page for the thrilling mystery of the . . .

Microbe Murder

<u>Prologue</u>

Enter Peddler, wearing sign "PEDDLER." He speaks:

> For many years I have traveled.
> There is much to learn:
> There is life to see,
> And death to cry about,
> And birth to be happy about.
>
> Now I am called the wise man
> Because I know stories of health and strength.
> Here is one of my stories.
>   (He holds up sign "SOAP.")
>
> With this in your hands
> You can kill microbes
>   That make boys sick
>   And give girls a cold,
>   That cause many pains
>   And sometimes death.

(Curtain Opens)
<u>Scene 1</u> Home of Davy Crockett in the mountains of Tennessee

Mrs. Crockett: There doesn't seem to be a thing we can do.
          Davy is sick and I'm afraid he's going to die!
Davy: Ma! Ma! Come and talk to me.
Mrs. Crockett: (She calls): I'll be there in a minute, Davy.
          (To herself): Oh, this work of mine seems without
          end. Everything is out of order. I can't even wash
          my dishes--and those flies on the dishes and gar-
          bage! My oh my!
     (Mrs. Crockett goes in to see Davy, but is called back by
          a knock on the door.)
Mrs. Crockett: (Hurries to the door.) My goodness! Who
          can that be? I do hope it's the peddler! Maybe he
          can give me some help for Davy. We must make
          Davy well!

Peddler: Hello! Mrs. Crockett. How are you and how is that
          fine son of yours? Yes, sir! That Davy Crockett is
          a fine boy!
          (To the audience): He can't die. He's got to fight at
          the Alamo.
          (To Mrs. Crockett, who is now crying): Say, there!
          Something is wrong! Tell me all about it.
Mrs. Crockett: Davy is very sick. His skin is hot and dry.
Peddler: I have just the thing for him. Here it is. (He
          hands her a bottle.)
Mrs. Crockett: Thank you, my friend. I'll give him some
          right now.
Peddler: But wait! There is something else you must do.
          Sit down. (Mrs. Crockett sits down.) Now I will
          tell you what I learned from a doctor:

               One must not drink water that has not
               been boiled.

Mrs. Crockett: Never?
Peddler: No. Never! Also, all dishes must be washed in hot
          water with soap. Then put them into hot water again.
Mrs. Crockett: Why bother with all that work and time?
Peddler: The lives of your family are dear to you. If one
          member of your family gets sick, you don't want all
          of your family to get sick, do you?
Mrs. Crockett: Of course not!
Peddler: Then listen closely to me:
          The dishes of a sick person should be kept separate.
          They should be washed separately, in very hot, soapy
          water. Then put them in boiling water.
Mrs. Crockett: Should I wash Davy's dishes separately? I
          have so much to do already.
Peddler: What would you do to keep those you love well?
Mrs. Crockett: Anything!
Peddler: Then never allow dishes to remain dirty. Never
          leave garbage on dishes. Never leave garbage with-
          out a cover. Because microbes grow in dead food.
Mrs. Crockett: Microbes? What are they?
Peddler: Microbes cause people to get sick. All garbage
          should be put deep in the ground and covered with
          soil.

Mrs. Crockett: I think I see what you mean. I should try to
keep everything in the kitchen so clean that microbes
won't live here. Then, even if we get sick, we will
get well quickly.

Peddler: That's right! But some people don't believe doing
these things will kill the microbes.

Mrs. Crockett: I believe you. I will try to do what you have
told me. Will you stay with Davy while I go to the
stream for water?

Peddler: Of course. I'll be glad to stay with my friend Davy.

(Curtain)

Scene 2   Ladies at a stream washing clothes and singing.

Verse. Ladies sing it once through, loud and cheerfully.

Born   on   a   moun - tain top   in   Tenn-e-ssee --

The, green - est state in the   Land of   the Free!

Raised in the for - est, he   knew every tree --

Killed him   a   bar --   When he was on-ly three!

Chorus. Ladies sing it several times, getting softer as
Fannie Belle begins to talk.

Da-vy, Da - vy Crockett, King of   the wild fron - tier!

Fannie Belle: Did you know that Granny and the peddler had
    a fight? Granny was so mad that she didn't even tell
    me what the fight was about. Granny doesn't like
    new ideas!
Ginny Jinks: I thought you were Granny's best friend.
Fannie Belle: I am, but I can't agree with her sometimes--
    Oh! Here she comes now! She looks as mad as she
    did this morning.

    (Granny enters. Girls go on with their washing.
    They pretend not to see Granny. Girls hum the
    tune once more, getting softer as Granny speaks.)

Granny: What are you all so happy about? That peddler
    makes me so mad! He tries to tell me how to wash
    my dishes. He even thinks he knows more about
    keeping my kitchen clean than I do myself.
Fannie Belle: You are right, Granny. The peddler does
    know what he's talking about. By the way, what did
    he say to you?
Granny: Oh, he told me . . .
Ginny Jinks: Here comes Annie Crockett. I saw the peddler
    heading towards her house.
Granny: Why all the hurry? What's on your mind, Annie?
Mrs. Crockett: Davy is ill. Mr. Peddler is with him. I have
    come for more water to boil.
Granny: Water to boil?
Mrs. Crockett: Yes. He tells me to wash all our dishes in
    hot, soapy water. Then put them in hot water again.
Granny: Too much work! Our own way is best!
Fannie Belle: What else did he tell you?
Mrs. Crockett: He said I shouldn't use a cloth to dry the
    dishes. Microbes are everywhere.
Granny: Nonsense!
Mrs. Crockett: Hot, soapy water will kill microbes.
Fannie Belle: What are microbes? And why kill them?
Mrs. Crockett: Microbes make people ill.
Granny: What does the peddler get out of this?
Mrs. Crockett: Nothing but the cost of the medicines he sells.
    He says that, all over the country, people are learning

to put garbage deep in the ground and to cover it with
soil.

Fannie Belle: Why?

Mrs. Crockett: To keep microbes away from dishes, food
and water. Dishes used by a sick person should be
kept separate. Wash them separately too. I am taking this water back to do as the peddler says.

Granny: You're a fool! You believe everything you hear. I
have lived long and know better. It's microbe murder!

(Mrs. Crockett leaves, as Granny laughs at her. The
curtain closes, but opens again quickly.)

Peddler Enters and Speaks: It is now one month later. Annie
Crockett did try my wise words. She boiled all her
water. She used soap to kill the microbes...
And here's the result!

Davy Enters and Speaks: I'm all well now. Here's a song I
wrote. (He whispers loudly to the audience): And
I'm only three!

(Davy sings, to the same tune):

Born on a mountain top in Tennessee,
A tiny microbe almost murdered me!
Thanks to the Peddler, my mother got wise--
Now we use soap and hot water,
And chase away the flies!

(Everyone sings the Chorus):

Microbe, microbe murder! That's what we all can do!

(They repeat the Chorus softly once or twice, as they
leave the stage or the curtain closes.)

The End

New Words
(Not on 1,700 Word List)
microbe   murder   peddler   garbage

HOW-TO-DO-IT ARTICLES

This type of article is meant to give precise information in clear steps. The how-to-do-it is basically a set of instructions. The instructions may be woven into a fictional story to make it more readable. More often than not, however, the story may obstruct the directness of the teaching. If the how-to-do-it is something which the reader needs to have done, then a few introductory words should suffice to arouse his interest and assure him that he can do it himself.

How-to-do-its can be of many kinds: helpful ideas around the farm and in the home, hints for the housewife, canning and cooking ideas, and even things for children to do.

The first example is written to serve two purposes: to show people one way of helping prevent disease in the village, and to show them how to enrich the soil. It is presented as one of a series of articles on village and farm improvement in Liberia.

How To Use Your Waste Material

By a Committee in a Class in Writing For New Literates

You can prevent disease in your village in two ways:

1. Put an end to places where flies pick up germs on their feet.

2. Gather waste material to put on the soil of your gardens.

Did you know that this waste material will make your garden grow better? Be sure to gather it far away from your house. Then you put it on your garden between crops.

What are some of these waste materials? Bones, fallen leaves, dead plants and skins from vegetables. All these can be used.

Put all these things in a pile. Add a little soil to the heap when it is about a foot high. Then add soil when it is about two feet high, and so on. Be sure the old food and dead animals are always under the soil.

A Compost Heap

We call this pile of soil and old waste material a "compost heap." You should always add all your new waste material to the compost heap. Make a fence of sticks or boards to keep the heap together. Cover it with long thatches such as you use to make your roof. Put a long stick down in the center of the heap.

After a few days pull the stick up. The end that was in the heap will be hot. This is because everything in the compost heap is rotting.

After a few weeks, turn the heap upside down. In this way the things that were on top will also rot.

The waste must rot before it can help the soil. In a year the compost heap will be much smaller than it was. When things rot, they grow smaller. They will not look the same.

Now the rotten waste materials in your compost heap will be food for your garden. This is food for the soil. These rotten waste materials we now call compost.

So, by making compost, you do two things:

1. You put the bad waste materials in a heap and cover it so the flies cannot get on it.

2. You are making wonderful food for your garden.

In the second how-to-do-it the instructions have been set free of their hiding places in the long paragraphs. By indenting clearly, and by starting each instruction on a new line, they are very easy to follow. This is the One-Two-Three technique mentioned in Chapter 20, even though in this example the steps are not numbered. This article on plastering, the class felt, would be of value in many parts of the world, as so many people build houses of mud, with some kind of plaster on the surface. The formula for the plaster would differ in various parts of the world, but the lesson remains the same: that the man-about-the-house can do a great deal himself to keep the home tidy and weatherproof.

Can I Do My Own Plastering?

By Ann Smith
Class Member in Writing for New Literates

Can I do my own plastering? Certainly! You can fix the walls of your own house. Learn by doing. Here is how.

You need the following tools and materials:

Tools

Plastering tool, called a trowel.

Materials

Plaster. You can buy ready-to-mix plaster from the store. Or the agricultural worker will show you how to mix your own.
Clean water.
Box for mixing.
Large box for walls.
Small box for cracks.
You may use any clean box that does not leak.
Tool for mixing.

How to prepare the wall for plastering:

Clean out all loose bits in the cracks.
Clean the mixing box.
Use clean water.
Wet all parts of cracks in wall before mixing plaster.
Wet the wall to be plastered before mixing plaster.

How to mix the plaster:

Put clean water in the mixing box.
Add dry plaster to the water.
Mix with the mixing tool.
Keep adding and mixing.
Mixture should be thick as paste.
Mixture should be smooth.

Now wet cracks on entire wall again.

Plastering at last!

> Use trowel to pick up the mixture.
> Make sure all parts of the cracks are filled.
> Use trowel to spread plaster evenly.
> Use trowel to smooth the plaster.
> Let it harden.

If you cannot buy plaster ready to use, do this:

> Use lime and sand (on wall of lime and sand).
> Mix 4 parts sand to 1 part lime.
> Mix with clean water until smooth.
> Mix until thick as paste.
> Use the same method as above.

THE SHORT SHORTS

Another type of how-to-do-it is often called the short short. These short shorts may range from 50 words or less to about 200. Several of them may be grouped on a page of Household Hints or Farm Hints. Or a short short may be tucked in at the end of a longer article to fill a page. Any number of short shorts are found in American farm, mechanics and household magazines. Each one can suggest only a very small but often important step to save the reader time or help him do a job more effectively. Ideas for short shorts abound everywhere, and can be adapted for every culture. These two have been found helpful in Africa.

Two Short Shorts

By Janice Timyan
Class Member in Writing for New Literates

Salt Helps Clean Your Pans

Women know that the food for their table must be cooked in clean pans. For many years women have used wood ashes to clean their pans. But do you know that you should add salt to the wood ashes? The salt will clean your pans much better.

This is how to do it:

Find a small can. Fill it four times with wood ashes. Place the wood ashes in another large can. Fill the small can with salt. Add the salt to the wood ashes. Salt cleans well. Salt added to your wood ashes will clean your pans better. Try cleaning your pans this way today.

Let A Nail Help Cook Your Fowl

Do you cook and cook an old fowl? And is it still not tender? Most women do not like to cook an old fowl because it takes so long to make it tender. You do not need to cook an old fowl so long.

Here is what you can do. This will help your old fowl get tender. And you will cook the fowl in much less time.

Place one large nail in the pan with your fowl. Or you may put in several small nails.

The nails should be new. The nails should be clean. You will find the nails will help your old fowl to become tender.

Now you know how to cook your fowl in less time. Now you know how to make it very tender. Use a large, clean nail. Or use several small nails.

New Words
(Not in 500 Word List)

cook   clean   pans   wood   fowl   nail   ashes   tender

FICTION WITH A LESSON

Stories with a moral are as old as the ages. New ones can be written, and old ones adapted from the fables of each culture. One of each kind is included here. Stories with a lesson serve a similar purpose to the stories of persuasion, except that they do not necessarily advocate specific steps to be taken. Stories with a lesson may be used along with the stories to persuade, for they set the attitudes of the readers. If the reader thinks about the lesson in the story, or talks about it with his neighbor, the story has accomplished its purpose.

Why Ramu Died

By T. V. Raghavan
Class Member in Writing Social Education Materials
Hislop College, Nagpur, India

Ramu was sick. He was lying on the floor of a hut. His cheeks were hot. He had high fever. Gopal was Ramu's father. The family lived in Rampur village.

Ramu's mother was weeping. Gopal was also weeping. They did not know what to do.

A man came into the hut. He was their neighbor. His name was Govind. He was an aged man. He had much experience.

Govind asked Gopal, "Why are you weeping?"

Gopal said, "My only son Ramu is sick. You touch him and see. His cheeks are hot. I do not know what to do. Ramu's mother is also weeping. I cannot stop her."

Govind felt sorry. He said to Gopal, "Let us go and bring a doctor."

Gopal asked Govind, "Is there a doctor here?"

Govind said, "Don't you know? There is a 'sarkari' (Government) doctor near the temple. Let us go and bring him."

Gopal said to Govind, "Alas, I have no money to pay the doctor."

Govind said, "You need not pay this doctor. He will come."

Then Gopal and Govind went to the doctor. "Namaste, Doctor Saheb," said Govind.

"Namaste, Govind. Who is sick at your house?" asked the doctor.

Govind said, "This is Gopal, Doctor. His son is sick. We came to take you home. Will you come?"

The Doctor Comes to Ramu

The doctor came. He examined Ramu. He said to Gopal, "Ramu has malaria."

Gopal asked the doctor, "What is that?"

Doctor said, "Malaria is a fever. I shall give you some quinine pills. You give Ramu one pill with water, one in the evening, one in the morning. The fever will go away." The doctor went away, and Govind went away.

Gopal gave the pills to his wife. He said, "You give one pill to Ramu with water, as the doctor said."

Gopal Must Go To Work

Gopal went to the fields to work. Without work he could not earn. He went to work with a heavy heart. Gopal's wife sat there watching her son Ramu. Gopal's wife did not like Govind. She thought Govind was doing some mischief. She did not trust the white pills. She threw the pills away.

Ramu was having high fever. He became worse. The fever touched his brain. He cried, "Mother, mother, where are you? Give me water, water!"

Ramu's mother gave him water. But she could not give the pills. She had thrown them away. Ramu died that evening.

Ramu's mother cried. Ramu's father cried. They wept. They wailed. Govind came in. He said to Gopal, "Crying does not bring back the dead. Take courage. Think of God."

Gopal's Wife Tells the Truth

Later in the night, Gopal asked his wife, "How many pills did you give Ramu?" She told the truth. Gopal became angry. He did not talk with his wife.

Gopal ran to Govind. He fell at his feet. Govind was surprised. Gopal told Govind what had happened.

The Doctor Tells Them What To Do

Gopal felt sorry. In the morning, Govind took Gopal to
the doctor. The doctor was a kind man. He told Gopal, "Do
not worry about the past. Now we shall work in the village
to wipe out malaria fever."

Gopal asked the doctor, "How can we do it?" He was
now prepared to do anything.

The doctor said, "Malaria is carried by mosquitoes. We
shall drive out the mosquitoes. We shall fill the ditches. We
shall burn the rubbish. We shall fill up the pools. We shall
not allow dirty water to stand."

The Villagers Work Together

The three men started work in the morning and evening.
They worked two hours daily. Gopal told the other villagers
about Ramu's death. He told them what they were doing.
Seeing them work, they also joined. They worked. They
cleaned. They filled up all pools. They filled up all ditches.
They put all the rubbish together and burned it.

The village became clean. Mosquitoes could not breed.
Gradually malaria was driven away from Rampur.

Ramu gave his life for malaria. Now there is no malaria
in Rampur. Rampur is clean. Rampur is free from dirty
standing water. The villagers have done it. Every village
can drive away malaria as Rampur did.

In this story, the new literate learns, as he reads about what
the hero of the story learns, of the danger of malaria and some ways
of getting rid of the danger. A good follow-up article would be like
the next one, "Stop Mosquitoes!" It might appear either in the same
pamphlet or periodical with the story, or it might be published in
the next issue. The value of such a follow-up article is that it gives
a few more specific points on which the new literate can act, and it
renews his determination to do something about the danger. None
of us--new literate or "old" literate--act generally upon one reading
concerning any subject. We need several reminders, and several
different approaches to the issue.

Stop Mosquitoes!

Pour oil on swamps.

Mosquitoes carry malaria. Malaria makes many people very sick. Malaria may make you sick. It may make your child very sick.

The best way to stop malaria is to kill the mosquitoes.

Cover all the wells.

Mosquitoes grow in still water. In the little streams and in the lakes the mosquitoes make their home. They like to live in the swamps too. They grow in wells that have no covers on them. And mosquitoes grow in old cans of water that lie around. These cans are filled with rain water.

Here are four ways you can kill mosquitoes:

1. Drain the swamps. Drain the old cans of water that are left after the rain. Drain wet spots of land. After you drain the wet spots, fill the spots with soil.

Put fish in the lakes.

2. If you can't drain swamps, pour oil on them. If you don't use the water, pour water on lakes. Pour oil on the wet spots of land.

3. Cover the wells. Cover all cans that hold the water you use.

4. Get fish for your lake. Get fish that eat mosquitoes. Put fish in the swamps too.

If you do these four things, soon the mosquitoes will die. You will not get sick with malaria. You will have good health. You will find that the work in killing mosquitoes will be worth the trouble.

Mosquitoes live in open cans of water.

Almost every culture has fables in which animals act and talk
very much like human beings. For centuries the stories and songs
of the animals have been kept alive by mothers telling them to their
children. The folklore has been added to by famous storytellers in
each generation. Putting them into print insures the fables against
loss in the rapidly changing cultures of the twentieth century.

Animal stories have a charm no other kind can match. Every
human quality can be given to the various animals, from the meanest
character to the noblest, without offense to anyone. The lessons in
the stories are sometimes trivial, sometimes valuable. But they
always stand out clearly. There is no pretense at being subtle and
trying to make the moral of the story sneak up on a reader's "blind
side" while he is engrossed in an interesting plot. The moral comes
right out in the open, and its charm lies in its being stated so plainly.

The following story is known among several tribes in West
Africa, and was written by a missionary in a class in Writing for
New Literates.

The Tortoise and the Mongoose

By Nancy Brooks
Class Member in Writing For New Literates

I want to tell you a story. The story is about a tortoise
and a mongoose. They lived long, long ago. Once upon a
time the tortoise gave the mongoose some food. It would
help him in catching animals. The mongoose ate the food.

"Now," the tortoise said, "you can catch many animals.
But one thing you cannot do. Do not catch animals that have
claws. Remember, don't catch animals with claws."

One day the mongoose went into the forest. He went into
the forest to catch animals. He suddenly saw where an animal had walked by. But it was an animal that had claws.
What had the tortoise said? "Do not catch animals that have
claws." But the mongoose was hungry. He wanted to eat.
He did not follow what the tortoise had told him.

So he went to the town and called to the people, "Help
me! Help me catch the animal."

They were hungry too. They all ran from the town. They went and waited where the animal was.

The mongoose went into the forest. He came almost to the place where the tortoise hid in the forest. Yes, it was the tortoise he had been following. Just then the tortoise made a sound. The mongoose was afraid. He ran and ran. He ran right into the people of the town.

They didn't see that he was the mongoose. They just saw an animal. They were hungry. Now they would eat. They wouldn't be hungry. They caught the mongoose. The mongoose died because he didn't follow what the tortoise said.

Remember, when you are given an order, be sure to follow it.

New Words

(Not on 1, 000 Word List)

tortoise   mongoose   claws   hungry

FICTION JUST FOR FUN

One of the greatest delights, for all of us who can read well, is reading just for the pure fun of it. Occasionally we enjoy a story where the moral doesn't jump out at us or where there is nothing in particular to learn. We just relax and let our minds go off in a dream world of the story. When the new literate reads for the fun of it, it is a pretty sure test that he has progressed to the point where reading is almost as important to him as eating and sleeping.

Stories just for the fun of it have great value, for they whet the appetite of the new reader for wholesome entertainment as well as for valuable information. Continued whetting of the reading appetite, by a diversity of styles and types of articles, will keep the new reader always on the quest for more to read. There is no joy to equal that of the writer, editor and publisher with an eager-reading public ready to grab up all the literature that comes off the presses.

Here is a story, just for the fun it it, from Anand the Wise Man, Volume II:

Anand Calls The Police

By a Committee led by Margaret Lee Runbeck

One night when Anand was in the city it began to rain. His umbrella was at home. So he went to the door of a shop to protect himself under the roof. He was standing outside when he heard someone inside the shop saying, "Cut his neck, cut his back, cut his arms, and cut his legs. I will give you money tomorrow."

Anand thought to himself, "What does that man mean? 'Cut his neck and cut his back. Cut his arms and cut his legs. I will give you money tomorrow.' What does he mean? There must be a very bad man in his shop. He must be killing another man."

Anand was frightened as he stood outside. He said to himself, "I will run to the police." He ran as fast as his legs could go. He told the police, "I was standing outside a shop door and I heard a man say, 'Cut his legs, cut his neck. Cut his arms, cut his back, I will pay you tomorrow.' I think someone is being killed."

The police took Anand to the police inspector and said, "Anand was standing outside the shop. He heard a man in the shop say, 'Cut his legs, cut his neck, cut his arms, cut his back. I will pay you tomorrow.' He believes a man is being killed."

The police inspector said, "You did right to run to us."

The police and the police inspector ran with Anand to the shop. The police inspector called out, "Open the door. Open it quickly. Open the door or you will be killed."

A small man opened the door, looking frightened. He was a modest little man who would not hurt anyone. He said, "What do you want?" The inspector said, "We want the body of the man you killed."

"I am a tailor," the little man said, "Why are the police here? What do you want?"

The inspector said, "What man did you kill? What man

promised to give you money for killing?''

The tailor said, ''I am not killing anyone. I was only telling this other man how to cut the neck of these clothes, how to cut the back, and how to cut the arms and legs.''

The inspector knew what Anand heard. Anand thought that a man, not clothes, was being cut up. He laughed at Anand. ''It is fine to call the police but you must have someone who has made a mistake.''

''Take me,'' Anand said laughing. ''I was the man who made the mistake.''

BIOGRAPHIES

True stories about people who have overcome great odds are always of interest and inspiration. The people may be famous, or they may be known only in their own community. In either case, there is a great deal about their lives which the writer can dramatize to thrill the new literate. In writing stories of real people, be sure to say that they are true, so as to distinguish them from the fictional stories.

Two types of biographies are included here. One is a fragment of a long, continued story about Gandhi. In a periodical, a chapter of about this length might appear in each issue. In a pamphlet, a series of chapters would complete the biography. It is best to have each chapter short, so that it can be read quickly without tiring.

When Gandhi Walked To The Sea

By Helen McMahon
Class Member in Writing For New Literates

Mahatma Gandhi often spoke to great crowds of people. He used to hold up his left hand. He would take hold of the thumb with his right hand and say, ''This is for the untouchables. They are on the same level as all of us.''

Then Gandhi would point to his first finger and say, ''This is spinning.'' Then the second finger, ''This means no alcohol and no opium.'' The third finger was for friendship between Hindus and Moslems. The fourth finger was for women being equal to men.

Then Gandhi would point to his wrist and say, "My wrist stands for non-violence. All the fingers are fastened to my wrist. So all good comes through non-violence."

What is non-violence? To Gandhi, non-violence meant that he would not fight with other men. Often when men cannot agree on something they will fight. But Gandhi would never fight. And he would not allow his followers to fight. They used non-violence.

Gandhi said, "There is a force greater than fighting. That great force is Truth."

In India they have a word, "satyagraha." Satyagraha means truth force. Satyagraha is what Gandhi and his followers used to meet all problems.

Gandhi used satyagraha in his Salt March in the spring of 1930. The British taxed salt. They also made a law that nobody could buy salt except from the British government.

Gandhi started out with 78 followers. He walked to the sea, 200 miles in 24 days. People from miles around came and watched on their knees, by the side of the road. Some of them joined in the march. By the time they reached the sea there were several thousand marching.

Gandhi and his followers spent the night praying beside the sea. Next morning they went down to the shore. Gandhi leaned over and picked up some salt that he found on the shore. It was against the law because he did not get the salt from the British government.

This was a sign for the people all over India to refuse to carry out the British laws. This was the beginning of India's working for her own government. It took 17 years of working through the power of satyagraha. Without an army, without battles -- by the power of Truth (Satyagraha) -- India at last got her own government.

New   Words
(Not in 1,700 Word List)

wrist   thumb   non-violence   untouchables   spinning   opium
    alcohol   satyagraha   Gandhi   Hindus   Moslems

A short biographical sketch follows. The short sketch has only enough details to help the reader get acquainted with a person whose name he may see or hear again. Persons prominent on the local scene, in the country, or around the world may be included in a column you might call "Get To Know Your Leaders," or "A Person You Should Know." And don't forget to include women, too!

Ralph Bunche

By a Class Committee in Writing for New Literates

Ralph Bunche is one of the world's greatest statesmen. A statesman is a leader of his state or nation. Ralph Bunche began his life in a very humble Negro home.

In America, every boy can have a good education. Ralph was very bright and went to many schools and colleges. Then he taught school, but continued to study.

As a statesman, Mr. Bunche worked for better conditions in America and in Africa. He has received many honors. Many of the honors were never before given to a Negro.

In the United Nations he was given the job of mediator of Palestine. As mediator he worked for peace in Palestine. The Jews of Palestine honored him as a statesman. The other side honored him too.

As United Nations mediator of Palestine, Ralph Bunche became famous. He did the best he knew how for the world. Ralph Bunche believes in the United Nations. He wants you to believe in the United Nations.

Ralph Bunche has shown that he is a friend to all the peoples of the world. He is patient and loving and kind. That is how he worked for peace in a troubled spot in the world. He stood up for what was right.

Can you do as much for the world? You can start by being patient and loving and kind. You can stand for what is right.

New Words
(Not in 1,700 Word List)

Ralph Bunche   statesman   Negro   United Nations
mediator   Palestine

INFORMATION AND INTERPRETATION

One of the most popular pages in <u>Lanao Progress</u>, the fortnightly magazine for the Maranaws of Lanao in the Philippines, was
the page of laws simply explained. Ignorance of the laws often led
to trouble for the Maranaws, as it does for many other peoples.
An understanding of laws, when they are presented in a readable
manner, leads to cooperation of people with their government and
to general civic pride.

Interpretive articles can be prepared on any number of subjects,
such as laws, government workings, what the schools do for the
people, what hospitals do, what government health programs do.
The writer can help make clear the people's relation to many organizations which they may not realize are working for their good. In
many instances it will be well to have an expert write the articles,
or at least have the articles appear as if written by the expert, even
though it has been simplified by the writer for new literates.

The following article was written by a member of a Syracuse
University School of Journalism class in writing for new literates.
On return to his native Liberia, Mr. Mentee was placed in charge
of literature production for the new literates.

Take Pride In Our Constitution

By Samuel Mentee
Class Member in Writing For New Literates

We are citizens of Liberia - a great country. As citizens
we ought to know our Constitution. What is in it? Why
should we know about it?

Every nation with an organized government has a Constitution. The Constitution contains our rights as citizens.
That is why we should now learn our rights. The Constitution sets and limits the power of our government officials.

Declaration of Rights

Our Constitution has a very important part. This is the
Declaration of Rights. The Declaration of Rights is the
heart of the Constitution. We call it the heart of the Constitution because the life of our country depends on it. And our
own lives depend on the Declaration of Rights.

Our freedom depends on the Declaration of Rights. Our Government knows that everyone in Liberia must be free.

The First Right

The first right in the Declaration of Rights is: "All men are born free." What does this mean? This means simply: since we were born in a free country, we have the right to stay free.

The Declaration of Rights also says that we "have certain natural rights." For example, we have the right to own our property. We have the right to buy property. We have the right to look for our happiness.

Another Of Our Rights

Another part of the Declaration of Rights says, " all power is in the people." The power of the Government is in the people. You are the people.

When the power of the Government is in the people, it is a Democracy. Our Government in Liberia is this kind. Liberia is a Democracy. In Democracy we put men in the Government to rule the nation. We put them there when we "elect" the men in Government. Our power to elect men to office is very important. It is a right to be very proud of.

Freedom of Worship

Our Declaration of Rights has another important part. This is the freedom of worship. This means that you can go to your own church and worship God in your own way. Many countries do not have freedom of worship. This is another right we in Liberia can be proud of.

Liberia has a fine Constitution. And the Declaration of Rights is the heart of our Constitution. Together, they make Liberia safe and free.

WRITING NEWS FOR NEW LITERATES

The motto of one of the leading newspapers in the United States
is "All The News That's Fit To Print." We can follow this standard,
except for the unlimited "all." In the first place, every publishing
concern for the new literates, whether mission or government, works
on a very limited budget. And presenting news is but one small part
of a total literature program for new literates.

In the second place, it would not be wise to present "all the news"
to the new literate, even if our facilities allowed us to. News of
crime, of disaster, of conflict between peoples and races, if presented in the "objective" manner of standard journalism practice,
would only confuse and bewilder the new literate.

The writer and editor must interpret what he presents to the new
literate. Interpretation begins with selection of news events to be
published. This is not censorship, but an evaluation of what is suitable for publishing. The philosophy of the editors will govern selection of news. And it is to be hoped that the emphasis will be on
events illustrating the good, the brave, the progressive, and the
cooperative nature of mankind. Events concerning the negative and
petty nature of man may have to be included occasionally, but only
if they point up, in contrast, the constructive, cooperative activities
of many other men and women in the news.

The well-prepared interpretations of the Christian Science
Monitor should be studied over a period of several months by prospective editors for new literates. For the Monitor does for the
American reading public the very job which we need to do on a
smaller scale for the new literates: constructive selection and
thoughtful news interpretation. (See Appendix A for periodicals
helpful to the editor for new literates.)

The following news story is presented in two ways. Each was
written by a class member in Writing for New Literates. The first
is written in a style reminiscent of the early chapters of the Anand
reader. Each sentence is very short. There is an attempt to relate
the organization of the churches to the village council, with which
readers would be familiar. This should be of value in areas where
the readers have had very little communication with the outside
world.

The Meeting Of The Churches

(The Story As It Appeared In American Newspapers)

Davos, Switzerland.

Faced with the task of laying down a Christian program of action
in world affairs, the World Council of Churches opened its annual
meeting today.

Dr. Franklin Clark Fry, president of the United Lutheran Church in America, who is chairman of the session, described it as one of the most important in the council's history.

Dr. Willem Visser 't Hooft, the World Council's general secretary, told the opening meeting that "to be in the church is to fulfill the calling of the watchman who speaks in the name of the Lord to the nations and to those in authority." He added, "We are not just people who want to propagate some of their own political notions, but we seek to be the spokesmen for the Highest Authority."

He also called on the council's 165 Protestant, Anglican and Orthodox churches to seek a joint approach to "the deepest human need...the evangelical task of the church."

The Meeting Of The Churches

First Re-written Version
By Marie Brock
Class Member in Writing For New Literates

There are many councils in the world.
You know about your village council.
There is also a council of churches.
There is a Council of Churches for the whole world.

The World Council of Churches has a chief just like your
    village council.
This chief is called the Council's Secretary.
The Council's Secretary told people this:

We church members are like watchmen.
We are like watchmen who speak to the nations of the
    world.
We also speak to the rulers of the world.
We do not speak only for our own nations.
We try to speak for God Himself.

At the Council meetings church leaders will talk about many
    things.

The leaders will ask,
    How can we best tell everyone about God?

They will talk about world peace.
They will ask,
    How can all church members work for world peace?

New Words
(Not on 1,000 Word List)

    secretary   council

The second version includes more details, like names and places, and is written in a slightly harder style. This would be of value to a reading public in the city where there is some contact with the world. In either situation, rural or city, the interpretation should aim at making the news more understandable to the average new literate.

There is an old adage, "names make news." How many names, especially with difficult spelling, should we try to keep when rewriting? Names complicate the story, and slow down the reading by the new literate. However, names are important, and they are interesting. In the first version you notice all the names were dropped, and in the second all kept in.

And how should names be spelled? Some periodicals, in an African language, for example, keep the entire name "World Council of Churches" in English. Others use equivalent terms in their own language to indicate an organization of churches.

Some periodicals keep English or European names exactly the same, without respelling. Others adopt the names into the spelling of the language. "Franklin Fry" might come out something like "Frankelin Frai." And what could be done with "Willem Visser 't Hooft! In a language that may not have a "v," it might come out something like "Wilem Wisa ta Hoof." These are but a few of the troubles in trying to handle foreign names!

Second Re-written Version
By Grace Flaten
Class Member in Writing For New Literates

Each year the World Council of Churches has a meeting. This year the meeting was in Switzerland. The World Council meets to make plans for Christian action.

Dr. Franklin C. Fry is the president of the World Council of Churches. He said that this meeting is one of the most important the council has ever had.

Dr. Willem Visser 't Hooft is the secretary of the World Council of Churches. He gave a talk at the first meeting. He said, "We church members are like men who watch for a chance to speak in the name of God. We must speak to the nations and to their leaders." He also said, "We are not just people who want to get across some ideas of our own nations. We seek to speak for God."

There are 165 different kinds of churches in the World Council of Churches. Dr. Visser 't Hooft also called on all of them to unite in our biggest job. Our job is to reach the hearts of the people with the story of Christ.

New Words
(Not on 1,700 Word List)

Switzerland   Franklin C. Fry   Willem Visser 't Hooft
                 council

Exploits of daring always thrill the reader. And the story of climbing Mt. Everest should be interesting to everyone, except perhaps in a country so flat the people have never seen a hill.

To The Top Of The World!

By a Committee in a Class of Writing For New Literates

When the world was made, some of the world was low ground. Some of the world was high ground. We call the high ground the mountains.

In the country of Nepal are the highest mountains in the world. They are named the Himalayas. The Himalayas are nearly six miles high. The Himalayas are 29 thousand feet high.

It is very cold on the top of the Himalayas. The water in the air there falls down like a white cover. This is called snow. The snow lies very deep. People sometimes get lost in the deep snow. Often the snow falls down the side of the mountain.

People like to do hard things. Many times men have tried to climb to the top of the Himalayas. Some died on the way. Some failed to reach the top.

Recently, another group tried to get to the highest point. The highest point in the Himalayas is Mount Everest.

Two men reached the top of Mount Everest. One man was from Nepal. The other was from New Zealand.

They climbed and climbed. Every day for one month they climbed. They suffered from the cold and the snow. The climbing was hard work for their hearts. But they had faith that they at last would reach the top.

Finally -- they were there! The man from Nepal held the flag. The man from New Zealand took his photo.

All the world heard the news with great joy. This was another victory of man over the mountains.

New Words

Nepal   Himalayas   New Zealand   Mount Everest
snow   photo

On the local scene many stories will fall into the simple an - nouncement class: meetings or conferences to come, or reports about conferences held. The value of these is in keeping readers up to date with the activities of the church, the literacy campaign and other organizations. The following news story is of an actual event in Liberia.

A New Training Center At Klay

By Samuel Mentee

During the last week of March and the first week of April, there were meetings at many towns of Liberia. These towns are Tchien, Zorzor, Bopolu, Voinjama, Webbo, Ganta.

The Department of Public Instruction in Monrovia sent a man around to all those towns. This man told them about the new training center. It will be opened at Klay soon. Literacy workers will be trained there.

At Klay, the Government will teach the young people health, agriculture, and how to teach children and adults to read and write. They will be taught how to use radios, too.

The chiefs were called in council. Each chief was asked to send someone of his chiefdom to take the training at Klay.

The training will begin on June 7, and will last for six months. When the men complete the training, they will go back to their home towns to teach. Then another training course will start at Klay. In this way all of Liberia will learn.

(All words except place names are on the 1,700 Word List)

THE ESSAY

The essay, with which we all remember struggling in composition classes in school, is generally the most overworked and least effective type of writing. You see long rambling essays in many periodicals and pamphlets for new and not-so-new literates in many countries. The master writer can turn out beautiful essays, where the thoughts stand out like sparkling diamonds. But the average writer hides his ideas, if there are any, in a foliage of flowery words and empty phrases. He brings in anything and everything, mostly abstract ideas, so his essay becomes an aimless rambling.

The good essay--preferably the short essay--has a place in literature for the new literates. Like a good sermon, the good essay should have a point (one is enough) and stick to it. When the point is made, stop.

The following essay was found in a periodical for readers of English in Africa. It is neither particularly good nor particularly bad, just an average essay.

What Is Civilization?

Civilization is an overworked word. It is also a word whose meaning is often not properly understood, although it is used so much.

You cannot buy civilization, nor can you be given it. You cannot say, "Yesterday I was not civilized; today I am." It is very difficult to know if this person is civilized and that one is not. For it certainly does not depend on how you are dressed, what language you speak, or even what education you have had. It is easier to decide whether a whole population is civilized or not, for its degree of civilization depends on how its ordinary men and women behave, particularly towards each other.

At one time the British were accounted uncivilized. The Romans thought them uncouth barbarians. But before that the Romans were themselves "uncouth barbarians" and civilization came to them from countries further east. Today, historians and archaeologists tell us of long-forgotten civilizations that flourished in lands which are now bare desert or are inhabited by people who seem to the rest of the world just as uncivilized as the Britons did to the Romans.

The founders of these ancient civilizations had no education as we know it today. They had no bicycles, motor cars or railways. Most of them could not even read or write, and slaves were common. Yet they left their mark on the world. Our way of life today owes much to their wisdom and constructive thought which have lived on, though their towns are often buried by many feet of earth.

Africans who visit Europe are shown the great cathedrals built hundreds of years ago. These churches, some with spires towering 400 feet into the sky, are more beautiful than most of our present day constructions, and yet they were built mainly by men who could neither read nor write and who were extremely poor.

This means that it is possible to be civilized, even today, without being educated and without being rich. On the other hand, people who are rich and educated may still be uncivilized. People believe, quite wrongly, that education and increased production will automatically bring civilization. If a country behaves in a civilized way, it means that the people as a whole have too much self-respect and pride to do many things which at present lower the African in the eyes of others. Self-respect is the root of an upright and honorable life. The next requirement is thought for your neighbor and fair and honorable treatment of women. These are the most important, and later come other conditions, such as cleanliness and a respect for the law. It is what is in the heart of the people that matters. On that depends the right of a people to be called civilized.

The class in writing for new literates gave this essay consider-able discussion and then rewrote it together. As you read the re-vision, keep in mind these notes which the class members made as they rewrote the essay:

1. Historical events of original are omitted, as they are meaningless to the new reader.

2. The ramblins of original are cut out.

3. It was felt that there was a core of important truth in the original. This the class attempted to keep.

4. Note the balance within the revised articles. Concepts are centered around the hand, head and heart. These are easily translated concepts (some areas might use liver instead of heart!).

5. Note the promise of another article. Some class members felt that this article should not stand alone without emphasizing that God is needed for civilization. However, this idea was not in the original, and so was omitted to keep article short. It certainly should be brought out in the next of a series of this nature.

What Is Civilization?

Class Revision

You have heard lots of talk about civilization. Some people say, "I am civilized because I have fine clothes. I have a bicycle. I have a car."

But such people don't really know what civilization is. You can be civilized without having these things.

Other people say, "I am civilized because I have much learning. I have been to the big city. I can speak English (or French, or some other "civilized" language)."

But such people don't really know what civilization is. Learning and travel are good. But you can learn much and travel far and still not be civilized.

Then, what is civilization? What makes people civilized?

Civilization is not only what you have in your hands. Not only what you have in your head. But civilization is what you have in your heart.

A person who is really civilized has concern for others in his heart. A person who is really civilized has a concern for his family. He has concern for his neighbors. He has concern for his people. A person who is really civilized shares what he has in his hands with others. He shares what he has in his head with others.

Civilization begins in your heart.

Next time: Can You Be Civilized Without God?

DEVOTIONS AND BIBLE STORIES

Devotional writing often falls into the same trap that the essay does--the trap of abstraction. Instead of sermonets couched in language reminiscent of the pulpit, the effective devotion stands on concrete--a concrete witness of the power of God. A short story of God working in and through others stirs a reader much more than long abstract preaching.

The classes in writing for new literates have been fortunate in having been requested to simplify some of the devotions from The Upper Room, the monthly Methodist booklet. The writing in most of them rates "Fairly Easy" on the Flesch readability scales in English. In the foreign language editions, of which there are almost 20, some complaints have been received that the translations are too difficult.

It was felt that if the English could be simplified, the translators would have an easier job keeping it simple. With this in mind, several of the devotions were rewritten by members of the classes in writing for new literates. Two are included here, with comments on the revision.

First Upper Room Devotion

(Original Version)

Having disobeyed his parents and broken a promise he had made them, a ten-year-old boy knew he should be punished. He was given a choice of a spanking or of remaining at home for two weeks--no visits to friends, no trips to the store. He chose to stay at home.

Like this boy, many of us are afraid of physical pain. We are afraid of war, of torture, of insecurity, of people, of death, of fear itself. Yet thousands of people today have lived through these experiences victoriously.

Another child broke one of her mother's treasures which had been used without permission. She brought the pieces to her mother with great fear. Her mother said the never-forgotten words: "Never mind, Dear, just so you don't break my heart."

In like manner, we come with fear to God. We find Him the forgiving Father. His perfect love casts out our fear. With the psalmist we then say, "The Lord is my light and my salvation; whom shall I fear? the Lord is the strength of my life; of whom shall I be afraid?"

Revision of First Upper Room Devotion

By Grace Chen

Comments

A ten-year-old boy did not obey his father and mother. He broke his promise. He knew he must be punished.

Really two stories in this devotion. Participial phrases of original avoided. Long sentences broken up.

His father said, "I will give you a choice. You must be spanked. Or you must stay at home for two weeks."

The boy was afraid of being spanked. He chose to stay at home. That meant he couldn't visit his friends or go to the store.

Conversation heightens interest.

Many of us are like this boy. We are afraid of many things. We are afraid of pain. We are afraid of war and death. We are afraid of other people. We are afraid of fear itself. Yet thousands of people find victory over their fears.

Short sentences make the fears stand out more clearly.

Another little girl broke one of her mother's treasures. She had used it without asking her mother. She brought the broken pieces to her mother. The little girl was in great fear. But her mother told her something she never forgot:

Second story starts here.

"Never mind, Dear. Just don't break my
heart."

Conversation of
original is retained.

In the same way we come with fear
to God. We need not fear Him. God is
our forgiving Father. His perfect love
makes us free from fear.

We can say the words of this psalm:
"The Lord is my light and my salvation;
whom shall I fear? The Lord is the
strength of my life; of whom shall I be
afraid?"

It was thought best
not to change the
words of the Bible
quotation.

New Words
(Not in 1,700 Word List)

spanked   psalm   salvation

Second Upper Room Devotion

(Original Version)

Confined to her bed for years, a dear friend of mine has
learned to be used of God in Kingdom work. Willing to serve God,
she daily finds contentment and satisfaction in living. Her prayers,
counsel, and cheerful spirit are an inspiration to all who know her.

A look at biography shows that physical environment, be it
influenced by wealth or poverty, health or illness, does not in itself
produce contentment. It is the willingness to surrender ourselves to
God. Then the miracle happens--peace in the midst of pain, the joy
of service to others found in the hard work of success, the thrill of
a closer fellowship with God. Just as Paul learned to be content, so
we learn contentment when we dedicate ourselves to God.

Today, we can find contentment by speaking of God's goodness
to us, by forgetting self and putting Him first in our lives, and by
being still and knowing that He is God. Today we can express our
contentment in the lives we live.

Revision of Second Upper Room Devotion

By Fran Brown

Comments

My friend is sick. She has been in
bed for many years. But she loves God
and is happy to serve God. She serves

Sentences shortened
and simplified.

Him by her happy life. She helps other
people to be happy.

We do not need to have money to be
happy. We do not need to be strong to be
happy. We are happy when we give ourselves to God. Then a miracle happens.

*Compare this per-
sonalized version
with the abstraction
of the original.*

The miracle brings peace though we
are sick.

The miracle makes us happy to serve
others.

*Could use fewer
paragraphs; they
waste space.*

The miracle brings us close to God.

Paul learned to have peace. We can
learn to have peace like Paul's.

Today we can find peace in these ways:

1. By speaking of God's love for us
2. By putting God first in our lives
3. By being still and knowing that He
   is God

*Do you like the "1,
2, 3" or does this
belong in a devo-
tional?*

Today we can show our peace in the
lives we live.

New Words

(Not in 1,000 Word List)

Paul   miracle   ourselves

There is a rich storehouse of stories in the Old and New
Testaments. In writing Bible stories for the new literates you may
go directly to the Bible. Or you may use as a source any one of
many collections of Bible stories. Some have been written for
children, others as popular literature for adults. Several writers
have become prominent for taking Bible stories and presenting them
in very readable fashion.

The writer of Bible stories for new literates would do well to
read a number of these popularized versions. Do not copy the
stories as others have written them, nor even approximate their
style of writing. Bible stories are not copyrighted, but another
person's style is copyrighted.

When you write Bible stories for new literates, don't fail to go
to the best source--the Bible itself. In classes over the past five
years we have discovered that this is, by far, the most popular of
all sources for stories. A series of graded Bible stories, Heroes
of Faith, is in print, published by the authors of this text.

The following story was written by a member of two successive
summer classes in Writing for New Literates, at Chautauqua, N.Y.:

Three Brave Men Who Loved God

By Marie Brock

Once there was a king. This king lived long, long ago.
He lived in a country far away.

Three young men also lived in this country. The three
young men were Shadrach, Meshach and Abednego.

The three young men loved God. But the king did not love
God. The king made an image of a man. The image was very
big. The image was made of gold.

Then the king's servants called out, ''Come everyone.
Come to the image of gold. You must worship the image of
gold. You must bow down before the image. The image is
God.''

(But we know the image of gold was not God.)

The king's servants called out again, ''Come everyone.
You must worship the image of gold. When you hear music,
then you must bow down before the image.''

The king's servants also said, ''The king has a great big
fire. His servants will throw you into the fire if you do not
worship the image of gold. You must bow down. Do not make
the king angry.''

Many, many people came to the image of gold. They wor-
shipped the image when they heard music. They bowed down
to the image.

The three young men came but they did not worship the
image. They did not bow down.

The king was very angry. The king said to the three young men, "Listen, Shadrach, Meshach and Abednego. When you hear the music again, you must worship the image of gold. If you do not bow down to the image, my servants will throw you into my great big fire."

The three young men said, "We will not worship the image of gold. We will not bow down before your image. Our God can save us if he wishes. Our God may not wish to save us. But we will worship only him."

The king was very, very angry. The king's servants threw the three young men into the great big fire. The fire was so hot it killed the king's servants.

Soon the king looked into the fire. He saw the three young men. They were walking in the great big fire.

The king saw another young man, also walking in the fire. The other young man was beautiful as an angel. This young man was an angel.

Now the king was not angry. He called out, "Shadrach, Meshach and Abednego. Come here."

The three young men came out of the fire. They were not burned. Even their hair was not burned.

The king said to all his people: "The God of Shadrach, Meshach and Abednego is very great. He sent an angel to save them from the fire. The angel walked in the fire. The angel saved the three young men. No other god is so great as the God of Shadrach, Meshach and Abednego."

That day the king began to see the truth. We know that the God of Shadrach, Meshach and Abednego is the only true God.

New Words
(Not in the 1,000 Word List
though every word except "image" is
on the 1,700 list)

bow   angel   angry   image   servants   throw   music
worship

POETRY FOR NEW LITERATES

Every cultural group on earth has a storehouse of poetry, handed
down through the generations by word-of-mouth, or more permanently
preserved in print. The two-year-old girl on her mother's lap listens
attentively while her mother reads the nursery rimes; several years
later she learns to read them by herself; and even later reads them
to her own two-year-old.

The Moros of Lanao province in the Philippines have age-old
legends in poetry form. Professional singers spend entire nights in
recitation, with improvised melodies, of the long stories about their
Ulysses-style hero, Bantugan, who went forth to slay dragons and
rescue beautiful princesses. When the "baioks" of Bantugan were
written down and printed in serial form on the back cover of the
fortnightly magazine Lanao Progress, they quickly became the most
popular feature for the new literates to read.

What is poetry? Like describing "beauty," describing "poetry"
is almost impossible. A dictionary definition seems barely adequate:
"The art of metrical composition; the art of exciting pleasure by
means of beautiful, imaginative, or elevated thought expressed in
appropriate words, usually in metrical form..."

The ingredients of poetry are rime and rhythm: rime, the re-
currence of similar sounds, usually at the end of lines; rhythm, the
pattern of beats, like the drum in an orchestra, which keeps the
reader going steadily forward. The rime and rhythm may be intri-
cately intertwined, or ever so simple. If words are woven together
with rime and rhythm, and if they communicate ideas while at the
same time touching the reader's heartstrings with joy, sadness or
quiet meditation--then those words have been woven into a poem.

Newspapers have brought the account of the death of America's
leading journalist-poet, Edgar A. Guest. For more than forty years
he wrote a daily column, all in verse. Perhaps none of Guest's lines
will achieve the immortality of those of Wordsworth, of Longfellow,
or of Tagore. But if the reader has been stirred by these lines,

>   It takes a heap o' living
>   In a house t' make it home,

then Edgar Guest, through his poetry--or "verse," if you prefer--
has served to make the lives of countless thousands of readers a
little brighter and a little happier.

Poetry for new literates need not follow any set pattern. Whether
the poet creates a sonnet or a jingle matters but little, if the thoughts
and the emotions stand out clear and sparkling. Writing poetry can
hardly be taught. But it can and should be encouraged. The teacher
of writing for new literates, the editor and the publisher, all should
try to discover poets. When a "discovery" is made, the best assur-

ance of a continuing flow of poems from the new poet is to publish
the best of his early works, then more each succeeding year, as his
verse grows in maturity and in beauty.

The authors of this book modestly claim such a "discovery." To
the 1958 Chautauqua summer course came a spry lady, well into what
poets call the "September years." She had written verse before, and
upon leaving three weeks later, she told the class she would write
"a few" poems, using the words in the Streamlined English word list.

Imagine our surprise the following summer, when she returned
with a portfolio of a hundred or more verses. Others at Chautauqua
have caught a similar vision. At the poetry writing classes, copies
of the word list were distributed, and several experienced writers
of poetry began writing for new literates.

To these, and to all future poets, we offer hearty encouragement.
We hope that their best efforts may be put into print for the eyes of
the new literates. Now, presented for the first time, are a few of
the poems by our discovery, "the Chautauqua lady from Toronto:"

Poems By Alice Grant

(All Written Within the 1,700 Word List)

Big Attraction

There is a big attraction
    At "each one teach one" place.
For everyone is learning;
    You see it on each face.

Words

I want to read
    So I can see
What each word has
    To say to me.

Each One Teach One

"Each one teach one,"
    How can it be?
I teach you,
    Since he taught me.

Try

Around us air is everywhere;
    The sky above is high.
The birds would never reach it
    If
They did not try to fly.
    And so
We try to learn to read.

The Truth

We need the truth
    With which to know
    And grow.
Be sure to read the truth.

How To Learn

The secret of learning
    Is often to do,
So we will remember
    By using it too.

She Was A Joy!

She was a joy!
She learned to read,
And taught a boy
So he was freed.

Now he can read
To learn!

Long And Short

The days seem long
  Which are not full enough
    To make them short.

The days seem short
  Which are so full
    They leave no time
      To make report.

New York

New York to you
  Seems very far,
Perhaps, no matter
  Where you are.

But people, though
  They may be far,
Are just as human
  As you are.

Old Path

That path goes to a garden
  Of many years ago.
What stories those old trees could tell
  We will never know.

Treasures

All of us have treasures
  We do not know we have--
A baby's smiling little face,
  Some happy children's laugh,
Freshness in the morning air
  Sky colors at sunset--

They all belong to all of us,
  So we must not forget.

New Year

Last year is gone,
  No matter how you used it--
If you have done your best
  Or if you have abused it.

This year is yours,
  To use well or abuse it--
Plan well and do your best;
  You never need excuse it.

Election

A president was elected
  The other night.
Now the voters are hoping
  Their choice was right.

If All Is Well

If we are rich or poor
God never looks to see.
He looks inside the hearts
  Of you and me.

He looks at what we are
And always he can tell,
With each of you and me,
  If all is well.

God Looks At Us

God looks at people, not at race or skin;
He looks at what we are: at souls within.

CARTOON STRIPS

The average home in the United States, by Sunday midafternoon, looks as if a playful tornado has swept through it, scattering sheets of gaudy "funny papers" into every room. For every member of the family, from three to ninety-three, carries the page with his favorite "comic" to his preferred place to read it. The comics (few of which are comical) have indeed invaded almost every home, in the color Sunday supplements (at least one big-city newspaper boasts of 100 different strips each Sunday), and in the black-and-white daily editions. Readership surveys consistently show that the comics rank high among the most-read pages of newspapers.

"Comic books," too, are being published on every conceivable subject, from nursery tales to the classis. Most of the stories of the Old and the New Testaments have been transferred to the comic strips--or, let's use a more accurate term, cartoon strips. These cartoon books, priced from a dime to a half dollar or more, are purchased by thousands, mostly young people. Surveys show that additional thousands more read each cartoon book, as they are traded by their original owners for others, then traded again until the flimsy paper on which they are printed starts to shred.

There is little doubt that the cartoon books would be popular if introduced into almost any literature program. A missionary from Haiti brought back an American-published cartoon book on the story of Christ. She bought it on a newsstand in Port-au-Prince, where hundreds are sold each month, even though they are in English. She hopes to arrange for an edition in the language of the people, Creole.

One can hardly bring up the subject of cartoon strips among educators without stirring up a tempest of debate. The detractors-- and they tend to be vehement in their condemnation of the cartoon strip--claim that "looking at" the strips is a poor substitute for real reading. Defenders of cartoon strips point to their documented popularity, and maintain that it isn't their form that is poor, but it's been the subject matter, which until recent years, has been inferior. Improve the content, they say, and the already popular form will be more acceptable, even to the critics of the cartoon strips.

When a child of ten or eleven reads a cartoon book about David Copperfield, will he be led to read, with greater enjoyment and understanding, the book in its original form a few years later? When a new literate reads, in cartoon strip form, stories of the life of Christ, will this create in him a desire to read the New Testament? --These are a couple of questions with which you can spring into the middle of a hot debate about the merits of the cartoon strip.

Presented here are two examples of the cartoon strip. They vary greatly in purpose, artist's approach and intended use. The first, on the following two pages, was prepared in a summer class

at Chautauqua, by a writer and artist team. The writer, Meta Kenan, is a school teacher with experience in writing for children, and the artist, Richard Hunter, is a former professional artist, now serving as a missionary in India. This one cartoon story has already proved its popularity, having been printed in six different languages, to our knowledge.

On the page opposite is an entirely different use of the cartoon strip. "Do You Sleep Well" has been adapted from a series of "jet cards," developed by Dr. Gladys Rutherford, a retired, outstanding village health specialist with a lifetime of service in India. She has prepared sets of jet cards on many health and sanitation problems. Normally a set of 25 or 30 or more jet cards is used to teach one lesson. They are printed on cards about 10 by 15 inches in size. The village nurse holds up each card in turn, reading the message on the back, which is printed in several languages for use in different areas.

These examples of cartoon strips are presented with our suggestion that this form be considered for more use in programs of literature for new literates. There is little danger that they will be used too much, for two factors help insure against this. First is the lack of the person who can both draw and write, or writer and artist who work as a team. Second is the cost of printing cartoons, unless suitable equipment, as offset presses, are available.

Undoubtedly, more important than the question of how much should pictures be used, either in cartoon form, or as illustrations for all types of articles, is the question what kind of illustration is best? Photograph? Realistic drawing, using shading? Stick people, as in the health cartoon?

These questions can't be answered one way or another at the present time. We do know, however, that new literates must learn to see pictures, as well as to read print. Research is needed to find out how new literates react to pictures. At least one man is making a genuine effort to find out how Africans respond to illustrations. Through efforts such as those of Hall Duncan, a missionary in South Africa, we may know much more, within a few years, and with that knowledge communicate more effectively with pictures.

WHAT DO AFRICANS SEE IN PICTURES?

By Hall Duncan

Is a picture worth a thousand words to an African? That all depends on the picture, the idea it is to convey and to whom it is shown. Some pictures need more than a thousand words to explain them to a person who has not seen many pictures or who has never been trained to see them.

Your Health

Do You Sleep Well?

A story told in pictures. Read from number 1 to number 6.

Africans who can comprehend pictures see
them in terms of their past experience and training. For example, a Chopi miner looked at a picture of an angel holding a sword (right) and said:

"It is a person with wings grasping an umbrella. The rain won't wet him and give him the
fever. His wings will help him get to school more
quickly."

In Africa you cannot assume anything as you
show a picture. You must first find out what is
seen, and then why these things are seen. Next
you must be prepared to explain and answer questions about pictures.

In Leopoldville, Belgian Congo, a well-dressed Christian African told me that he resented a particular picture of Christ. This picture showed Christ extending his right hand with the palm down as in
blessing. The African said it meant to him: "Stay in your place.
There's no room for development for you."

Another picture of Christ blessing children of various races is
rejected by some African people because the African child in the picture seems to be pushed out of the inner circle of children that are
grouped about Christ.

Yes, arrangement of people and objects, gestures, colors,
clothes and many other details play a very important part in perception. A person who uses pictures blindly in Africa and does not explain them fully to his audience can run into real trouble.

Education Doesn't Always Teach About Pictures

We are becoming aware that education in Africa has overlooked
the fact that people must be taught to see pictures. I shall never
forget the day when an African with a degree in education from an
overseas university gave the same answers to a particular perception test as a non-literate woman. Because
of his advanced education I expected him to
be aware of certain pictorial factors. But
he wasn't.

Some Africans do not
see a head in profile
as being natural un-
less it has two eyes.

Sometimes Africans do see what Euro-
peans see in a picture but the reasons differ. In experimenting with two simple drawings of a house, one in perspective and the
other not, an African in Rhodesia chose the
house in perspective. I thought to myself,
this man has a sense of depth as he per-
ceives this picture. Further questioning revealed that he had made his choice because
the roof appeared steeper and would most

This poster was designed for Africans who cannot see depth in pictures, so positioning of objects plays a key role. The picture took months of work to produce, and is used in Sunday schools to teach stewardship.

likely shed the rain better. A group of teen-age girls who had had
considerable training in art and perspective chose the house not in
perspective because it seemed larger, although both houses were
drawn to the same scale.

Much research and intelligent listening are required in Africa
before we really begin to make headway into understanding some of
the problems of perception. Fortunately, scientific and religious
groups are taking definite steps to study the problem.

A psychologist is directing a research program to discover the
general principles involved in the construction of drawings for different groups of Africans. Experiments are now being conducted in
depth perception. Other experiments will follow, dealing with the
drawing of the human body, the positioning of objects in a drawing,
and the use of color. The results of these studies will provide information necessary to produce pictures which will be better understood
by Africans.

Symbolism to the African

In this field of research, RAVEMCCO (Radio, Visual Education
and Mass Communication Committee of the Christian Council of
South Africa) is piloting an inquiry into the meaning of Christian symbolism to Africans, both Christian and non-Christian. In time, we
should be able to increase the effectiveness of our Sunday school
posters and church materials as a result of this study.

The present RAVEMCCO study is concerned only with symbols
of good and evil. Most of the pictures used in the questionnaires
have been taken directly from Christian publications. Others have
been invented to probe deeply certain
reactions.

One such test shows an African
carrying a brief case and wearing a
smart European suit with hat. A halo
has been drawn around his head.
Some Africans see only Western
attire as being suitable when preaching the Gospel. The psychological
effect of clothing is in itself a very
involved study, of the greatest important to us who design and produce pictures.

In a few symbolism tests that
have been given among Christian

A confusing picture, because
some Africans see a woman
carrying a house on her head.

groups, the answers are very interesting. Some Africans see a halo as
a line, a shadow, a crown, a hat or

This is part of an experimental perception test. A well-educated African pastor saw the man trying to uproot trees and catch birds while sitting on another man's head.

nothing at all. An angel may be seen as two people, the wings somehow resembling the human form. A young African man with well-rounded muscles and straight stature wearing a loin cloth is sometimes seen as an old man because of his primitive dress, or as a sick person because the lines drawn to indicate muscles are seen as sores or scars.

One well-educated African Christian education director, seeing neck muscles in a picture of a half-naked goat herder, exclaimed: "I see his collar, but where is his shirt?" A sword may be seen as a cross, an umbrella, a walking stick or some other object. The devil may appear as nothing more than an unusual animal. Even the use of a European name on a drawing can hamper a picture's effect on an African.

From these few examples it can be seen how pictures take on various meanings, sometimes the very opposite of what is intended.

The African's appetite for literature is increasing. He wants pictures in his books and magazines. He wants to be able to identify himself with the pictures and gain meaning from them. Visual aids used haphazardly in a literature program may only confuse the new literate. Illustrations used skillfully, anticipating reactions to them, will lead the new literate to greater understanding of the printed page.

IN SUMMARY

This long chapter has provided a sampling of the possibilities of articles and stories for new literates, and a glimpse at some of the research still needed.

You may be able to think of other types of writing which do not fit neatly into the categories suggested here. There is editorial comment, for example, which the journalist would consider to be distinct from news interpretation. There are a variety of games with words to add to the entertainment and learning value of periodicals. Crossword puzzles, word matching games, spelling games, the rebus (in which pictures are substituted for some of the words)-- these are but a few of the word games. Writers will find a wealth of ideas in books for children, and in collections of games and puzzles, about which any librarian can tell you.

A Recipe for You: Read and Write

For success in writing for new literates, we've a two-part recipe. The first part is to read something simple every day. Don't be afraid to read the "comic books," especially those of classical works. Read the "boy's life" of Edison, and the "girl's life" of Florence Nightingale. Read Sunday School materials and study guides for young adults. In your reading of newspapers and magazines, always be on the lookout for the writer who can say it simply.

And the second part of the recipe is to write. Avoid copying the style of any other writer, for the style that you may develop may be far better. Write something every day, and don't be concerned if every word isn't rushed immediately into print. Mastery of writing, like mastery of the piano, takes practice--and more practice. How many thousands of practice notes are struck by the pianist's fingers, to be heard by no one, for each beautiful note heard by hundreds or thousands of people when mastery is achieved?

Mastery of writing simple and effective articles like the examples in this chapter--and far better than these examples--is within your power. When you master writing for new literates, there is a public of millions, waiting for the words of entertainment, of information and of inspiration to come from your pen or your typewriter. Of all the jobs needed to get literature to the new literates--the editor, the artist, the printer, the publisher--your job of writing is the most important. Keep writing!

Chapter 23

The Last Thirty Years—And the Next?

What is the state of world literacy in the mid-20th century? The keen, not too sympathetic, observer might be quick to penetrate the veils of attention-calling drum thumping and padded literacy statistics. He would declare that literacy around the world is much the same as it was when Each One Teach One began.

We might agree--except for two things: we now have the technical know-how to make illiterates literate on a large scale, and experience has demonstrated that mass literacy campaigns will work.

What, then is missing? Can it be that the fires of enthusiasm and vision for literacy are still mere flickers in the hearts of too many of the world's leaders?

In no one is the fire of literacy burning more passionately than in the heart of Dr. Laubach. This, as his son, I can say with authority, for I have seen his zeal develop from the start. And, it is not surprising if more than one ember from the overflowing fire of the father dropped to kindle the still small glow of the son.

His enthusiasm for the world's silent billion perhaps reached a peak, at which it has since remained, right after the World Christian Conference at Tambaram, India, in December of 1938. No sooner had the conference ended than he wrote a letter to all the delegates. Passages from that letter, which still seem to smolder on the yellowing, twenty-year-old paper, inspire me--and I hope you, also--more than anything else I can here copy or compose:

"Eleven hundred million people, almost two-thirds of the world, never have had a delegate anywhere, are voiceless, for they cannot read nor write nor vote. In Asia and Africa, over a billion people are illiterate-- over half the human race. This cold paper cannot tell you what that means. You think it is a pity they cannot

293

read, but the real tragedy is that they cannot speak.
They are the silent victims, the forgotten men, driven
like animals, mutely submitting in every age before
and since the pyramids were built. ... It is a human
weakness not to realize suffering unless we hear a cry.
The illiterate majority of the human race does not
know how to make their cry reach us.

"... They are enslaved for life. More than half the
human race are slaves--hungry, driven, diseased,
afraid of this world, and of the demons in the next.
Yet they can be set free.

"I have not only seen these people across Asia and
Africa, but I have sat beside many of them, and taught
them one by one. I have seen a new light kindle in
their eyes; love and hope dawn as they begin to step
out of their blindness. I know that we can lift this
tragic multitude out of their curse, by caring and knowing and doing our part.

"... As millions become literate there looms up the
staggering task of providing them with enough good
literature. Literacy campaigns are going to double
the world's readers. A mighty tide has begun to rise.
I am aghast to comprehend what a terrifying task we
confront as these millions begin to read. Are we going
to give them reading matter--or who? Will it be clean
or rot? Will they be flooded with the message of democracy or communism, of God or atheism? Will they
read love or hate?

"Whatsoever is sown in their minds the world will
reap. What will happen when this dumb two-thirds
shall speak 'after the silence of the centuries?'"

But, perhaps it's too late to put the inspiration of this book in
the last chapter. Certainly you, who have studied this text, are
among those who least need inspiring.

We have tried to inspire by presenting what in educational terms
are called the "materials and methods" with which to fight illiteracy.
The ideas described here are those which we believe, from our experience, will help make new literates--and keep them literate--in the
quickest, most effective way.

There are undoubtedly other materials and methods still to be developed. It is our fervent hope and prayer that the student of this text will go on to find and perfect some of these--and when he has done so, will share his experience for the good of illiterates the world around.

Take this book, as the harvester takes his tools to the harvest. His harvest: rippling stalks of grain. Yours: the uncounted, yearning illiterates. His tools: the sickle or mower, powered by muscle or fuel. Yours: books and methods, powered with zeal and motivated by love.

Your harvest grows greater every year. So, whet your tools with practice, sharpen and refine them with experience. And enlist others, for

> The harvest is truly plentiful,
>
> But the laborers are few.

APPENDIXES

APPENDIX A

BOOKS, PERIODICALS AND OTHER MATERIALS HELPFUL TO THE LITERACY
WORKER AND TO THE WRITER AND PUBLISHER FOR NEW LITERATES

This bibliography is practical, rather than exhaustive. Almost every item has been
found useful in training programs. Each individual should become familiar with
two or three titles in each of the first nine groups. This list forms a nucleus for
a minimum adequate library in a permanent literacy-literature training center.

GROUP 1

BOOKS ON LITERACY AND FUNDAMENTAL EDUCATION

Angelica Cass and Arthur Crabtree. Adult Elementary Education. New York: Noble &
        Noble. 1956.

Peter du Sautoy. Community Development in Ghana. London: Oxford University Press. 1958.

Davida Finney and Adib Galdas. Village Reborn. New York: Committee on World
        Literacy and Christian Literature, 475 Riverside Drive. 1958.

Eli Ginzburg and Douglas Gray. The Uneducated. New York: Columbia U. Press. 1953.

Williams S. Gray. The Teaching of Reading and Writing (An International Survey).
        New York: UNESCO Publications Center, 152 W. 42 St. 1956.

Sarah Gudchinsky. Handbook of Literacy. Norman, Oklahoma: Summer Institute of
        Linguistics, University of Oklahoma. 1957.

Hope Hay. Northern Rhodesia Learns to Read. London: 2 Eaton Gate, S.W. 1. 1947.

Frank C. Laubach. Toward a Literate World. New York: Columbia University Press. 1938.

_____. India Shall Be Literate. Nagpur, India: National Christian Council. 1940.

_____. The Silent Billion Speak. New York: Friendship Press. 1945.

_____. Teaching the World to Read. New York: Friendship Press. 1947.

_____. Wake Up Or Blow Up. Westwood, New Jersey: Fleming Revell. 1951.

_____. The World Is Learning Compassion. Westwood: Fleming Revell. 1958.

_____. How It Can Be Done. Syracuse, New York: Laubach Literacy and Mission
        Fund, Box 131, Syracuse 10. 1958.

_____. English Spelling Made Easy for the World. Syracuse: Laubach Literacy
        and Mission Fund, Box 131, Syracuse 10. 1959.

_____. Thirty Years with the Silent Billion. Westwood, New Jersey: Fleming
        Revell. 1960.

_____. Devotional pamphlets by Dr. Laubach, included because of their significance
        in the development of his literacy work. From Box 131, Syracuse 10, N.Y.:
        Letters by a Modern Mystic, Learning the Vocabulary of God.

Marjorie Medary. Each One Teach One. New York: Longmans, Green & Co. 1953.
        A sprightly-written account of literacy and Dr. Laubach's part in it.

Karel Neijs. Literacy Training for Adults (in New Caledonia). New York: Committee
        on World Literacy and Christian Literature, 475 Riverside Drive. 1958.

Mary Nussbaum. A Selected Bibliography of Literacy Materials (with special reference
        to Africa). Hartford, Conn.: Hartford Seminary Foundation. 1958.

Philip Penning. The Christian Bookseller. Madras: Christian Literature Soc., P.O.Box 501.

Seth Spaulding and David M. White (Editors). Publishing for the New Reading Audience.
        Rangoon, Burma: Burma Translation Society. 1958. Also, Box 131, Syracuse
        10, N.Y. A report of a UNESCO Regional Seminar held in Burma.

Pan American Union. The Americas and Illiteracy. Washington, D. C.: Pan American
          Union. 1951.

Trevor and Grace Shaw. Through Ebony Eyes. London: Lutterworth Press, 2 Eaton
          Gate, London S. W. 1. 1956.

UNESCO (United Nations Educational, Scientific and Cultural Organization).

          All UNESCO materials available from:
          United Nations Bookstore, United Nations, New York, N. Y.

_____. Illiteracy at Mid-Century. 1957.

_____. Fundamental Education. Macmillan Co. 1947.

_____. Learn and Live, A Way out of Ignorance for 1, 200, 000 People.   1951.

_____. Literacy Teaching: A Selected Bibliography. UNESCO Educational Studies
          and Document No. XVIII. 1956.

          Other valuable studies in this series (new ones published continually):

          II   African Languages and English in Education
          III   How to Print Posters
          VII   Education for Community Development
          IX   Experiments in Fundamental Education in French African Territory
          X   The Use of Research in a Community Education Programme
          XI   Some Methods of Printing and Reproduction
          XIII   A Bibliography on the Teaching of Modern Languages
          XIV   Adult Education in Turkey
          XV   Fundamental, Adult Literacy and Community Development in the
                      West Indies
          XVI   Some Studies in the Education of Immigrants for Citizenship
          XXIII Editing the Magazine for New Literates
                      By Robert S. Laubach
          XXIV Periodicals for New Literates: Seven Case Studies

_____. Monographs on Fundamental Education. These are of interest:

          No. 1 Fundamental Education: Description and Programme
          No. 2 Co-operatives and Fundamental Education
          No. 3 Mexican Cultural Mission Programme
          No. 4 The Haiti Pilot Project
          No. 5 The Healthy Village

U. S. Dep't. of Health, Education, and Welfare. Education for Better Living.
          Washington, D. C.: Sup't. of Documents. 1957. $1. 50

Ruth Ure (now Ruth Warren). The Highway of Print. New York: Friendship Press. 1946.

_____. Literacy. London: Edinburgh House, 2 Eaton Gate, London S. W. 1. 1956.

GROUP 2

TEACHING OF SPEAKING AND READING ENGLISH TO ADULTS

Angelica Cass. How We Live. New York: Noble & Noble. $1. 50.
          For first-year students, beginners, and semi-literate adults.

_____. Your Family and Your Job. New York: Noble & Noble. $1. 25.
          For beginners or intermediate students.

_____. Write Your Own Letters. New York: Noble & Noble. $. 50.
          Describes in simple language and with many examples how to write
          all types of business and social letters.

_____. Americanization Helpbook. New York: Noble & Noble. $. 75.
          Provides the foreign-born adult with the essential information that
          he needs to become a good American citizen.

Robert J. Dixson. Dixson's English Series. New York: Regents Publ. Co., 200 4th Ave.
 Fourteen books in a series for foreign-born adults learning English.

_____. American Classics Graded Readers. New York: Regents Publ. Co.
 Ten classics by American authors, simplified and arranged in ascend-
 ing order of difficulty. Publisher will send complete lists on request.

C. M. Gibson and I. A. Richards. First Steps in Reading English. New York: Pocket
 Books, Inc. 1957. $.35.

Emma Lewis Bright (and others). The Brown Family. New London, Conn.: Arthur
 Croft, Publ. 1957.
 Series intended for semi-literate American, English-speaking adults.

Robert Lado. English Language Tests for Foreign Students. Ann Arbor, Michigan:
 George Wahr Publ. Co. 1957.

_____, and Charles C. Fries. Intensive Course in English. Pittsburgh, Pa.:
 University of Pittsburgh Press. 1958.

 In Four Volumes ($2.25 each volume): 1. English Sentence Patterns
 2. English Pattern Practices 3. English Pronunciation 4. Vocabulary

Frank C. Laubach. Streamlined English. New York: Macmillan Co. 1956. $1.25.
 For adults beginning to learn to read. Used as basis for television
 teaching as developed in Memphis, Tenn.; now used in other cities.

_____. Teacher's Manual for Streamlined English. New York: Macmillan Co. $1.75.
 Detailed instructions for use of Streamlined English for teaching either:
 1. English-speaking illiterates, 2. Foreign-born learning English.

_____. Reading Readiness Charts (to precede Streamlined English). Memphis, Tenn:
 Foundation on World Literacy, Hickman Bldg.
 Set of ten charts, in two sizes:
  1. 8 by 10 inches (for individual use) $.25 a set.
  2. 20 by 30 inches (for group use) $2.25 a set.

_____. How to Make Everybody's World Safe. New York: Committee on World
 Literacy and Christian Literature, 475 Riverside Drive. $1.
 A second reader in Streamlined English series. Especially helpful for
 the person educated in another language who is learning to read English.

_____. The Story of Jesus. New York: Committee on World Literacy and Christian
 Literature, 475 Riverside Drive. Set of three booklets, $1. per set.
 A second reader in Streamlined English series. Building upon vocabu-
 lary in Streamlined English, it tells the story and teachings of Jesus.

_____. The Inspired Letters. New York: Thomas Nelson & Sons. 1956. $1.50.
 Can be used as a third reader in Streamlined English series. It is an
 easy-reading version of the Letters of the New Testament.

_____. Learn English the New Way. Book I, "New English in Twelve Lessons" (50¢),
 Book II, "Bridges to the Old Spelling" ($1). Box 131, Syracuse 10, N.Y.
 Used in experimental classes for foreign born; teaches reading of new,
 revised English spelling first, then bridges to traditional spelling

I. A. Richards and C. M. Gibson. English Through Pictures. (Also French, German,
 Hebrew, Italian and Spanish Through Pictures.) New York: Pocket Books, Inc.
 1952. Each book 35¢.

 The Basic English approach to reading English (and the other languages
 mentioned) with pictures and short text. Almost a self-taught method.

Herbert Scheuler and Harold Lenz. Practical American English for Students from other
 Lands. New York: Longmans, Green & Co. 1956. $3.25.

 Developed for Americanization programs; suited for persons educated in
 another language.

Harley A. Smith and Ida Lee King. I Want to Learn English. Austin, Texas: Steck Co., 1951.

GROUP 3

EASY-READING MATERIALS FOR NEW LITERATES

This list is short, reflecting: 1. That there aren't many materials in
English suitable for adult new literates, and 2. There is inadequate
information on materials in other languages--research badly needed.

Committee on World Literacy and Christian Literature, 475 Riverside Drive, New York
27, N.Y. This Committee aids in publishing materials in many languages, working mainly through mission boards affiliated with the National Council of Churches
of Christ in the U.S.A. Information on publications will be sent on request.

Foundation for World Literacy. A Door Opens. Hickman Bldg., Memphis, Tenn.
A second reader in the TV English reading series. Request lists of other materials.

Jamaica Social Welfare Commission, Kingston, Jamaica, B.W.I. Publishes numerous
practical booklets in easy English, also a magazine, News for Adult Readers.

Materials Preparation Department, Intermountain School, Brigham City, Utah. Publishes
many text-type booklets for use with teaching Indians.

Pan American Union. Biblioteca Popular (Popular Library, in Spanish). Washington, D.C.
Has published about 75 booklets in easy-reading Spanish; useful in Latin America.

Reader's Digest. Adult Education Readers (Level A and B). Also Reader's Digest
Readings (Part 1 and 2). Reader's Digest, Pleasantville, N.Y.
Four booklets which resemble copies of the Digest. Suitable for intermediate
and advanced students. $.75 each booklet.

Reading-For-You Publications, Box 131, Syracuse 10, N.Y. (Robert Laubach, Publisher)
Customs and Courtesies in the U.S.A., Trouble and the Police, How to Find A
Job, Why You Need Insurance. $.30 each booklet. Four booklets written in
lively, easy manner on topics of interest to immigrants to the United States.

Heroes of Faith. $1.20. Stories of fifteen heroes from the Old Testament. Starts
with 500-word vocabulary. Suitable for intermediates and advanced students.

Jeanette Smith (Compiler). Bibliography of Reading Materials for Adults with Limited
Reading Ability. Foundation for World Literacy, Hickman Bldg., Memphis, Tenn.

Angelica Cass (Compiler). Bibliography of Materials for Americanization and Adult Elem-
tary Education. Bureau of Adult Education, Education Dep't, Albany, N.Y.

GROUP 4

MATERIALS IN ENGLISH HELPFUL IN

PREPARATION OF GRADED SERIES IN OTHER LANGUAGES

E. C. Baity and committee. Tanganyika Reading Series.

Frank C. Laubach and committee. U Sein, the Wise Man. Translation, from Burmese,
of the second reader.
_____. Anand, the Wise Man. (Vol. 1). Translation of second reader in Hindi.

Margaret Lee Runbeck and committee. Anand, the Wise Man (Vol. 2). Continuation of
second reader in Hindi.

India Village Service. The Moti-Maya Series. Translation of third reader in Hindi.

Frank C. Laubach. The Story of Jesus. Useful as second reader; now in 80 languages.

All of above materials available from Committee on World Literacy and
Christian Literature, 475 Riverside Drive, New York 27, N.Y.

Robert S. Laubach (Editor). Read and Grow (No. 1). Box 131, Syracuse 10, N.Y.
Stories and articles (illustrated) of many kinds. Useful for English reading and
for translation. Other numbers in Read and Grow series being published.

GROUP 5

HOW-TO-WRITE BOOKS

WRITING FOR AMERICAN MAGAZINES

George L. Bird. Article Writing and Marketing. New York: Rinehart & Co., Inc. 1956.

Edith T. Osteyee. Writing for Christian Publications. Philadelphia: Judson Press. 1953.

Roland E. Wolseley. Writing for the Religious Market. New York: Association Press. 1956.

DISCUSSIONS BY NOTED WRITERS ABOUT THEIR CRAFT

Benjamin Brown (Ed.). Writer's Conference Comes to You. Philadelphia: Judson Press.

Norman Cousines (Ed.). Writing for Love or Money. New York: Longmans,Green & Co. 1949.

BOOKS TO HELP YOU MAKE YOUR WRITING EASY AND FASCINATING

> The person who really wants to write should study at least one
> of these books carefully. All are good; choose any one of them.

Robert Crawford. The Technique of Creative Thinking. New York: Hawthorn Books.

Rudolf Flesch and A. H. Lass. The Way to Write. New York: McGraw-Hill Co. 1955.

Roger H. Garrison. A Guide to Creative Writing. New York: Henry Holt & Co. 1952.

Sir Ernest Gowers. Plain Words, their ABC. New York: Alfred Knopf. 1955.

Frank H. McCloskey. How to Write Clearly and Effectively. New York: Garden City
Books. 1951.

R. G. Ralph. Put It Plainly. New York: Thomas Crowell Co. 1953.

Irving Rosenthal and Morton Yarmon. Writing Made Simple. New York: Made Simple
Books, Inc., 220 Fifth Ave. 1956.

Norman G. Shidle. Clear Writing for Easy Reading. New York: McGraw-Hill Co. 1951.

GROUP 6

THEORY AND TECHNIQUES OF READABILITY

Jeanne S. Chall. Readability: An Appraisal of Research and Application. Columbus,
Ohio: Bureau of Educational Research, Ohio State University. 1958.
Very thorough, though technical analysis and history of readabilty.

Edgar Dale. How to Read a Newspaper. Chicago: Scott, Foresman & Co. 1941.
Though aimed, as title implies, at the reader, also of aid to the writer.

William S. Gray and Bernice Leary. What Makes a Book Readable. Chicago: University
of Chicago Press. 1935. Old, but reliable, with ideas on readability
which have evolved into newer formulas and theories.

Robert Gunning. The Technique of Clear Writing. New York: McGraw-Hill. 1952.
Presents the "Fog Index" for measuring readability. Also a good book
on how-to-write, with many practical suggestions.

Seth Spaulding. A Readability Formula for Spanish. Privately printed by author, available
from Robert Laubach, Box 131, Syracuse 10, N. Y.

Rudolf Flesch. Five books, published by Harper & Bros., New York: (1.-1946) The Art
of Plain Talk, (2.-1949) The Art of Readable Writing, (3.-1951 The Art of
Clear Thinking, (4.-1951) How to Test Readability , (5.-1954) How to Make
Sense. No. 4 is a handy reference book, with the Reading Ease and Human
Interest formulas explained. Read No. 2 for amplification of use of these
formulas and for excellent hints on writing. No. 1 is excellent reading for
someone who knows nothing about readabilty. No. 3 and No. 5 set forth his
later ideas on what makes for easy and interesting writing.

GROUP 7

BOOKS ABOUT SPOKEN AND WRITTEN LANGUAGES

TECHNICAL--RECOMMENDED FOR CLASS ASSIGNMENT AND STUDY

H. A. Gleason. An Introduction to Descriptive Linguistics. New York: Henry Holt. 1955.

_____ . Workbook in Descriptive Linguistics. New York: Henry Holt. 1955.

Eugene Nida. Learning a Foreign Language. 475 Riverside Drive, New York 27. 1950.

Edward Sapir. Language. New York: Harcourt, Brace & Co. 1949.

SEMI-TECHNICAL--SOME LINGUISTIC BACKGROUND HELPFUL IN READING

Ruth Nanda Anshen (Editor). Language: An Inquiry into its Meaning and Function.
        New York: Harper & Bros. 1957.

Charles C. Fries. The Structure of English. New York: Harcourt, Brace & Co. 1952.

_____ . The Structure of Language. New York: Harcourt, Brace & Co. 1952.
        The linguist's approach to understanding English and other languages.

I. J. Gelb. A Study of Writing. Chicago: University of Chicago Press. 1952.
        Absorbing history of writing, from cave man's scratches to electronic age.

Robert A. Hall. Leave Your Language Alone! Ithaca, N.Y.: Linguistica. 1950.

S. I. Hayakawa. Language in Thought and Action. New York: Harcourt, Brace & Co. 1949.

Robert Lado. Linguistics Across Cultures. Ann Arbor: University of Michigan Press. 1957.

A. C. Moorhouse. The Triumph of the Alphabet. New York: Henry Schuman. 1953.

Paul Roberts. Patterns of English. New York: Harcourt, Brace & Co. 1956.

Margaret Schlauch. The Gift of Languages. New York: Dover Publ. 1955.

NON-TECHNICAL--GENERALLY FASCINATING BOOKS ON LANGUAGE

Roger W. Brown. Words and Things. Chicago: The Free Press. 1958.

Edward T. Hall. The Silent Language. New York: Doubleday & Co. 1959.

J. Maurice Hohlfeld (Chairman). Language Preparation and the Communication of the
        Gospel. Hartford, Conn.: Hartford Seminary Foundation. 1957.
        A book resulting from special study seminars held at Hartford Seminary.

Charlton Laird. Miracle of Language. New York: World Publishing Co. 1953.

Donald J. Lloyd and Harry R. Warfel. American English in its Cultural Setting.
        New York: Alfred Knopf. 1956.

Eugene Nida. God's Word and Man's Language. New York: Harper & Bros. 1952.
        Every mission literacy worker should read this, on problems of translation.

Mario Pei. The Story of Language. New York: J. B. Lippincott. 1949.

_____ . The Story of English.   New York: J. B. Lippincott. 1952.

_____ . Language for Everybody. New York: The Devin-Adair Co. 1956.
        Three books by a most prolific writer; you'll enjoy any one of these.

Thomas Pyles. Words and Ways of American English. New York: Random House. 1952.

Edwin Smith. The Shrine of a People's Soul. New York: Friendship Press. 1947.
        A moving book, showing what a dear possession is a people's own tongue.

GROUP 8

REFERENCE BOOKS HELPFUL TO THE WRITER, EDITOR AND
PUBLISHER OF MATERIALS FOR NEW LITERATES

Rowena Ferguson. Editing the Small Magazine. New York: Columbia University Press. 1958.

Randolph Karch. Basic Lessons in Printing Layout. Milwaukee: Bruce Publ. 1955.

Louis A. Leslie. 20,000 Words, Spelled, Divided and Accented. New York: McGraw-Hill.
1951. Easier to use than a dictionary for spelling and dividing words.

Thorndike-Barnhart Dictionary. New York: Scott-Foresman & Co. 1951. Also Bantam
Books. Cost of various editions range from paperback ($.50) upward. The
paperback has all the "common words" and many more. Excellent for writing
for new literates because the most common meaning of each word is given first.

Edward L. Thorndike and Irving Lorge. Teacher's Wordbook of 30,000 Words. New York:
Columbia University Press. 1952.

Michael West. A General Service List of English Words. New York: Longmans, Green &
Co. This book gives meanings of words and indicates frequencies of most
common meanings. Oriented towards Great Britain rather than the U.S.

The two books just mentioned are indispensable for the person doing a great
deal of writing in English, though too expensive for the occasional user.

Robert Root, Earl Roe and John Smith. A Religious Style Manual. Syracuse: Syracuse
University School of Journalism. A guide to terminology of many religions.

Edith Hay Wycoff. Editing and Producing the Small Publication. New York: D. Van
Nostrand Co., Inc. 1956.

GROUP 9

PERIODICALS FOR THE LIBRARY OF A PERMANENT TRAINING CENTER

PERIODICALS CONCERNED WITH LITERACY, LANGUAGE AND PUBLISHING

Adult Education News. Nagpur 1, B.S., India. Bi-monthly $1. a year.
Official organ of the Central Adult Education Comm., National Christian Council.

Adult Leadership. Adult Education Association of the U.S.A.   743 N. Wabash St., Chicago, Ill.
Ten times yearly, $5 ($6 abroad).

African Features. 2 Eaton Gate, London S.W.1.   Monthly; articles of many kinds suitable for
translation. Cuts (blocks) also available. Inquire costs of various services.

Books for Africa. 2 Eaton Gate, London S.W.1. Quarterly book lists and reviews. $.50 yearly.

Bulletin. Evangelical Literature Overseas. 1825 College Ave., Wheaton, Ill. Quarterly. Free.

Community Development Bulletin. Mass Education Clearing House. University of London
Institute of Education, Malet St., London W.C.1. Monthly. Price on request.

Education Abstracts. UNESCO Publications Center, 152 W. 42 St., New York. Ten for $1.75.

Fundamental and Adult Education. UNESCO, same address. Quarterly. $1.

Floodtide. Christian Literature Crusade, Fort Washington, Pennsylvania. Price on request.

Information Bulletin on Reading Materials. UNESCO Regional Centre, 26-A Drigh Road,
Karachi 29, West Pakistan. Quarterly. Free.

Koinonia Magazine. Koinonia Foundation, Pikesville Box 5744, Baltimore 8, Md. Bi-monthly.
Articles on technical aid, literacy, community development programs. Free.

Mountain Life & Work. Council of Southern Mts., Box 2000, Berea, Ky. Quarterly, $1.

Multiplier. Overseas Audiovisual Service Division, International Cooperation Administration,
Washington, D.C. Monthly, free. Obtain from U.S. Information Offices abroad.

Newsletter. Committee on World Literacy and Christian Literature, 475 Riverside Drive,
New York 27, N.Y. Eight times a year, $1.

Newsletter. Laubach Literacy and Mission Fund, Box 131, Syracuse 10, N.Y. Free.

Newsletter. World Education, Inc., 45 E. 65 St., New York, N.Y. Free.

Newsletter. World Neighbors, Inc., 1145-19th St. N.W., Washington, D.C. Free.

Newsletter. U.S. National Commission to UNESCO. Department of State, Washington. Free.

Service. Baptist Mission Press, 41 A Lower Circular Rd., Calcutta 16. Free; publishing tips.

Reproductions Review.   101 W. 31 St., New York 1, N.Y. Monthly, $4.50 (in U.S.),
           ($5.50, Canada; $6.50 elsewhere). Very helpful for small offset print shop.

Word at Work. Committee on World Literacy and Christian Literature, 475 Riverside Drive,
           New York 27, N.Y. Occasional, free. Many tips to writers, editors.

PERIODICALS FOR NEW LITERATES

     This list undoubtedly incomplete; research is being undertaken to determine more of
     these. For later information, inquire of the authors, Box 131, Syracuse 10, N.Y.

El Nur (In Arabic). Literacy House, Minia, Egypt. Monthly, price on request.

The Key. Kenya Adult Literacy Office, P.O. Box 30040, Nairobi, Kenya. Price on request.

Light. American Mission, Malakal, Sudan, East Africa. Monthly, $1.50.

Light (Ajvaliu, in Gujerati). Mission Press, Surat, India. Monthly, $1 foreign subscription.

Light of Life (Divan Prakash, in Marathi). Christ Church, Nana Peth, Poona, India. Monthly.

New Day. Nat'l. Literacy Campaign, Dep't. of Publ. Instruction, Monrovia, Liberia. Monthly.

News for Adult Readers. Jamaica Social Welfare Commission, Kingston, Jamaica. Monthly.

News for You. Reading-For-You Publ., Box 131, Syracuse 10, N.Y. Weekly, price on request.

PERIODICALS READABLE IN PART BY NEW LITERATES

African Challenge. Private Post Bag, Lagos, Nigeria. Monthly, $1.

Caribbean Challenge. Box 186, Kingston, Jamaica. Monthly, $1.50.

Dengta (In Chinese). P.O. Box 5364, Kowloon, Hong Kong. Price on request.

Envol (In French), Oyebi? (In Lingala), Sankai (In Kinguana), Sikama (In Kikongo). B.P. 2309,
           Leopoldville, Belgian Congo. Each magazine monthly, $1.50 a year abroad.

Neno La Imani (In Congo Swahili). B.P. 52, Bunia, Belgian Congo. Monthly, price on request.

AMERICAN YOUTH PERIODICALS--MANY IDEAS FOR WRITERS, EDITORS

American Education Publishers, 1250 Fairwood Ave, Columbus, Ohio: My Weekly Reader.
           In six editions, grades 3-8, $1 school year. Also Braille edition.

Civic Education Service, 1733 K St., N.W., Washington 6, D.C. Four weekly periodicals:
           American Observer (Grades 10-12, $1.50 school year), Weekly News Review (Gr. 9-11,
           $1.20), Junior Review (Gr. 7-9, $1.20), Young Citizen (Gr. 5 and 6, $.80).

Scholastic Corp. Publ., 33 W. 42 St., New York 36, N.Y. Four editions of Scholastic (weekly):
           Teacher's, Senior High School, Junior High, Senior and Junior combined. $2, each edition.

GROUP 10   AUDIO-VISUAL AIDS

Each One Teach One. 16mm color film, 25 minutes long. Story of literacy in Indian village.
           Free loan from Box 131, Syracuse 10, N.Y.

The Word. 16mm color, 25 minutes long. Shows literacy's role in technical aid; thrilling
           scenes from New Guinea Laubach tour. $10 rental, Films, In., Wilmete, Illinois.

Frank Laubach. Color film strip with long-play record. For sale only, $9 strip and record.
           Society for Visual Education, 1345 Diversey Parkway, Chicago 14, Illinois.

For other film strips, inquire of Committee on World Literacy, 475 Riverside Dr., New York.

Wake Up Or Blow Up. 16mm, 28 min. Shows need for self-help programs abroad. Contri-
           butions appreciated in return for loan of film. World Neighbors, 1145-19 St., Washington.

Ray of Hope. 16mm film, 28 min, b & w. Shows how TV Streamlined Reading is taught; also
           the Memphis story. World Literacy Foundation, Hickman Bldg., Memphis, Tenn. Free.

APPENDIX B

SOURCES OF INFORMATION

Where You Can Get Facts Useful in Writing for New Literates

Compiled by Marie Foust

The sources of information in the following lists offer, at nominal cost or without cost pamphlets, magazines and other literature on a host of subjects. These agencies, schools, companies and government departments are listed under the following headings:

General Sources   United States Federal Government

Church Publishers   Supplies And Equipment

College Extension Services   Miscellaneous Suggestions

International Sources   Publishers of Pamphlets And Manuals

This list makes no claim to being complete, for it is a skimming of the hundreds of sources; your own state, and your own country will have many more.

In most cases, each listing includes a key number and letter which are a clue to the kind of information available. The clues are in this code:

THE CODE

With each listing there is a number and/or a letter. The numbers mean:

1 Good source miscellaneous materials
2 Some FREE material
3 Supplies--Library, Printing, etc.
4 Periodical material--magazine or mailing
5 Catalog of materials available
6 Government, or other agency, sources; often with catalog provided
7 Materials especially useful in literacy and missions project

The letters mean:

A Agriculture & Farming Information
C Crafts & Home Repairs
F Food
G General Information & History, usually about company's products
H Home & Family (Includes child care, teen-age problems, etc.)
I Industry & Labor
L Of a Religious Nature
M Miscellaneous--All sorts of good ideas!
N Nature
O Old Folks
P Peace
R Race and Intergroup Relations
S Safety and Health
T Mental Health
W Library Supplies
X We can't classify it, but there's some good "stuff" available!
Y Printing supplies

GENERAL SOURCES

Aetna Life Affiliated Companies   2 S
   151 Farmington Avenue
   Hartford 15, Conn.

Agricultural Missions, Inc.   2 A
   475 Riverside Drive
   New York 27, N. Y.

American Automobile Assoc.   2 S
   Washington, D. C.

American Medical Ass'n.   2 S
   535 N. Dearborn St.
   Chicago, Ill.

American Nat'l. Red Cross   2 H S
   Washington, D. C.

American Nature Association   2 N
   1214 Sixteenth St. , N. W.
   Washington, D. C.

American Pencil Co.   2 G
   Hoboken, New Jersey

American Telephone & Telegraph   2 G
   195 Broadway
   New York, N. Y.

Armour & Company   2 F
   Public Relations Div.
   Chicago, Ill.

Assoc. Childhood Education   H
   1201 Sixteenth St. , N. W.
   Washington 6, D. C.

Assoc. Childhood Ed. Internatl.   H
   1200 Fifteenth St. , N. W.
   Washington 5, D. C.

Blue Cross Commission   2 S
   American Hosp. Assoc.
   425 N. Michigan Avenue
   Chicago 11, Ill.

Board of Nat'l. Missions   L
   Division of Evangelism
   475 Riverside Drive
   New York 27, N.Y.

Bristol Myers Company   2 G S
   45 Rockefeller Plaza
   New York 20, N. Y.

   Educational Service Dept. GT-29
   630 Fifth Ave.,
   New York 20, N. Y.

Brown & Sharpe Mfg. Company   2 C
   Dept. 43
   Providence 1, R. I.

Bureau for Intercultural Educ.   2 C
   119 W. 57th St.
   New York 19, N. Y.

Bureau of Educational Services   2 S
   401 Broadway
   New York 13, N. Y.

Carnegie Endowment for Inter-   P
national Peace
   405 W. 117th St.
   New York 27, N. Y.

Celotex Corporation   A
   120 S. LaSalle St.
   Chicago 3, Ill.

Chamber of Commerce of USA   1
   1615 H St. , N. W.
   Washington 6, D. C.

Child Development Publications   5 H
of the Soc'y. for Research in
Child Development, Inc.
   1341 Euclid Avenue, Un. of Ill.
   Champaign, Ill.

Child Study Assoc. of America   5 H
   132 E. 74th St.
   New York 21, N. Y.

Chilean Nitrate Educational   2 A
Bureau, Inc.
   120 Broadway
   New York, N. Y.

Chrysler Corporation   2 G
   Detroit, Michigan

Civic Education Service
   1733 K St. N. W.
   Washington 6, D. C.

"Classics Illustrated"
   Gilberton Co. , Inc., Pub.
   101 Fifth Ave.
   New York, N. Y.

Committee on World Literacy &   7 L
Christian Literature
   475 Riverside Drive
   New York 27, N. Y.

Congress of Industrial Organizations
   Publicity Dept.
   718 Jackson Place, N. W.
   Washington 6, D. C.

David C. Cook Publishing Co.   4 R L
   Elgin, Ill.

The George F. Cramm Co., Inc. 730 E. Washington St. Indianapolis, Indiana	2 5 M	Industrial Arts Cooperative Serv. 519 W. 121st St. New York, N. Y.	C G
Disston & Sons, Inc. Philadelphia 35, Pa.	2 C	Institute for American Democracy Inc. New York, N. Y.	R
Dow Chemical Co. Dept. P. E. N. Midland, Mich.	2 C	Internat'l. Business Machines 590 Madison Ave. New York, N. Y.	1
Educational Comics, Inc. 225 Lafayette St. New York 12, N. Y.		Johnson & Johnson New Brunswick New Jersey	2 S
Firth Carpet Company 295 Fifth Avenue New York, N. Y.	2 G	Johnson Publishing Co. Atlanta Dallas New York Chicago	2 S
Foreign Policy Ass'n., Inc. National Headquarters 22 E. 38th St. New York 16, N. Y.		Julius Rosenwald Fund 4901 Ellis Ave. Chicago 15, Ill.	2 R
Ford Foundation Offices 477 Madison Ave. New York 22, N. Y.	P	Kennecott Copper Corpor. Dept. S6, Box 238 New York 46, N. Y.	2 C
Friendship Press, Inc. 475 Riverside Drive New York 27, N. Y.	R	Koinonia Foundation Pikesville Box 5744 Baltimore 8, Md.	7 M
General Electric Company Education Service Schenectady 5, N. Y.	2 G	Korea Pacific Press 1828 Jefferson Place, N. W. Washington 6, D. C.	2
General Mills, Inc. Dept. of Public Service Minneapolis 15, Minn.	2 F G S	Laubach Literacy & Mission Fund Box 131, Syracuse 10, N. Y.	7 M
General Motors Men & Women Employee Relations Staff Detroit, Michigan	2 O	Metropolitan Life Insurance Co. 1 Madison Ave. New York 10, N. Y.	1 2 M
The B. F. Goodrich Company Public Relations Staff Akron, Ohio	2 H	Natl. Board Fire Underwriters 85 John St. New York 7, N. Y.	2 S
Goodyear Tire & Rubber Co. Public Relations Dept. Akron, Ohio	2 G	Natl. Commission for the Defense of Democracy through Education 1201 16 St., N. W. Washington 6, D. C.	2 R
H. J. Heinz Company Pittsburgh 30, Pa.	2 F	Natl. Committee for Mental Hygiene 1790 Broadway New York, N. Y.	2 T
Hogg Foundation Univ. of Texas Austin, Texas	T		
Home Missions Council 287 Fourth Ave New York 10, N. Y.	7 M	Natl. Cotton Council of America P. O. Box 18 Memphis 1, Tenn.	2 G
"I Dare You" Committee 835 Checkerboard Square St. Louis, Missouri	L	Natl. Conf. of Christians & Jews 43 West 57 St. New York 19, N. Y.	2 R

National Dairy Council   2 F S
   111 N. Canal St.
   Chicago 6, Ill.

Natl. Education Assoc. of U.S.   1 2 M
   1201 16th St. N.W.
   Washington 6, D.C.

National Geographic Magazine   5 M
   1146 16th St. N.W.
   Washington 6, D.C.

Natl. Industrial Conf. Board   I
   247 Park Ave.
   New York 17, N.Y.

Natl. Livestock & Meat Board   2 F
   Dept. of Home Economics
   407 S. Dearborn St.
   Chicago, Ill.

Natl. Recreation Assoc.   1 2 5 M
   315 Fourth Ave.
   New York 10, N.Y.

New York State Joint Legislative   2 O
   Comm. on Problems of Aging
   94 Broadway, Newburgh, N.Y.

Pan-American World Airways   2 G
   135 E. 42 St., New York, N.Y.

Parent Education Project   H
   University of Chicago
   Chicago 37, Ill.

Pepperell Mfg. Company   2 G
   160 State St.
   Boston, Mass.

Proctor & Gamble   2 G S
   Educational Dept., Box 599
   Cincinnati 1, Ohio

Public Affairs Pamphlets   1 7
   22 E. 38 St.
   New York 16, N.Y.

Reader's Digest Ed. Service   4 7 X
   Pleasantville, N.Y.

Science Research Associates   H M
   57 W. Grand Ave.
   Chicago 10, Ill.

Social Science Research Council   R
   230 Park Ave., New York, N.Y.

Society for the Psychological   R
   Study of Social Issues
   Association Press
   347 Madison Ave., New York

Spencerian Pen Company   2 G
   434 Broadway
   New York 13, N.Y.

"South Today" Press   R
   Clayton, Georgia

"Steelways"   2 G
   American Iron & Steel Institute
   350 Fifth Ave., New York, N.Y.

Superior Coach Corporation   2 S
   Lima, Ohio

The School Executive   E
   470 Fourth Ave., New York

The Tropical Paint & Oil Co.   2 C G
   1134-1246 W. 70 St.
   Cleveland 2, Ohio

Turtex Service Dept.   G
   Gen. Biological Supply House
   761-763 E. 69 Place
   Chicago 37, Ill.

UAW-CIO Education Dept.   G I
   8000 E. Jefferson
   Detroit 14, Michigan

UNESCO Publications Service   5 7
   152 W. 42 St., New York 36

U.S. Beet Sugar Association   2 A
   Tower Building, Washington, D.C.

United States Gypsum Company   2 A
   Publications Dept.
   300 W. Adams St., Chicago, Ill.

Welfare Council of New York City   O
   44 E. 23 St., New York 10

Westinghouse Electric Corp.   2 G
   306 Fourth Ave., P.O. Box 1017
   Pittsburgh 30, Pa.

Wheat Flour Institute   2 F G
   309 W. Jackson Blvd.
   Chicago, Ill.

World Education, Inc.   7
   45 E. 65 St., New York, N.Y.

World Neighbors, Inc.   7
   1145-19th St., N.W.
   Washington 6, D.C.

CHURCH PUBLICATIONS

Christian Herald
   27 E. 39 St.
   New York 16, N.Y.

Christian Life
   434 S. Wabash Ave.
   Chicago 5, Ill

Gospel Trumpet Co.
   1303 E. Fifth St.
   Anderson, Indiana

Internatl. Journal Religious Education
   79 E. Adams St.
   Chicago 3, Ill.

Methodist Church Editorial Division
   810 Broadway
   Nashville 2, Tennessee

Presbyterian Story Papers
   Witherspoon Building
   Philadelphia 7, Pa.

Yearbook of American Churches
   National Council of Churches
   475 Riverside Drive
   New York 27, N.Y.

Youth
   1505 Race St.
   Philadelphia, Pa.

COLLEGE EXTENSION SERVICES

Bureau of Publications   2 F X
   State Education Dept.
   Albany 1, N.Y.

Bureau of Publications   2 H X
   Teachers College, Columbia U.
   New York, N.Y.

Bureau Secondary Curriculum   2 X
   Development, State Ed. Dept.
   Albany 1, N.Y.

Dept. of Forestry Extension   2 A
   State U., College of Forestry
   Syracuse 10, N.Y.

N.Y. State College of Agriculture   2 X
   Cornell University
   Ithaca, N.Y.

N.Y. State College of Home Eco-   2 X
   nomics, Cornell University
   Ithaca, N.Y.

N.Y. State Education Dept.   2 H
   Bureau of Adult Education
   Albany 1, N.Y.

Ohio State University   2 H
   Columbus, Ohio

"University of Chicago Roundtable"   2 H
   University of Chicago
   Chicago 37, Ill.

University of Florida   2 C
   Tallahassee, Florida

University of Kentucky   2 F A H
   Bureau of School Service
   Lexington, Kentucky

University of West Virginia   2 F A H
   Extension Service
   Morgantown, West Virginia

University of State of New York   2 H W
   Albany, N.Y.

     - - - -

The Extension Service of almost
   every State University in the
   United States has similar
   publications on farming, food
   preparation, nutrition, health.

INTERNATIONAL SOURCES

Government of India
   Information Service
   Washington, D.C.

Puerto Rico Department of Labor
   Division of Migration
   21 W. 60 St.
   New York 23, N.Y.

Indian Council of Agricultural Research
   New Delhi, India

     - - - -

The Ministry of Education, and of
   Agriculture, and of other Departments of many countries may be
   contacted for source materials.

     - - - -

Popular Library of Fundamental Education
   Pan American Union
   Washington 6, D.C.

U.S. FEDERAL GOVERNMENT

Superintendent of Documents
   Federal Security Agency
   Public Health Service
   Division of Housing Research
   U.S. Gov't Printing Office
   U.S. Dept. of Agriculture
   U.S. Dept. of Commerce
   U.S. Dept. Health, Ed. & Welfare

(Materials by each Dept. available from
Supt. of Documents, Washington 25,
D.C.; request catalog.)

U. S. Dept. of Interior.
  Bureau of Indian Affairs
  Bringham City, Utah

Materials Preparation Dept.
  Intermountain School
  Brigham City, Utah

Office of Internatl. Information
  Dept. of State, U. S. Gov't.
  Washington, D. C.

Corresponding departments in many
other governments undoubtedly can
be of great help when requests reach
the correct office.

SUPPLIES AND EQUIPMENT

Bausch & Lomb Optical Co.   G
  619 St. Paul Street
  Rochester 2, N. Y.

Bro-Dart Industries   3 W
  59 E. Alpine St.
  Newark 5, N. J.

Demco Library Supplies   3 W
  Box 1070
  Madison 1, Wisconsin

A. B. Dick Company   3 Y
  5700 Touhy Ave.
  Chicago 31, Ill.

Ditto, Inc.   3 Y
  2243 W. Harrison St.
  Chicago 12, Ill.

Gaylord Bros. (Library Supplies)   3 W
  155 Gifford St.
  Syracuse, N. Y.

Remington Rand, Inc.   3 W
  Library Bureau Division
  Buffalo, N. Y.

MISCELLANEOUS SUGGESTIONS

To receive all U. S. public document
lists, subscribe to:

  Monthly Catalog of U. S. Public
  Documents, $3 a year ($3.75 if
  mailed abroad). Supt. of Documents, Washington 25, D. C.

Book lists, annotated, available from:

  U. S. Office of Ed., Washington, D. C.
  Natl. Ed. Assn., Washington, D. C.
  American Library Assn., Chicago, Ill.
  Pan-American Union, Washington, D. C.

Supt. of Documents, Washington, D. C.
  will send free bi-weekly list of its
  "Selected U. S. Gov't. Publications."
  (Foreign postage may be extra.)

The U. S. Information Agency in any
  country will be helpful.

PUBLISHERS OF PAMPHLETS, MANUALS
AND PAPERBACK BOOKS

Technical Books and Manuals

Fawcett Publications
  67 West 44 St.
  New York 36, N. Y.

Grossett's Library of Practical Handbooks
  Grossett & Dunlap
  1107 Broadway
  New York 10, N. Y.

Made Simple Books, Inc.
  220 Fifth Ave.
  New York 10, N. Y.

Pamphlets on Many Subjects

Alumni Publications, Inc.
  10 Columbus Circle
  New York 19, N. Y.

Good Reading Rack Service
  76 Ninth Ave.
  New York 11, N. Y.

Modess Family Life Institute
  Box 1000
  Milltown, N. J.

Public Affairs Pamphlets
  22 E. 38 St.
  New York 16, N. Y.

Paperback Books

Bantam Books, Inc.
  25 West 45 St.
  New York 36, N. Y.

Pelican Books (and Penguin Books)
  3300 Clipper Mill Road
  Baltimore 11, Md.

Pocket Books, Inc. (Perma Books)
  630 Fifth Ave.
  New York 20, N. Y.

New American Library of World Literature
  501 Madison Ave.
  New York 22, N. Y.

For Additional Information, See

Literary Market Place (Annual Book)
  R.R. Bowker Co., 62 West 45 St.
  New York 36, N. Y.

APPENDIX C
The Streamlined English Combined Word Lists

(Thorndike-Lorge List of 1,000 most used words, plus some 700 other useful words)

These combined word lists are valuable to writers of adult graded materials in English. Use of these lists will help you write for adults with different ranges of experience in reading English.

Here are the Stages of reading, and their corresponding lists:

Stage II   Use list 1-500 (left-hand column in alphabetical listing). These are the first 500 most used words in English, according to the Thorndike-Lorge word count. Materials in Stage II are for the adult foreigner or English-speaking "new literate" who has finished Stage I (Streamlined English or equivalent English primer).

Stage III   Use words found in both lists, 1-500 and 500-1,000 (first two columns), which are the 1,000 most used words in the Thorndike-Lorge word count. Materials in Stage III are for adults who have read considerably in Stage II, or equivalent materials.

Stage IV   Use words in any of these combined lists. The column called "Others" consists of words found useful in writing materials on many non-technical subjects. We sometimes call this the "Reader's Digest" Stage for new literates, and we feel that a sizeable body of literature should be developed in Stage IV.

SOME RULES TO GUIDE YOU IN USING THESE LISTS

When writing on any one of the above stages, you will need to use a few words not found on the corresponding list. These are the "new words" in your article. Introduce them very gradually--three, if possible, certainly no more than five new words to each 100 words you write. Every new word should be repeated five times, including, if you wish, its use in the title, with a picture illustrating the article, or in a list of new words.

Can you vary the form of the word as you find it in these lists? Yes--and no. Let these rules guide you.

You may add "regular" endings to words, such as:

    1. Plurals: -s, -es ("book" to "books," "box" to "boxes");
             -y to -ies ("enemy" to "enemies).
    2. Tenses: -s ("say" to "says"); -ed ("hunt" to "hunted"); -ing ("go" to "going").
    3. Adverb forms: -y ("wind" to "windy"); -ly ("careful" to "carefully").
    4. Comparatives: -er, -est ("big" to "bigger" or "biggest").
    5. "One who does:" -er ("sing" to "singer").
    6. Possessives: -'s ("girl" to "girl's"); -s' ("boys" to "boys' ").

You may not add any prefixes (un-, in-, ir-, etc.) unless you find the word listed with the prefix ("less" and "unless," for example, are both on the list.

You may not add -less, -ness and -tion, unless you find the word listed with the ending. These endings make easy, concrete words more abstract and harder.

If words change form with plurals, or with different tenses, be sure the form you use is in the proper list ("feet" is in 1-500, "foot" in 500-1,000; "fly" is in 1-500, "flew" in Others list, but "flown" is not listed).

Beware of combining words on these lists. "State" and "man" and "ship" are all listed, but "statesmanship" would certainly be a new, much more difficult concept. If the thought is not greatly changed, you may combine words. "Mail" and "man" are listed, so "mailman" would not be too hard for Stage IV.

Be careful to use the more common meanings of words listed. "Fast" may be used to mean "speedy" (go fast), or "tight" (hold fast). But if used to mean "stop eating" (to fast), it would have to be counted as a new word.

In case of doubt, use your best judgment; the word lists are meant to serve you, not to be your master.

1-500	500-1,000	Others

A

1-500	500-1,000	Others
a	able	acid
about	accept	accident
above	according	active
across	account	addition
act	action	adjust
add	admit	advantage
after	advance	adventure
again	affair	Africa
against	afternoon	agree
age	afraid	agriculture
ago	agree	airplane
air	allow	a. m.
all	although	angel
almost	amount	angle
alone	animal	angry
along	arrive	anybody
already	art	anyone
also	Arthur	anyway
always	article	apart
am	attempt	apple
America		approve
American		April
among		arch
an		argue
and		Asia
another		asleep
answer		ate
any		atom
anything		attack
appear		attend
are		attention
arm		attraction
army		August
around		aunt
as		auto(mobile)
ask		author
at		average
away		awake

B

1-500	500-1,000	Others
back	baby	bake
bank	bad	balance
be	bag	band
became	ball	base
because	battle	basin
become	bay	basket
been	bear	bath
before	beat	beast
began	beautiful	bee
begin	beauty	beg
being	bed	begun
believe	behind	behave
best	belong	belief
better	below	bell
between	beside	bent

1-500	500-1,000	Others
big	beyond	berry
bill	bird	Bible
Bill	bit	birth
body	black	bite
book	blood	bitter
both	blow	blame
boy	blue	bless
bring	board	blind
brought	boat	boil
built	born	bomb
business	box	bone
but	branch	boot
by	break	bottle
	bridge	bottom
	bright	bought
	British	bow
	broken	brake
	brother	brass
	brown	brave
	build	bread
	building	breakfast
	burn	breath(e)
	busy	brick
	buy	bride
		broad
		brook
		brush
		bulb
		burst
		bury
		bush
		butter
		button

C

1-500	500-1,000	Others
call	cannot	cake
came	can't	capital
can	captain	carbon
car	catch	card
care	caught	careful
carry	cent	carpenter
case	center	carriage
cause	century	cart
chance	certain	cat
change	certainly	cattle
child	chain	central
children	chair	chalk
city	character	chapter
close	charge	cheap
color	Chicago	chemical
come	chief	chest
coming	church	chicken
company	circle	China
condition	class	choice
consider	clean	choose
continue	clear	chose
cost	clothes	Christ

1-500	500-1,000	Others		1-500	500-1,000	Others
could	cloud	Christian		direction	department	
country	club	Christmas		discover	depend	
course	coal	civilization		distance	describe	
court	coat	clerk		dog	desert	
cover	cold	climb		double	design	
cry	college	clock		doubt	detail	
cut	command	closet		draw	develop(ment)	
	common	cloth		dream	devil	
	complete	clothing		drink	devote	
	contain	coin		drive	difficult(y)	
	control	collar		dry	dig	
	cook	collect		due	dirty	
	cool	comfort(able)		duty	disappear	
	corner	committee			discuss(ion)	
	count	compare			disease	
	cross	compete(ition)			dish	
	crowd	congress(man)			distant	
	cup	connect(ion)			distribute	
		cooperate			district	
		copper			divide	
		copy			divorce	
		corn			doll	
		cotton			dozen	
		courage			Dr.	
		cow			drag	
		crack			drain	
		credit			drove	
		cried			dust	
		crime				
		crooked			**E**	
		crop				
		crown		each	ear	earn
		cruel		early	earth	easily
		crush		either	east	education
		cure		end	easy	effect
		current		enough	eat	elect
		curtain		even	edge	electric(ity)
		curve		evening	effort	eleven
		custom		ever	egg	employ
				every	eight	empty
	D			everything	else	engine
				eye	enemy	entertain
day	dance	daily			England	entire
dear	dare	dam			English	equal
demand	dark	damage			enjoy	error
did	date	danger			enter	event
die	daughter	dangerous			escape	everyone
different	dead	darkness			especially	everybody
do	deal	debt			Europe	everywhere
doctor	death	December			except	evil
does	decide	decision			expect	exact
dollar	declare	deed			experience	example
done	deep	defend			explain	exchange
don't	degree	delay			express	excuse
door	desire	delegate				exercise
down	destroy	delicate				exist
dress	difference	delight				expert
drop	dinner	deliver				expose
during	direct	deny				

1-500	500-1,000	Others		1-500	500-1,000	Others

F

1-500	500-1,000	Others
		group
		grow
face	fail	faith
fact	fair	false
fall	famous	familiar
family	farm	fat
far	farmer	fault
father	fast	February
fear	favor	feed
feel	fell	female
feet	fellow	fence
felt	field	fertile
few	finally	fiction
fight	finger	file
figure	finish	firm
fill	fish	fix
find	fit	flag
fine	floor	flame
fire	flower	flat
first	fly	flew
five	fool	flight
follow	foot	flour
food	foreign	flow
for	forest	fold
force	forget	foolish
found	form	forgive
four	forth	former
friend	forward	foundation
from	France	fourth
front	free	frame
full	French	freedom
	fresh	frequent
	fruit	Friday
	further	friendship
	future	fun(ny)
		fur
		furnish
		furniture

G

1-500	500-1,000	Others
garden	gain	gay
gave	game	germ
get	gate	gentle
girl	gather	gift
give	general	glasses
given	gentleman	globe
go	George	glory
god(G)	German(y)	glove
gone	glad	goat
good	glass	goods
got	going	governor
government	gold(en)	grain
great	grant	greet
green	grass	growth
	gray	guest
	grew	gun
	ground	

group
grow
guard
guess
guide

H

1-500	500-1,000	Others
had	hair	habit
half	hall	hadn't
hand	hang	handle
happen	hat	handsome
happy	health	happiness
hard	heat	harbor
has	heaven	harm
have	heavy	harmony
he	height	hasn't
head	Henry	hate
hear	hill	haven't
heard	history	healthy
heart	hole	hide
held	honor	hire
help	hot	hit
her	hurry	hollow
here	hurt	holy
herself		honest
high		honey
him		hook
himself		horn
his		hospital
hold		hotel
home		huge
hope		humor
horse		hung
hour		hungry
house		hunt
how		
however		
human		
hundred		
husband		

I

1-500	500-1,000	Others
I	ice	immediate
idea	ill	impossible
if	inch	improve
I'll	include	income
important	indeed	India
in	Indian	influence
increase	industry	ink
interest	instead	inside
into	iron	inspire
is	island	instrument
it	issue	introduce
its		invent(ion)
itself		invite
		isn't

1-500	500-1,000	Others

J

1-500	500-1,000	Others
John	job	January
just	join	jar
	joy	jelly
	judge	Jesus
		jewel
		journal
		journey
		judgment
		July
		jump
		June

K

1-500	500-1,000	Others
keep	kill	kettle
kept	kiss	key
kind	kitchen	kick
king	knee	kindness
knew	knight	kingdom
know	known	knife
		knock
		knowledge

L

1-500	500-1,000	Others
labor	laid	lamp
lady	lake	language
land	lay	laughter
large	lead	lawyer
last	led	lazy
late	leg	leaf
laugh	length	lean
law	lift	leather
learn	lip	lend
least	listen	lesson
leave	London	level
left	lord	liberty
less	lose	library
let	loss	limit
letter	lot	lion
lie	lower	liquid
life		list
light		load
like		local
line		locate
little		lock
live		Lord
long		loose
look		loud
lost		luck
love		lying
low		

M

1-500	500-1,000	Others
made	manner	machine
make	march	magazine
man	market	mail
many	Mary	male
mark	master	manage
marry	material	mankind
matter	measure	map
may(M)	meat	March
me	meet	marriage
mean	meeting	mass
men	member	match
might	met	maybe
mile	method	meal
mind	middle	meant
miss(M)	milk	medical
moment	million	medicine
money	mine	melt
month	minute	memory
more	modern	merchant
morning	mount	mercy
most	mountain	message
mother	mouth	metal
move	movement	midnight
Mr.	music	military
Mrs.		mill
much		mineral
must		mission
my		mistake
myself		mix
		Monday
		monkey
		moon
		moral
		motion
		mystery

N

1-500	500-1,000	Others
name	nation	nail
national	natural	narrow
near	nature	navy
need	nearly	needle
never	necessary	nerve(ous)
new	neck	nest
New York	neighbor	net
next	neither	newspaper
night	news	nobody
no	nice	noise
nor	nine	noon
not	none	normal
note	north	November
nothing	nose	nurse
now	notice	nut
number		

1-500	500-1,000	Others		1-500	500-1,000	Others
						pray
						precious
						prefer

O

1-500	500-1,000	Others
of	O	oak
off	object	obey
office	obtain	observe
often	ocean	o'clock
old	offer	October
on	officer	official
once	oh	operate(ation)
one	oil	opportunity
only	opinion	opposite
open	ought	orange
or	outside	ordinary
order		organization
other		organize
our		original
out		ourself(ves)
over		oven
own		overcoat

Others (continued): prevent, print, private, prize, process, product(ion), profit, progress, proper(ty), protect, protest, proud, punish, pure, push

Q

1-500	500-1,000	Others
question	quarter	quality
quite	queen	quantity
	quickly	quarrel
		queer
		quick
		quiet

P

1-500	500-1,000	Others
paper	page	pan
part	paid	parent
party	pain	particular
pass	paint	path
pay	pair	payment
people	past	pearl
perhaps	peace	pen
person	period	pencil
picture	pick	per cent
place	piece	perfect
plan	plain	perform
plant	pleasant	permit
play	please	personal
point	pleasure	physical
poor	position	pile
possible	post	pin
power	pound	pipe
present	practice	pity
president	prepare	plane
price	press	plate
produce	pretty	plenty
public	prince	plow
put	probably	p. m.
	problem	poison
	promise	pole
	prove	police
	provide	political
	pull	popular
	purpose	possess
		pot
		potato
		pour
		powder
		practical
		praise

R

1-500	500-1,000	Others
rather	race	radio
reach	rain	rail(road)
read	raise	rank
real	ran	rapid
reason	ready	rate
receive	realize	raw
red	really	ray
remain	record	recent
remember	refuse	recognize
rest	regard	regular
result	reply	relief
return	report	religion(ious)
right	require	remove
river	rich	repeat
road	ride	represent(ative)
room	ring	request
round	rise	respect
run	rock	reward
	roll	rice
	rose	ripe
	rule	rode
	rush	roof
		root
		rope
		rough
		row
		rub
		rubber

1-500	500-1,000	Others

S

1-500	500-1,000	Others
said	safe	sad
same	sail	sailor
sat	salt	saint
saw	save	sale
say	scene	sand
school	season	sang
sea	seat	satisfy(ied)
second	seek	Saturday
see	sell	scale
seem	send	science
seen	sense	score
serve	sent	secret
set	service	secretary
several	settle	seed
shall	seven	seize
she	shade	seldom
ship	shape	select
short	share	self
should	shoe	selfish
show	shop	senate(or)
side	shore	sentence
since	shot	separate
sir	shoulder	September
small	shout	serious
smile	sick	servant
so	sight	sew
some	sign	sex
something	silver	shadow
son	simple	shake
soon	sing	shame
sort	single	sharp
sound	sister	sheep
speak	sit	sheet
stand	six	shine
start	size	shirt
state	skin	shock
step	sky	shook
still	sleep	shoot
stood	smoke	shut
stop	snow	silent(ce)
story	soft	silk
street	soil	sin
strong	sold	sink
such	soldier	skirt
sun	sometimes	slept
supply	song	slip
suppose	soul	slope
sure	south	slow
system	space	smell
	special	smooth
	spend	soap
	spirit	social
	spoke	society
	spot	solid
	spread	someone
	spring	somewhere

1-500	500-1,000	Others
	square	sore
	St.	sorry(ow)
	star	soup
	station	speed
	stay	spent
	stick	spite
	stock	spoil
	stone	stage
	store	stamp
	storm	statement
	straight	steal
	strange	steam
	stream	steel
	strength	stiff
	study	stir
	subject	stove
	success	street
	sudden	stretch
	suddenly	strike
	suffer	string
	sugar	strip
	suit	struggle
	summer	student
	surprise	style
	sweet	substance
		succeed
		suggest(ion)
		Sunday
		supper
		support
		swing

T

1-500	500-1,000	Others
table	tall	tail
take	taste	talent
taken	teach	taught
talk	tear	tax
tell	thank	teacher
ten	thee	team
than	therefore	teeth
that	thin	telephone
the	third	temple
their	thirty	tend
them	thou	terrible
themselves	tie	test
then	till	theory
there	tire(d)	thick
these	tomorrow	thread
they	top	threw
thing	touch	throat
think	trade	throw(n)
this	train	Thursday
those	travel	thy
though	trip	ticket
thought	trouble	tight
thousand	trust	tiny
three	truth	tip

1-500	500-1,000	Others
thus		tone
time		tongue
to		tonight
today		tool
together		tooth
told		total
too		tower
took		track
toward		treasure
town		treat
tree		trick
tried		truly
true		Tuesday
try		twice
turn		type
twenty		typewriter
two		

U

1-500	500-1,000	Others
under	uncle	understood
until	understand	unhappy
up	usually	uniform
upon		union
us		unite
use		United States
		unknown
		unless
		useful
		usual

V

1-500	500-1,000	Others
very	valley	valuable
voice	value	variety
	various	vegetable
	view	victory
	village	vine
	visit	virtue
		visitor
		vote

W

1-500	500-1,000	Others
wait	warm	wage
walk	wave	wake
wall	wear	warn
want	weather	wash
war	weight	wasn't
was	west	waste
Washington	wide	weak
watch	wild	weapon
water	wing(ed)	wedding
way	winter	Wednesday
we	wise	weed
week	wonderful	welcome
well	won't	western
went	wood	wet
were	worth	whatever

1-500	500-1,000	Others
what		wheat
when		wheel
where		whenever
whether		wherever
which		whip
while		whisper
white		whistle
who		wicked
whole		win
whom		wine
whose		wipe
why		wire
wife		witness
will		won
wind		wood
window		wool
wish		wore
with		worn
within		worry
without		worse
woman		worship
women		worst
wonder		worthy
word		wound
work		wreck
world		written
would		wrote
write		
wrong		

Y

1-500	500-1,000	Others
year	yard	yell
yes	yellow	yesterday
yet	yourself(ves)	yield
you		you're
young		youth
your		

Z

1-500	500-1,000	Others
		zero
		zipper
		zone

(These lists are printed separately in an eight-page, handy booklet. Inquire about them from the authors, Box 131, Syracuse 10, N.Y.)

APPENDIX D

LANGUAGES AND COUNTRIES IN WHICH LITERACY TEAMS HAVE HELPED TO
PREPARE EACH ONE TEACH ONE LESSONS

To October 1959

The 65 Countries In Which Dr. Frank Laubach And Team Have Worked
Officially With Departments Of Education And With
Other Governmental Departments

1. Afghanistan	23. Honduras	45. Pakistan (East and West)
2. Algeria	24. India	46. Paraguay
3. Angola	25. Indonesia	47. Peru
4. Australia	26. Iran	48. Philippines
5. Basutoland	27. Iraq	49. Portugal
6. Belgian Congo	28. Italian Somaliland	50. Puerto Rico
7. Brazil	29. Italy	51. Saudi Arabia
8. British Guiana	30. Jamaica	52. Sierra Leone
9. British Somaliland	31. Jordan	53. Singapore
10. Burma	32. Kenya	54. South Africa
11. Ceylon	33. Korea	55. Southern Rhodesia
12. Colombia	34. Lebanon	56. Spain
13. Cuba	35. Liberia	57. Sudan
14. Dominican Republic	36. Libya	58. Tanganyika
15. Egypt	37. Malaya	59. Thailand
16. Ethiopia.	38. Mexico	60. Trinidad
17. French Cameroun	39. Nepal	61. Turkey
18. Ghana	40. New Guinea (British)	62. Uganda
19. Greece	41. Nicaragua	63. United States
20. Guatemala	42. Nigeria	64. Venezuela
21. Haiti	43. Northern Rhodesia	65. Viet Nam
22. Hawaii	44. Nyasaland	

The 96 Countries For Which Laubach Literacy Teams Have Helped
To Prepare Lessons in 274 Languages And Dialects

1. Afghanistan 1951

  Persian
  Pushtu

2. Algeria 1951, '58

  Arabic
  French
  Kabyle

3. Alaska 1949

  Esquimo

4. Angola 1950

  Chokwe
  Kimbundu
  Ngangela
  Ocipama
  Nyemba

  Portuguese
  Umbundu

5. Argentina 1944

  Spanish

6. Australia 1949, '51

  Aranda
  Mowung
  Nungubuyu
  Pitjantjatjara

7. Basutoland 1948

  South Sotho

8. Bechuanaland 1948

  Tsonga

9. Belgian Congo 1948, '50

  Bwikalebwe
  Congo Swahili
  French
  Kihungana
  Kikongo
  Kimbala
  Kimanga
  Kingwana
  Kituba
  Lingala
  Lokele
  Otetela
  Tshiluba

10. Bolivia 1943, '44

  Aymara
  Quechua
  Spanish

11. Brazil 1943, '44

    Portuguese

12. British Cameroun
    1951

    Bali

13. British Guiana 1948

    English

14. British Somaliland
    1958

    Somali

15. Burma 1951, '56

    Akha
    Burmese
    Hoka Chin
    Ganung
    Kachin
    Karen Pwa
    Karen Sgaw
    Lahu
    Rawang
    Taung Thu

16. Ceylon 1938, '39

    Singhalese
    Tamil

17. Chili 1944

    Spanish

18. China 1936, '50

    Amoy
    Cantonese
    Fukienese
    Hokkien
    Mandarin
    National Phonetic

19. Colombia 1943, '44

    Spanish

20. Cuba 1943, '44

    Spanish

21. Dominican Republic
    1943

    Spanish

22. Ecuador 1943, '44

    Kechua
    Spanish

23. Egypt 1935, '47, '51,
    '54, '55, '58

    Arabic

24. Ethiopia 1947, '56

    Amharic
    Anuak
    Coptic
    Gala

25. France 1950, '58

    French

26. French Cameroun
    1948, '50

    Bafia
    Bali
    Banok
    Basa Cameroun
    Bulu
    Douala
    French
    Kaka
    Mabea
    Mekae
    Yambassa
    Yaounde

27. French Equatorial Africa
    1950

    Nanjeri

28. Ghana 1948

    Ahanta
    Ashanti
    Ewe
    Fanti
    Ga
    Twi

29. Goa 1952

    Malayalam
    Portuguese

30. Greece 1956

    Greek

31. Guatemala 1943, '44

    Cakchiquel
    Conob
    Kekchi
    Mam
    Quiche
    Spanish

32. Haiti 1943, '44

    Creole
    French

33. Hawaii 1935, '38, '47,
    '48, '49, '51

    English
    Hawaiian
    Ilocano
    Polynesian
    Tagalog
    Visayan

34. Honduras 1944

    Miskito
    Spanish

35. Hong Kong 1936

    Cantonese

36. India 1935, '36, '37,
    '38, '39, '49, '51,
    '52, '53, '55, '56

    Assamese
    Bengali
    Chatisgarhi
    Garo
    Gond
    Gujerati
    Gurmuki
    Hindi
    Hindustani
    Kabui Naga
    Kanarese
    Malayalam
    Marathi
    Mundari
    Oriya
    Punjabi
    Santali
    Saora (Orissa)
    Tamil
    Telegu
    Urdu (Allahabad)
    Urdu (Bombay)
    Urdu (Madras)

37. Indonesia 1935, '51, '56

    Bali
    Buginese
    Buton
    Donggo
    Dyak

Indonesia (Con't.)

Indonesian
Javanese
Karo Batak
Makassar
Posso
Simalungan Batak
Sumatran Malay
Sumba
Sundanese
Toba
Toradja

38. Iran 1947, '56

Persian

39. Iraq 1947

Arabic
Armenian

40. Israel 1935, '55

Arabic
Hebrew

41. Italian Somaliland 1958

Somali
Arabic

42. Italy 1953, '56

Italian

43. Ivory Coast 1954

Baouli

44. Jamaica 1943

English

45. Jordan 1950, '56

Arabic

46. Kenya 1938, '56, '58

Dhuluo
Kalinga
Kamba
Kenya Swahili
Kukuyu
Luganda
Masai
Olunyore

47. Korea 1949

Korean

48. Laos 1956

Lao

49. Lebanon 1935, '48, '51, '56

Arabic

50. Liberia 1948, '50

Bassa
Gio
Gola
Grebo
Kissi (Gissi)
Kpelle
Kru
Loma
Mandingo
Mano
Sapo
Tchien
Vai

51. Libya 1951, '56

Arabic
Italian

52. Madagascar 1948

Malagasy

53. Malaya 1935, '51

Malay
Arabic

54. Mexico 1942, '43, '44

Aztec
Camomilpa Aztec
Eastern Aztec
Maya
Nawatl
Spanish
Tarascan

55. Morocco 1951, '58

Arabic
Spanish

56. Mozambique 1950

Chopi
Elombe
Gitonga
Shanga
Tsongo
Tswa
Xironga

57. Natal 1950

Zulu

58. Nepal 1953

Nawari
Nepali

59. New Britain 1949

Kuanua

60. New Guinea (British) 1949

Amele
Azera
Gedeged
Gogodala
Hula
Jabem
Kate
Kuman
Medlpa
Mekeo
Motu
Orokaiva
Pidgin English
Purari
Roro
Sinangoro

61. New Guinea (Dutch) 1957

Kapauku

62. Nicaragua 1942

Spanish

63. Nigeria 1948, '50

Bushanti
Ewe
Hausa
Kafanchan
Iregwe
Jaba
Rukuba
Tiv
Yoruba

64. Northern Rhodesia 1948

Bemba
Lunda

65. Nyasaland 1948

Elombe
Nyanja
Yao

66. Pakistan 1939, '50,
    '53, '55, '56

    Baluchi
    Iqbal
    Punjabi
    Pushtu
    Sindhi
    Urdu (Lahore)

67. Panama 1943

    Spanish

68. Paraguay 1943

    Guarani
    Spanish

69. Peru 1942, '43

    Cuzco-Quechua
    Quechua
    Spanish

70. Philippines 1929 to
    '40, '52, '56

    Bagobo
    Bantok
    Benguet
    Bicol
    Bilaan
    Bukidnon
    Cebuano
    Gedang
    Ibannag
    Ifugao
    Igorot
    Ilocano
    Ilongo
    Isanay
    Joloano
    Kalinga
    Madayan
    Magindanaw
    Manobo
    Maranaw
    Paganadan
    Pampangan
    Panayan
    Pangasinan
    Samar
    Spanish
    Subano
    Tagalog
    Visayan
    Zamboangan

71. Portugal 1949, '56

    Portuguese

72. Puerto Rico 1942

    Spanish

73. Ruanda-Urundi 1949

    Kirundi
    Urundi Swahili

74. Saudi Arabia 1950, '58

    Arabic

75. Sierra Leone 1947

    Kisi
    Kono
    Kru
    Kuranko
    Limba
    Mende
    Patua
    Susu
    Temne

76. Singapore 1935, '48

    Arabic
    English
    Hokkien
    Malayan

77. Solomon Islands 1947

    Kwara'ae

78. South Africa 1948

    Afrikaans
    North Sotho
    Sotho
    Tsonga
    Tswana
    Vende
    Xhosa

79. Southern Rhodesia 1948

    Nyanja
    Shona
    Sindebele

80. Spain 1956

    Spanish

81. Spanish Guinea 1948

    Bulu

82. Sudan 1947, '55, '58

    Anuak
    Arabic
    Bari
    Dinka

    Moru
    Nuer
    Shilluk
    Sande

83. Syria 1947

    Arabic

84. Taiwan 1939, '50

    Hokkien

85. Tanganyika 1939, '50

    Arabic
    Cigogo
    Swahili
    Sukuma

86. Thailand 1949, '50, '56

    Thai

87. Togoland 1949

    Ga

88. Trinidad 1943

    English

89. Tunisia 1951, '58

    Arabic

90. Turkey 1935, '55, '56

    Turkish

91. Uganda 1948

    Luganda
    Swahili

92. United States 1935,
    '54, '57, '59

    English
    Navaho
    Sioux
    Ukrainian
    Yiddish

93. Uruguay 1944

    Spanish

94. Venezuela 1944

    Spanish

95. Viet Nam 1956

    Koho
    Jarai
    Raday
    Vietnamese

96. Zanzibar 1938

    Arabic
    Swahili

Alphabetical Listing Of Languages In Which Lessons
Have Been Prepared By Laubach Teams

Language	Country	Language	Country
1. Afrikaans	South Africa	50. Creole	Haiti
2. Ahanta	Ghana	51. Cuzco-Quechua	Peru
3. Akha	Burma	52. Dinka	Sudan
4. Algerian Arabic	Algeria	53. Dhuluo	Kenya
5. Amele	New Guinea	54. Donggo	Indonesia
6. Amharic	Ethiopia	55. Douala	French Cameroun
7. Amoy	China	56. Dyak	Indonesia
8. Anuak	Ethiopia , Sudan	57. Eastern Aztec	Mexico
9. Arabic	Arabia, Egypt, Sudan, British Somaliland, Italian Somaliland, Syria	58. Elombe	Mozambique, Nyasaland
		59. English	United States, other countries
10. Aranda	Australia	60. Esquimo	Alaska
11. Armenian	Iraq	61. Ewe	Ghana
12. Ashanti	Ghana	62. Fanti	Ghana
13. Assamese	India	63. French	France, French Cameroun, Haiti, French Equatorial Africa
14. Aymara	Bolivia		
15. Azera	New Guinea		
16. Aztec	Mexico	64. Fukienese	China
17. Bafia	French Cameroun	65. Ga	Ghana
18. Bagobo	Philippines	66. Gala	Ethiopia
19. Bali	French Cameroun	67. Ganung	Burma
20. Bali	Indonesia	68. Garo	India
21. Baluchi	Pakistan	69. Gedang	Philippines
22. Baouli	Ivory Coast	70. Gedeged	New Guinea
23. Banok	French Cameroun	71. Gio	Liberia
24. Bantok	Philippines	72. Gitonga	Mozambique
25. Bari	Sudan	73. Gogodala	New Guinea
26. Basa Cameroun	French Cameroun	74. Gola	Liberia
27. Bassa	Liberia	75. Gond	India
28. Bemba	Northern Rhodesia	76. Grebo	Liberia
29. Bengali	India	77. Greek	Greece
30. Benguet	Philippines	78. Guarani	Paraguay
31. Bicol	Philippines	79. Gujerati	India
32. Bilaan	Philippines	80. Gurmuki	India
33. Buginese	Indonesia	81. Hausa	Nigeria
34. Bukidnon	Philippines	82. Hawaiian	Hawaii
35. Bulu	French Cameroun, Spanish Guinea	83. Hebrew	Israel
		84. Hoka Chin	Burma
36. Burmese	Burma	85. Hokkien	China
37. Bushanti	Nigeria	86. Hindi	India
38. Buton	Indonesia	87. Hindustani	India
39. Bwikalebwe	Belgian Congo	88. Hula	New Guinea
40. Cakchiquel	Guatemala	89. Ibanag	Philippines
41. Camomilpa Aztec	Mexico	90. Ifugao	Philippines
42. Cantonese	China	91. Igorot	Philippines
43. Cebuano	Philippines	92. Ilocano	Philippines, Hawaii
44. Chatisgari	India		
45. Chokwe	Angola	93. Ilongo	Philippines
46. Chopi	Mozambique	94. Indonesian	Indonesia
47. Cigogo	Tanganyika	95. Iqbal	Pakistan
48. Conob	Guatemala	96. Iregwe	Nigeria
49. Coptic	Ethiopia	97. Isanay	Philippines

98.	Italian	Italy, Libya	155.	Malayalam	Goa, India
99.	Jaba	Nigeria	156.	Mam	Guatemala
100.	Jabem	New Guinea	157.	Mandarin	China
101.	Jarai	Viet Nam	158.	Mandingo	Liberia
102.	Javanese	Indonesia	159.	Mano	Liberia
103.	Joloano	Philippines	160.	Manobo	Philippines
104.	Kabui Naga	India	161.	Maranaw	Philippines
105.	Kabyle	Algeria	162.	Marathi	India
106.	Kachin	Burma	163.	Masai	Kenya
107.	Kafanchan	Nigeria	164.	Maya	Mexico
108.	Kaka	French Cameroun	165.	Medlpa	New Guinea
109.	Kalinga	Kenya	166.	Mekae	French Cameroun
110.	Kalinga	Philippines	167.	Mekeo	New Guinea
111.	Kamba	Kenya	168.	Mende	Sierra Leone
112.	Kanarese	India	169.	Miskito	Honduras
113.	Kapauku	New Guinea (Dutch)	170.	Moru	Sudan
114.	Karen Pwa	Burma	171.	Motu	New Guinea
115.	Karen Sgaw	Burma	172.	Mowung	Australia
116.	Karo Batak	Indonesia	173.	Mundari	India
117.	Kate	New Guinea	174.	Nanjeri	French Equatorial Africa
118.	Kechua	Ecuador			
119.	Kekchi	Guatemala	175.	National Phonetic	China
120.	Kenya Swahili	Kenya			
121.	Kihungana	Belgian Congo	176.	Navaho	United States
122.	Kikongo	Belgian Congo	177.	Nawari	Nepal
123.	Kikwango	Belgian Congo	178.	Nawatl	Mexico
124.	Kimanga	Belgian Congo	179.	Nepali	Nepal
125.	Kimbala	Belgian Congo	180.	Ngangela	Angola
126.	Kimbundu	Angola	181.	North Sotho	South Africa
127.	Kingwana	Belgian Congo	182.	Nuer	Sudan
128.	Kirundi	Ruanda-Urundi	183.	Nungubuyu	Australia
129.	Kissi (Gissi)	Liberia, Sierra Leone	184.	Nyanja	Nyasaland
			185.	Nyemba	Angola
130.	Kituba	Belgian Congo	186.	Ocipama	Angola
131.	Koho	Viet Nam	187.	Olunyore	Kenya
132.	Kono	Sierra Leone	188.	Oriya	India
133.	Korean	Korea	189.	Orokaiva	New Guinea
134.	Kpelle	Liberia	190.	Otetela	Belgian Congo
135.	Kru	Liberia, Sierra Leone	191.	Paganadan	Philippines
			192.	Pampangan	Philippines
136.	Kuanua	New Britain	193.	Panayan	Philippines
137.	Kukuyu	Kenya	194.	Pangasinan	Philippines
138.	Kuman	New Guinea	195.	Patua	Sierra Leone
139.	Kuranko	Sierra Leone	196.	Persian	Afghanistan, Iran
140.	Kwara'ae	Solomon Islands	197.	Pidgin English	New Guinea
141.	Lao	Laos	198.	Pitjantjatjara	Australia
142.	Lahu	Burma	199.	Polynesian	Hawaii
143.	Limba	Sierra Leone	200.	Portuguese	Angola, Brazil, Mozambique, Portugal
144.	Lingala	Belgian Congo			
145.	Lokele	Belgian Congo			
146.	Loma	Liberia	201.	Posso	Indonesia
147.	Lunda	Northern Rhodesia	202.	Punjabi	India, Pakistan
148.	Luganda	Uganda	203.	Purari	New Guinea
149.	Mabea	French Cameroun	204.	Pushtu	Afghanistan
150.	Madayan	Philippines	205.	Quechua	Bolivia
151.	Magindanaw	Philippines	206.	Quechua	Peru
152.	Makassar	Indonesia	207.	Quiche	Guatemala
153.	Malagasy	Madagascar	208.	Raday	Viet Nam
154.	Malay	Malaya, Singapore	209.	Rawang	Burma
			210.	Roro	New Guinea

211. Rukuba	Nigeria	241. Telegu	India
212. Samar	Philippines	242. Temne	Sierra Leone
213. Santali	India	243. Thai	Thailand
214. Saora (Orissa)	India	244. Tiv	Nigeria
215. Sapo	Liberia	245. Toba	Indonesia
216. Shanga	Mozambique	246. Toradja	Indonesia
217. Shilluk	Sudan	247. Tshiluba	Belgian Congo
218. Shona	Southern Rhodesia	248. Tsonga	Bechuanaland
219. Simalungan Batak	Indonesia	249. Tsonga(o)	Mozambique, South Africa
220. Sinangoro	New Guinea	250. Tswa	Mozambique
221. Sindebele	Southern Rhodesia	251. Tswana	South Africa
222. Sindhi	Pakistan	252. Turkish	Turkey
223. Singhalese	Ceylon	253. Twi	Ghana
224. Sioux	United States	254. Ukrainian	United States
225. Somali	British Somaliland, Italian Somaliland	255. Umbundu	Angola
226. Sotho	South Africa	256. Urdu (Allahabad)	India
227. South Sotho	Basutoland	257. Urdu (Bombay)	India
228. Spanish	Latin and South America, Spain, Spanish Guinea	258. Urdu (Lahore)	Pakistan
		259. Urdu (Madras)	India
		260. Urundi Swahili	Ruanda-Urundi
229. Subano	Philippines	261. Vai	Liberia
230. Sukuma	Tanganyika	262. Vende	South Africa
231. Sumatran Malay	Indonesia	263. Vietnamese	Viet Nam
232. Sumba	Indonesia	264. Visayan	Hawaii, Philippines
233. Sundanese	Indonesia		
234. Susu	Sierra Leone	265. Xhosa	South Africa
235. Swahili	Tanganyika, Zanzibar	266. Xironga	Mozambique
		267. Yambassa	French Cameroun
		268. Yao	Nyasaland
236. Tagalog	Hawaii, Philippines	269. Yaounde	French Cameroun
		270. Yiddish	United States
237. Tamil	Ceylon, India	271. Yoruba	Nigeria
238. Tarascan	Mexico	272. Zamboangan	Philippines
239. Taung Thu	Burma	273. Zanda	Sudan
240. Tchien	Liberia	274. Zulu	Philippines

Literacy Tours, With Dates, Places And Names
Of Members Of Laubach Teams

Year	Places Visited	Persons Accompanying Dr. Laubach
1935	Far East, Near East	Unaccompanied
1936-'37	India, East Africa	Unaccompanied
1938-'39	Philippines, Far East	Unaccompanied
1942-'43	Central and South America	Unaccompanied
1943-'44	West Indies, South America	Maria Dayoan, of the Philippines; Theodore Fricke, now Foreign Mission Secretary of American Lutheran Church; Jerry Reisner, now Presbyterian missionary in Mexico
1946-'47	Near East	Mrs. Frank C. Laubach; Jane Barclay, artist

1947-'48	Africa	Robert S. Laubach; Mr. and Mrs. Herold Olsen, artists, of Denmark
1949	India, Far East	Robert S. Laubach; Mr. and Mrs. Phil Gray, artists
1950	Africa	Phil Gray, artist; Robert S. Laubach; Dr. and Mrs. J. Maurice Hohlfeld, literacy professor, Hartford Seminary Foundation
1951	North Africa, Far East	Phil Gray, artist; Mrs. Frank C. Laubach; Dr. Frederick Rex, Committee on World Literacy and Christian Literature; Dr. Christy Wilson, professor, Princeton Theological Seminary; Robert S. Laubach
1952-'53	India (Project with TCA-- U.S. Technical Cooperation Admini- stration)	Mrs. Frank C. Laubach; Mr. and Mrs. Phil Gray, artists; Richard Cortright, literacy teacher, now of Baylor University; Betty Mooney, literacy teacher; Margaret Lee Run- beck, writer; Mrs. Welthy Fisher, Literacy House, India; June Dohse, secretary
1954-'55	Pakistan, Egypt, Sudan	Mr. and Mrs. Richard Cortright; Mrs. Frank C. Laubach; Mrs. E. C. Baity, writer, of Switzerland; Phil Gray, artist
1956	Near East, Far East	Richard Cortright
1958	France, Italy, Tunis, Egypt, Kenya, Sudan, British and Italian Somaliland, Yemen, Saudi Arabia, Lebanon	Unaccompanied

Recent Teams Sponsored By
The Committee On World Literacy And Christian Literature
475 Riverside Drive, New York, N.Y.

1954-'55	Iran, Egypt	Dr. and Mrs. J. Maurice Hohlfeld; Garner Hoyt, literacy teacher; Phil Gray, artist
1956	East Africa	Dr. and Mrs. Wesley Sadler, literacy experts; Mrs. E. C. Baity; James Carty, journalist, Nashville Tennesseean; Enoch Mulira, literacy teacher, Uganda; Phil Gray, artist
1957	Mexico, Guatemala, Honduras, Nicaragua, El Salvador	Dr. Frederick J. Rex
1958	Nepal, West Pakistan, Egypt	Dr. Frederick J. Rex
1959	Haiti	Dr. Wesley Sadler, Dr. Frederick J. Rex
	Togoland, Ivory Coast	Dr. Wesley Sadler, Dr. Floyd Shacklock
	Cuba	Rev. Raul Fernandez

(These lists are printed in a free booklet, "Each One Teach One Around the World. Order from Box 131, Syracuse 10, N.Y.)

APPENDIX E

AIDS FOR LITERACY CONFERENCES

<u>Themes for Discussion</u>

What are the themes which a literacy conference should discuss? This will depend upon the purpose of the Conference and the time at your disposal. Below is a suggested agenda for a four-day conference. If a shorter conference is planned, the most vital themes may be selected out of this list.

1. Literacy situation in our country, statistics, etc. Have we been gaining or or losing ground?

2. Obstacles to literacy--a most baffling problem
    Alphabet, literary language, lapsing into illiteracy, powerty, indifference, lack of literature--the vicious circles which a literacy campaign must break.

3. Successful campaigns--Philippines, Mexico, Brazil, Turkey.

4. Why our country needs literacy:
    Economic progress, unification, social reconstruction, national character and strength.

5. Type of literacy campaigns.
    Government.
    Private organizations--religious, secular.

6. Literacy as a servant of social reconstruction.
    Agriculture, health, economic betterment, beautification, cooperatives.

7. How to organize a campaign:
    In country.
    In city.
    Promotion of campaign, use of propaganda-like placards, radio, newspapers, cinema.

8. Financing a campaign, from:
    Government, will it be profitable investment?
    Individuals.
    Charitable sources.
    Others who might help.

9. Need of coordination.
    Government to have special department of adult education.

10. Need of full-time trained director for region:
    To organize, stimulate, coordinate, direct.

11. Preparing or selecting lessons.
    Aims: easy to learn, interesting to the adult, easy to teach.
    Methods: letter, keyword, story, picture-word-syllable.
        Phonetic review panel.
        Need for further exploration.

12. Basic word lists, how to prepare these.
    Shall colloquial unwritten words be tolerated?
    Necessity of beginning within vocabulary of illiterates.
    How much does spoken and written language overlap?

13. Who will teach?
    Shall day school teachers teach adults at night?
        Is it too much work for them?
        Do they make good teachers of adults?

Do they like to do it? Reports of grumbling.
Will they do it on volunteer basis?
Method which enables student to teach himself.
Could colleges and school give credit for teaching?
Should children be sent home to teach?
Should each student be required to teach one for promotion?
Could people be pledged to vote one month to teaching?
Types of people for volunteer teaching service:
    Students--high school, college, middle school, training school.
    Retired men, unemployed teachers, religious leaders, Imams, priests, pastors, evangelists, deaconesses, constables, all village officials, cooperative supervisors, former students, professors, mayors, women.

14. Training teachers; is it organized sufficiently?
    How much training is needed?
    Local conferences, by a local director.
    Careful instruction printed.
    Course should enable teacher merely to "follow the line."

15. Incentives to teach:
    Patriotism public spirit.
    Shall government require each literate to teach or be taxed?
    Shall government require employees to teach six each?
    Shall diplomas and medals be offered to those who teach?
    Shall each one who teaches one be paid a small sum?
    Shall regular teachers of adults be paid on a daily, weekly or monthly basis?
    Propaganda to arouse enthusiasm among teachers.
    Letters of appreciation from high officials.
    Example set in teaching by governors, premiers, rajas.
    Many articles in newspapers inspiring to teach.
    Goals--"this village literate by 19__."
    Slogans--"each one teach one" (or more). "No more thumb prints in this village."

16. Persuading adults to study--psychology of adults.
    Are they unwilling or in despair? What are their excuses for not wanting to learn?
    Difference between adults and children:
        Better reasoning, memory less keen.
        Desire adult reading matter.
        Wish to lead and be independent and express themselves.
        Will not be treated like children--treat them like rajas.
    Effective motivation.
        Make them see economic advantage of literacy.
        Picture secrets in agriculture, health, trades, etc.
        Protection from being defrauded.
        Franchise, ability to write name.
        Religious motive, desire to read sacred books.
        Shall we pay learner?
        Shall we furnish free lessons?
        Shall we offer free subscription to periodical?
        Shall we entertain with slides, film strips, moving pictures?
        Telling stories before teaching?
        Distribute in market place or homes pamphlets on chickens, cows, wells, rice, babies?
        Wall newspapers with valuable advice.
        Frequent graduation exercises and much praise.
        Information about their particular trade.
        Pride in their children.
        Have mela to arouse enthusiasm.
        Use of ridicule?
        Love and friendship. Personality of teacher. Praise.

Information about their particular trade.

Pride in their children.

Have mela to arouse enthusiasm.

Use of ridicule?

Love and friendship.   Personality of teacher.   Praise.

Arousing new hope, dispel sense of inferiority.

A successful demonstration before the people.

17. Successful teaching--advantages of each one teach one.

Choosing the brightest student first to inspire hope.

Why pupils do not stay in a class.

Scolding, unpleasant experiences with teacher.

Work too difficult, no progress.

Material strange and uninteresting--not life centered.

Too busy, too tired, wrong time of day, too many distractions.

Letting pupils have their own way.

Much praise.

Go swiftly, but do not push student.

Don't watch for mistakes.

Really love the students.

When to teach:

Women: 12 - 2 p.m. ? Men: 7 - 10 p.m. ?

One minute or ten minutes--any time they are ready.

The idle period in the year.

Try to make a fast friend while teaching.

Short periods are best, with no wasted moment.

Have the phonetic charts for students to carry with them and review anywhere.

18. How colleges can cooperate.

Department of Adult Education to train directors, expecially in Teacher Training Schools.

Department in journalism for writing within basic word list.

Student organizations to teach.

Research in word lists, what illiterates like to read, new methods of teaching.

Training students before vacation.

Meeting after vacation to hear reports.

Schools near college like Hislop College, Nagpur, writing for new literates.

A journal for new literates.

Colleges with courses in literacy and writing.

19. Women

A nation is as high as its womanhood.

Special urgency and special difficulties:

Low percentage of literate women; what are the statistics in our country?

Obstacles:

Opposition of some men.

Inability to leave homes.

Paucity of teachers.

Lack of lessons adapted to their needs.

Their sense of futility and despair.

Where to teach them?

In homes, hours 12 - 2 or 2 - 4 p.m. ? Behind Purday.

Must cook and care for children at night.

Schools for women.

Need of special women's organization to parallel men's.

Need of women directors.

20. Communal questions

Why religion desires literacy removed.

Shall we feel responsible beyond our own religion, beyond our own caste?
Can teaching pass the caste and religion boundaries?

21. Need of literature for new literates.
    Graded books above the primer.
    Variety of literature needed to meet each need.
    A bibliography needed for each language.
    What the villages are interested in. Let the conference prepare list,
    all participating. Put the list on blackboard.
    Periodical needed. Large type, short sentences, limited word list:
        Short articles, packed with interesting facts.
        Examine and criticize papers on hand.
    Secure articles from schools:
        Pay for articles?
        Shall school children be required to write these for credit?
    Need of a source paper in English for others to use.
    Types of literature:
        Fiction, interesting inventions, important secrets, poetry,
        picture booklets, folklore, songs, inspirational articles, etc.
    Desirability of translating:
        Not exact translations but paragraphs.
        Making illustrations indigenous.
    Bad literature--what is to be done? Should laws be passed against it?
    Libraries:
        Small villages reading rooms.
          Phonetic chart.
          Periodical.
        A few simple books.
        Good light.
        Somebody to help to write letters.
        Probable cost.
        Secure patrons to pay. Libraries for other countries like
        Carnegie for America.
    Keeping reprints of periodical articles for binding.
    Salesmanship of literature.
        Seventh-Day Adventist ideas.
        Salesmanship methods in the West.
        Shall we require subscription to paper?
        Can government add to taxation and pay for this paper.
        "We have much literature--it is not being sold."
        How to train salesmen. How to pay salesmen.

22. Follow Up. Have we a definite plan for the next conference?
    Have we a continuation committee that will work?
    Is the magazine for new literates provided for?
    Are we going home to sell books?
    Are we going to teach?
    Have we provided for a local organization in your community?
    Have we a set-up of local boards for your whole field, with names?
    Will the secretary and president and director PUSH vigorously?
    What do YOU propose to do? Each delegate to write this out and
    send to the secretary.
    Is a basic word list being prepared, if not in existence?
    Do all delegates have lessons? If not, get them straight away.
    Will you make a drive for writers in schools, churches, etc.?
    Will you paste many placards on the walls?
    Have you chosen YOUR village, to be its patron and make it literate?

In a final message, the chairman should remind the delegates that the success
of the conference is assured <u>after</u> it is over, when each delegate does his part.

APPENDIX F

TABLES FOR USE WITH THE FLESCH READABILITY FORMULAS

By James N. Farr and James J. Jenkins

Courtesy Journal of Applied Psychology, Vol. 33, No. 3, June 1949

Table To Determine HUMAN INTEREST Score

Directions:
Refer to the sample on pages 223-224. The Per Cent of Personal Words is 14. Find the vertical column under 14 at the top of the scale. The Per Cent of Personal Sentences is 7. In the left-hand column find the next highest number, 8 (only even numbers appear, to save space). Let your eye travel to the right along row 8 until it meets the column under 14. There you see 53--your Human Interest Score. All scores are found in the same manner.

_____ Per Cent of Personal Words _____

	0	1	2	3	4	5	6	7	8	9	10	11	12	13	14	15	16	17	18	19	20
0	00	04	07	11	15	18	22	25	29	33	36	40	44	47	51	55	58	62	65	69	73
2	01	04	08	12	15	19	22	26	30	33	37	41	44	48	52	55	59	62	66	70	73
4	01	05	09	12	16	19	23	27	30	34	38	41	45	49	52	56	59	63	67	70	74
6	02	06	09	13	16	20	24	27	31	35	38	42	46	49	53	56	60	64	67	71	75
8	03	06	10	13	17	21	24	28	32	35	39	42	46	50	53	57	61	64	68	72	75
10	03	07	10	14	18	21	25	29	32	36	39	43	47	50	54	58	61	65	69	72	76
12	04	07	11	15	18	22	26	29	33	36	40	44	47	51	55	58	62	66	69	73	76
14	04	08	12	15	19	23	26	30	33	37	41	44	48	52	55	59	63	66	70	73	77
16	05	09	12	16	20	23	27	30	34	38	41	45	49	52	56	60	63	67	70	74	78
18	06	09	13	17	20	24	27	31	35	38	42	46	49	53	57	60	64	67	71	75	78
20	06	10	14	17	21	24	28	32	35	39	43	46	50	54	57	61	64	68	72	75	79
22	07	11	14	18	21	25	29	32	36	40	43	47	51	54	58	61	65	69	72	76	80
24	08	11	15	18	22	26	29	33	37	40	44	48	51	55	58	62	66	69	73	77	80
26	08	12	15	19	23	26	30	34	37	41	45	48	52	55	59	63	66	60	74	77	81
28	09	12	16	20	23	27	31	34	38	42	45	49	52	56	60	63	67	71	74	78	81
30	09	12	17	20	24	28	31	35	39	42	46	49	53	57	60	64	68	71	75	78	82
32	10	14	17	21	25	28	32	35	39	43	46	50	54	57	61	65	68	72	75	79	83
34	11	14	18	22	25	29	32	36	40	43	47	51	54	58	62	65	69	72	76	80	83
36	11	15	19	22	26	29	33	37	40	44	48	51	55	59	62	66	69	73	77	80	84
38	12	16	19	23	26	30	34	37	41	45	48	52	56	59	63	66	70	74	77	81	85
40	13	16	20	23	27	31	34	38	42	45	49	53	56	60	63	67	71	74	78	82	85
42	13	17	20	24	28	31	35	39	42	46	50	53	57	60	64	68	71	75	79	82	86
44	14	17	21	25	28	32	36	39	43	47	50	54	57	61	65	68	72	76	79	83	87
46	12	18	22	25	29	33	36	40	44	47	51	54	58	62	65	69	73	76	80	84	87
48	15	19	22	26	30	33	37	41	44	48	51	55	59	62	66	70	73	77	81	84	88
50	16	19	23	27	30	34	38	41	45	48	52	56	59	63	67	70	74	77	81	85	88
60	19	23	26	30	33	37	41	44	48	52	55	59	62	66	70	73	77	81	83	88	92
70	22	26	29	33	37	40	44	47	51	55	58	62	66	69	73	77	80	84	87	91	95
80	25	29	32	36	40	43	47	51	54	58	62	65	69	72	76	80	83	87	91	94	98
90	28	32	36	39	43	46	50	54	57	61	65	68	72	76	79	83	86	90	94	97	*
100	31	35	39	42	46	50	53	57	60	64	68	71	75	79	82	86	90	93	97	*	*

Per Cent of Personal Sentences (left-hand column)

* Indicates 100 or over.

Table to Determine <u>READING EASE</u> Score

(Continued on Opposite Page)

Directions:

Refer to the sample on pages 212-213. The Number of Syllables Per 100 Words in 128. Find the vertical column under 128 at the top of the scale. The Average Sentence Length is 8. Find the row beside 8 in the left-hand column. Let your eye travel to the right along row 8 until it meets the column under 128. There you see 90--your Reading Ease Score.

After having counted other samples, find their Reading Ease Scores in the same manner.

_____Number of Syllables Per 100 Words_____

	120	121	122	123	124	125	126	127	128	129	130	131	132	133	134	135	136	137	138	139	140
4	*	*	*	99	98	97	96	95	94	94	93	92	91	90	89	88	88	87	86	85	84
5	*	*	99	98	97	96	95	94	93	93	92	91	90	89	88	87	87	86	85	84	83
6	*	99	98	97	96	95	94	93	92	92	91	90	89	88	87	86	86	85	84	83	82
7	98	97	96	96	95	94	93	92	91	91	90	89	88	87	86	85	85	84	83	82	81
8	97	96	95	95	94	93	92	91	90	90	89	88	87	86	85	84	84	83	82	81	80
9	96	95	94	94	93	92	91	90	89	89	88	87	86	85	84	83	83	82	81	80	79
10	95	94	93	93	92	91	90	89	88	88	87	86	85	84	83	82	82	81	80	79	78
11	94	93	92	92	91	90	89	88	87	87	86	85	84	83	82	81	81	80	79	78	77
12	93	92	91	91	90	89	88	87	86	86	85	84	83	82	81	80	80	79	78	77	76
13	92	91	90	90	89	88	87	86	85	85	84	83	82	81	80	79	79	78	77	76	75
14	91	90	89	89	88	87	86	85	84	83	83	82	81	80	79	78	78	77	76	75	74
15	90	89	88	88	87	86	85	84	83	82	82	81	80	79	78	77	77	76	75	74	73
16	89	88	87	87	86	85	84	83	82	81	81	80	79	78	77	76	76	75	74	73	72
17	88	87	86	86	85	84	83	82	81	80	80	79	78	77	76	75	75	74	73	72	71
18	87	86	85	85	84	83	82	81	80	79	79	78	77	76	75	74	74	73	72	71	70
19	86	85	84	83	83	82	81	80	79	78	78	77	76	75	74	73	72	72	71	70	69
20	85	84	83	82	82	81	80	79	78	77	77	76	75	74	73	72	71	71	70	69	68
21	84	83	82	81	81	80	79	78	77	76	76	75	74	73	72	71	70	70	69	68	67
22	83	82	81	80	80	79	78	77	76	75	75	74	73	72	71	70	69	69	68	67	66
23	82	81	80	79	79	78	77	76	75	74	74	73	72	71	70	69	68	68	67	66	65
24	81	80	79	78	78	77	76	75	74	73	73	72	71	70	69	68	67	67	66	65	64
25	80	79	78	77	77	76	75	74	73	72	71	71	70	69	68	67	66	66	65	64	63
26	79	78	77	76	76	75	74	73	72	71	70	70	69	68	67	66	65	65	64	63	62
27	78	77	76	75	75	74	73	72	71	70	69	69	68	67	66	65	64	64	63	62	61
28	77	76	75	74	74	73	72	71	70	69	68	68	67	66	65	64	63	63	62	61	60
29	76	75	74	73	72	72	71	70	69	68	67	67	66	65	64	63	62	61	61	60	59
30	75	74	73	72	71	71	70	69	68	67	66	66	65	64	63	62	61	60	60	59	58
31	74	73	72	71	70	70	69	68	67	66	65	65	64	63	62	61	60	59	59	58	57
32	73	72	71	70	69	69	68	67	66	65	64	64	63	62	61	60	59	58	58	57	56
33	72	71	70	69	68	68	67	66	65	64	63	63	62	61	60	59	58	57	57	56	55
34	71	70	69	68	67	67	66	65	64	63	62	61	61	60	59	58	57	56	56	55	54
35	70	69	68	67	66	66	65	64	63	62	61	60	60	59	58	57	56	55	55	54	53
36	69	68	67	66	65	65	64	63	62	61	60	59	59	58	57	56	55	54	54	53	52
37	68	67	66	65	64	64	63	62	61	60	59	58	58	57	56	55	54	53	53	52	51
38	67	66	65	64	63	63	62	61	60	59	58	57	57	56	55	54	53	52	52	51	50

Average Number of Words Per Sentence

* Indicates 100 or over.

Table to Determine <u>READING EASE</u> Score

(Continued from Opposite Page)

This is the "hard" side of the Reading Ease Scale.　If your writing is scored on this side, you had better try again. See the Recommended Readability Ranges, on page 214.　If you are measuring other materials in English, you may come across writing which scores 33 (the lowest on this page) or lower. To measure those, see Flesch's <u>How to Test Readability</u> (Appendix A).

Number of Syllables Per 100 Words

Average Number of Words Per Sentence

	141	142	143	144	145	146	147	148	149	150	151	152	153	154	155	156	157	158	159	160
4	83	83	82	81	80	79	78	77	77	76	75	74	73	72	72	71	70	69	68	67
5	82	82	81	80	79	78	77	76	76	75	74	73	72	71	71	70	69	68	67	66
6	81	81	80	79	78	77	76	75	75	74	73	72	71	70	70	69	68	67	66	65
7	80	80	79	78	77	76	75	74	74	73	72	71	70	69	69	68	67	66	65	64
8	79	79	78	77	76	75	74	73	73	72	71	70	69	68	68	67	66	65	64	63
9	78	78	77	76	75	74	73	72	72	71	70	69	68	67	67	66	65	64	63	62
10	77	77	76	75	74	73	72	71	71	70	69	68	67	66	66	65	64	63	62	61
11	76	76	75	74	73	72	71	70	70	69	68	67	66	65	65	64	63	62	61	60
12	75	75	74	73	72	71	70	69	69	68	67	66	65	64	64	63	62	61	60	59
13	74	74	73	72	71	70	69	68	68	67	66	65	64	63	63	62	61	60	59	58
14	73	72	72	71	70	69	68	67	67	66	65	64	63	62	61	61	60	59	58	57
15	72	71	71	70	69	68	67	66	66	65	64	63	62	61	60	60	59	58	57	56
16	71	70	70	69	68	67	66	65	65	64	63	62	61	60	59	59	58	57	56	55
17	70	69	69	68	67	66	65	64	64	63	62	61	60	59	58	58	57	56	55	54
18	69	68	68	67	66	65	64	63	63	62	61	60	59	58	57	57	56	55	54	53
19	68	67	67	66	65	64	63	62	61	61	60	59	58	57	56	56	55	54	53	52
20	67	66	66	65	64	63	62	61	60	60	59	58	57	56	55	55	54	53	52	51
21	66	65	65	64	63	62	61	60	59	59	58	57	56	55	54	54	53	52	51	50
22	65	64	64	63	62	61	60	59	58	58	57	56	55	54	53	53	52	51	50	49
23	64	63	63	62	61	60	69	58	57	57	56	55	54	53	52	52	51	50	49	48
24	63	62	61	61	60	59	58	57	56	56	55	54	53	52	51	50	50	49	48	47
25	62	61	60	60	59	58	57	56	55	55	54	53	52	51	50	49	49	48	47	46
26	61	60	59	59	58	57	56	55	54	54	53	52	51	50	49	48	48	47	46	45
27	60	59	58	58	57	56	55	54	53	53	52	51	50	49	48	47	47	46	45	44
28	59	58	57	57	56	55	54	53	52	52	51	50	49	48	47	46	46	45	44	43
29	58	57	56	56	55	54	53	52	51	51	50	49	48	47	46	45	45	44	43	42
30	57	56	55	55	54	53	52	51	50	49	49	48	47	46	45	44	44	43	42	41
31	56	55	54	54	53	52	51	50	49	48	48	47	46	45	44	43	43	42	41	40
32	55	54	53	53	52	51	50	49	48	47	47	46	45	44	43	42	42	41	40	39
33	54	53	52	52	51	50	49	48	47	46	46	45	44	43	42	41	41	40	39	38
34	53	52	51	51	50	49	48	47	46	45	45	44	43	42	41	40	40	39	38	37
35	52	51	50	49	49	48	47	46	45	44	44	43	42	41	40	39	38	38	37	36
36	51	50	49	48	48	47	46	45	44	43	43	42	41	40	39	38	37	37	36	35
37	50	49	48	47	47	46	45	44	43	42	41	40	39	38	37	36	36	35	35	34
38	49	48	47	46	46	45	44	43	42	41	41	40	39	38	37	36	35	35	34	33